W9-BXH-318

Books
by John Langone

Death Is a Noun
A View of the End of Life

Goodbye to Bedlam
Understanding Mental Illness and Retardation

VITAL SIGNS

VITAL SIGNS

The Way We Die in America

John Langone

Little, Brown and Company — Boston – Toronto

ST. PHILIPS COLLEGE LIBRARY

616.07
L284v

COPYRIGHT © 1974 BY JOHN LANGONE

ALL RIGHTS RESERVED. NO PART OF THIS BOOK MAY BE REPRO-
DUCED IN ANY FORM OR BY ANY ELECTRONIC OR MECHANICAL
MEANS INCLUDING INFORMATION STORAGE AND RETRIEVAL SYS-
TEMS WITHOUT PERMISSION IN WRITING FROM THE PUBLISHER,
EXCEPT BY A REVIEWER WHO MAY QUOTE BRIEF PASSAGES IN
A REVIEW.

SECOND PRINTING

T 06/74

The author is grateful to The Associated Press
and United Press International for permission
to quote from their news stories and to F. A.
Davis Company, Philadelphia, for permission to
quote from *Taber's Cyclopedic Medical Dictionary,* 6th Edition, 1955.

Library of Congress Cataloging in Publication Data

Langone, John, 1929-
    Vital signs; the way we die in America.

    1. Terminal care. 2. Death. I. Title.
[DNLM: 1. Attitude to death. 2. Death. 3. Philoso-
phy, Medical. W61 L284v 1974]
RC49.L36   616.07   74-929
ISBN 0-316-51422-5

*Published simultaneously in Canada
by Little, Brown & Company (Canada) Limited*

PRINTED IN THE UNITED STATES OF AMERICA

For Mark, Luke, John, and Lucia
— who never made it home.

33088

Contents

Acknowledgments

A book of this sort, much of it a work of assembly, relies heavily on many sources — personal contacts as well as previously published material.

Among the former, and aside from the patients and caretakers quoted, I am most indebted to James F. Holzer, director of public relations at Youville Hospital in Cambridge, Massachusetts.

I also would like to acknowledge that the interview with Mrs. Antonia Faliconi (a pseudonym) was conducted by Dr. Gerald Adler of Boston and is published with the permission of the hospital where it took place. A shorter version of the interview, on videotape, has subsequently been shown at medical conventions and hospitals throughout the country.

My special thanks also to Dr. Blaise F. Alfano, executive secretary of the American Society of Abdominal Surgeons; Herb Shaw, director of medical information at Harvard Medical School; Lawrence Strum, public relations director at Boston University Medical Center; Cynthia Bailey, occupational therapist par excellence; and to my many other friends in medicine, science, and journalism without whose help I would be adrift.

I thank also my editors, Bill Phillips and Dick McDonough, for their open-mindedness and their encouragement, and my wife, Dolores, for her patience and her love.

While I am grateful to all who have helped, I alone am responsible for the book's point of view and any errors it contains.

John Langone
Hingham, Massachusetts
October 1973

Introduction

This book focuses on a universal human experience. It does not pretend to be a definitive survey of attitudes toward death and dying, nor does it provide a solution to the dilemma of those who must balance their growing concern for the human needs of the dying patients against the pressure for long, continued intervention. It is not a bedside adviser on how best to face death, nor do I care to add to the heady debate on death as process or event. Neither will it put forth any new definition of death in an age of transplantation and nuclear-powered hearts. These things are touched upon, but only as the underlying theme of what is simply a piece of journalism bent on saying something about communication and caring, two ideals supposedly central to medicine. It is less a book about death and dying (which, for better or worse, should be left to the new breed of professional deathwatcher, the thanatologist) than, I hope, one about how those ideals are practiced and preached. It is also about those ideals forgotten, about dehumanization spawned by a preoccupation with defining death and the precise moment it occurs, by man's quest for immortality, by fear, by a simple failure to see the terminally ill — and for that matter all of the ailing in our society — as ordinary human beings with emotional as well as physical needs.

The health professionals, from the occupational therapist trying to help a person nearly killed by a stroke to use a weakened hand again to the neurosurgeon who sees potentially fatal afflictions nearly every day of his practice, have not been adequately educated about death. That deficit, coupled with the self-indulgent, cerebral approaches that mar much of health care today, has served to buttress the attitude of detached concern to which the dying patient and the aged are subjected.

Much has been made in recent years over the sad state of American medicine. And while this is true to some extent — particularly with regard to the unequal distribution of health services — America still has, to my mind, more medical expertise and talent than any other nation in the world. But witness the fact that American doctors and nurses, equipped with the best that modern technology can produce, are trained to treat only a small percentage of man's ills while neglecting the simple primary health care that most people require. Medical schools have concentrated on training specialists and on research. More than half of what a doctor used to do can now be performed by paramedics and other allied health workers, some ill-trained and lacking even a trace of human understanding and compassion. Nurses have slowly begun to move away from the bedside and are taking up the cudgel for "professionalism," which is settling them into positions in academic nursing and in hospital management and which views the nondegree school of nursing as an anachronism. If the American health care system is deficient, it is because it has not yet heard the words one dying patient put to her doctor: "All I want to know is that there is someone to hold my hand when I need it. Death may be routine to you, but it is new to me."

A word, here, about how this book took shape. Much of it was written inadvertently, by people unconsciously articulate who will never see their thoughts in print, for they were dying when it was begun and are dead now, and by others who did or did not care for them as they died or cried out softly for help. Some of their names — the caretakers with specific positions and hospital and university affiliations — are genuine. I have given pseudonyms to others and have also altered various signposts in their lives; the people in the chapter "The Dying" fall into this category. Still others are composites, but no less real to me, and I hope to the reader, than those from whom they were assembled.

Several of the caretakers were known to me because of their stature in the field: Dr. Elisabeth K. Ross, Dr. Ned Cassem, the Reverend Carl Nighswonger. Their work is familiar to professionals and to a large segment of the public. Tips, friends in hospitals, a casual meeting at a medical convention, a telephone call from someone who knew I was looking for material and had a friend or had heard an interesting story — these were the other avenues to interviews. I participated in interviewing three terminally ill patients with Dr. Cassem, observed two, and conducted all the other interviews recorded here myself. I found it was generally unnecessary, and indeed inadvisable, to ask a series of specific questions. The result would have been a grocery list. It was more a matter of talking, of listening, of taking an interest. Out of it came not only this book but several warm friendships that I hope will endure for my lifetime.

What the new thanatologists quoted here are advocating — caring and participation — are, of course, not new concepts. But their application to the terminal patient is. And I realized, during the research, that it is entirely possible that the recent emphasis on the simple technique of being a good listener when a dying patient talks — thereby reinforcing his self-image, helping him hold onto his dignity and self-respect — may set a mood of change in a vaunted medical system that has too long treated the disease and not the whole person, and regarded the patient as an organism, not a human being. The drug addict, the alcoholic, the emotionally disturbed individual, the geriatric patient, the unwed, pregnant teenager — all desperately need to be reassured that they still have worth, that they have pasts that were worthwhile.

I have come to believe, also, that these other patients should serve as teacher, too, as the dying patient has, for it may well be that all the research into death and dying that can and should be done has already been accomplished, even in the brief time in which it has been undertaken. There is, even now, a general acceptance and understanding of the style and pattern of "appropriate" dying, and it may be time to move on, to broaden the patient base, using the techniques and the information arising from dealing with the terminally ill.

There may be, also, an element of risk in continuing, unbridled focus on the dying. Conceivably, as more and more academics become involved in the subject, excessive exploitation of the patient as research tool could result, relegating him once again to a junior partnership in the health care industry. As it is, too many patients from society's less-favored strata are already under the microscope; the dying patients interviewed here are not bank presidents or philanthropists, a situation not contrived by the author, who attended many seminars on death and dying. Impatient to get on with their work, some researchers may find it easy to wink at the requisites to be met before choosing a patient to participate in a seminar: the assessment of each patient, his or her relatives' permission, the support of hospital personnel. Bent on adding to the literature of a discipline that has become as challenging as the laboratory quest for the secret of aging, those who work with the terminally ill — particularly those armed with credentials that say "Only the bearer admitted" — face the same danger that all professional students of human behavior face: in their efforts to probe its complexities they become far too objective, and in that is dehumanization. Despite admirable intentions, the dying patient could well end up merely another forgotten individual, forgotten as he was before, as his caretakers, ostensibly working for him, help themselves to government and private foundation grants to gain stature in a frontier field. What should be of concern is that opportunists and science for science's sake may undo all that has already been learned from the dying patient and force us back to a Dark Age where the mechanistic approach will prevail, and the patient seen as teacher first and patient second. The reversal of that, an attitude that has only recently resurfaced, must continue to be the rule, even though potentially valuable teaching cases may be lost.

None of this is to suggest that death and dying patients should be ignored, for that would be regressive and there would be no point in the pages ahead. Only that thanatology must not become a fad, like white buck shoes, the female orgasm, and the male menopause. Nor simply one more tiresome addition to the health professionals' current lexicon of input, interaction, interface, health care consumer, team effort, crisis orientation, health syllabi, manpower cadre, population base, HMO, outcome variable, role model, and catchment area.

"My impression is that much of the 'thanatology' that is going on across the country is counterphobic," observes the Reverend Allan W. Reed, Protestant chaplain and supervisor of the School of Pastoral Care at the Massachusetts General Hospital. "No harm in this. But I have seen and heard of nurses, physicians, ministers, and social workers going around trying to fit their patients into Kübler-Ross's five stages; I see them eagerly offering help in the form of information statistics, the latest sociological observations on a surgical floor, or an ethics professor's pronouncements on the state of modern man. Living and dying isn't that easy. I'd like to see fewer courses and lectures (including my own) and see more painful waits beside the bed, more agonizing silences in the waiting room — followed by sustained introspection and group sharing of the feelings brought to awareness by such attention to the death that is around us."

ONE

The Right Definition

Marley was dead: to begin with. There is no doubt whatever about that. The register of his burial was signed by the clergyman, the clerk, the undertaker, and the chief mourner. Scrooge signed it: and Scrooge's name was good upon 'Change, for anything he chose to put his hand to. Old Marley was as dead as a door-nail. Mind! I don't mean to say that I know, of my own knowledge, what there is particularly dead about a door-nail. I might have been inclined, myself, to regard a coffin-nail as the deadest piece of ironmongery in the trade.

— Charles Dickens,
A Christmas Carol

(From *The Century Dictionary and Cyclopedia*, A Work of
Universal Reference in All Departments of Knowledge, Prepared Under the Superintendence of William Dwight Whit-
ney, Ph.D., LL.D., Professor of Comparative Philology and
Sanskrit in Yale University, 1904.)

> **death** (deth), n. [Early mod E., also *deth* (dial. also
> *dead, deid,* etc.), <ME *deth, deeth,* often *ded, dede,*
> <AS. *death* = OFries. *dath, dad* = OS. *doth, dod* =
> D. *dood* = MLG. *dode* = LG. *dod* = OHG. *tod, tot,*
> MHG. *tot,* G. *tod* = Icel. *daudhr* = SW. Dan. *dod* =
> Goth. *dauthus,* death; from the strong verb represented
> by Goth. °*diwan* (pret. °*dau*), die, seen also in Goth.
> *dauths,* etc., E. *dead,* with suffix — *th* (orig. — *thu,* L.
> *-tu-s*), formative of nouns: see *dead* and *die*.] 1. Cessa-
> tion of life; that state of a being, animal or vegetable,
> in which there is a total and permanent cessation of all
> the vital functions. (a) In the abstract.
>
>> *Death,* dreadfull *Death* shall plague
>> Thee and Thy Seed.
>>> *Sylvester,* tr. of Du Bartas's Weeks,
>>> ii., Eden.

3

ST PHILLIPS COLLEGE LIBRARY

(b) Actual.

> Than scholde alle the Lond to make Sorwe for
> his *Dethe*, and else nought.
>
> > *Mandeville*, Travels, p. 89.

(c) Figurative or poetical.

> Sleep, that knits up the ravell'd sleave of care,
> The *death* of each day's life.
>
> > *Shak.*, Macbeth, ii. 2.

2. A general mortality; a deadly plague; a fatal epidemic: as the black *death*. 3. The cessation of life in a particular part of an organic body, as a bone.

> The *death* is seen to extend about an
> inch from the end of each fragment,
> and from the living bone in the im-
> mediate vicinity an abundant effusion
> of callus was thrown in a ferule-like
> form, bridging over the space oc-
> cupied by the sequestra.
>
> > *Buck's Handbook of Md.*
> > *Sciences*, V. 127.

death-agony (deth ag o-ni), n. The agony or struggle which sometimes immediately precedes death.

death-bell (deth bel), n. 1. The bell that announces a death; the passing-bell. 2. A sound in the ears like that of a tolling bell, supposed by the superstitious to presage death.

> O lady, 'tis dark, an' I heard the *death-
> bell*,
> An' darena gae yonder for gowd nor
> fee.
>
> > *Hogg*, Mountain Bard.

death-damp (deth damp), n. The cold, clammy sweat which precedes death.

death-fire (deth fir), n. A luminous appearance or flame, as the ignis fatuus, supposed by the superstitious to presage death.

> About, about, in reel and rout,
> The *death-fires* danced at night.
> > *Coleridge*, Ancient
> > Mariner, ii.

4

death-point (deth point), n. The limit of the time during which an animal organism can live in a certain degree of heat; specifically, the point of time, from the beginning of the immersion, when an organism is killed by water at a temperature of 212° F.

death-rattle (deth rat l), n. A rattling sound heard in the last labored breathing of a dying person,

> There was a sound in her convulsed
> throat like the *death-rattle*.
>> *J. Wilson*, Lights and Shadows
>> of Scottish Life, p. 194.

Death's-head moth, or **death's-head hawk-moth,** n. Acherontia atropos, the largest species of lepidopterous insects found in Great Britain. The markings on the back of the thorax very closely resemble a skull or death's-head; hence the English name. It measures from 4 to 5 inches in expanse of the wings. It emits peculiar sounds, somewhat resembling the squeaking of a mouse, but how these sounds are produced naturalists have not been able to explain satisfactorily. It attacks beehives, pillages the honey, and disperses the bees. It is regarded by the superstitious as the forerunner of death or some other calamity. Also called *death-bird.*

death-sough (deth such), n. The last heavy breathings or sighings of a dying person. (Scotch.)

> Heard na ye the lang-drawn *death-
> sough?* The *death-sough* of the Mori-
> sons is as hollow as a groan frae the
> grave.
>> Blackwood's Mag., Sept., 1820,
>> p. 652.

death-throe (deth thro), n. The struggle which accompanies death.

death-token (deth to kn), n. That which indicates approaching death.

> He is so plaguy proud, that the
> *death-tokens* of it
> Cry — "No recovery."
>> *Shak.*, T. and C., ii. 3.

5

death-watch (deth woch), n. 1. A vigil beside a dying person. 2. A guard set over a condemned criminal for some time prior to his execution. 3. The popular name of several small beetles which make a ticking or clicking sound, supposed by superstitious persons to be ominous of death. (a) Some species of the genus *Anobium,* or serricorn beetles, of the family *Ptinidoe,* as *A. domesticum, A. tessellatum,* and *A. striatum.* These insects abound in old houses, where they get into the wood by boring, and make a clicking sound by standing up on their hind legs and knocking their heads against the wood quickly and forcibly several times in succession, the number of distinct strokes being in general from seven to eleven. This is the call of the sexes. Few ears have escaped the noise of the *death-watch:* that is, the little clicking sound heard often in many rooms, somewhat resembling that of a watch; and this is conceived to be of an evil omen or prediction of some person's death.

> "Alas! the poor gentleman will never get from hence," said the landlady to me — "for I heard the *death-watch* all night long."
>
> *Sterne,* Tristram Shandy, vi. 6.

death (deth), n. The apparent extinction of life as manifested by absence of heartbeat and respiration. *cell d.* Complete degeneration or necrosis of cells. *fetal d.* Death of a fetus in utero; failure of the product of conception to show evidence of respiration, heartbeat or definite movement of a voluntary muscle after expulsion from the uterus. *fetal d., early.* Fetal death occurring during the first 20 weeks of gestation. *fetal d., intermediate.* Fetal death occurring during the 21st to 28th week of gestation. *fetal d., late.* Fetal death occurring after 28 weeks of gestation. *liver d.,* Sudden death following surgical procedures on the gallbladder and bile tracts. *local d.,* Death of a part of the body.

molecular *d.*, Caries, catastasis, or the last stage of a
catabolic process. *somatic d.* Death of the whole body.
　　　　　　　— *Dorland's Illustrated Medical
　　　　　　　Dictionary,* 23rd edition.

And King Lear said, "She's dead as earth. Lend me a
looking glass. If that her breath will mist or stain the stone,
why, then she lives." And Dr. Hugo Manus, assistant
physician to the hospital at Breslau, suggests that the tying
of a tight ligature around one of the fingers will determine
whether a person supposed to be dead is so in reality, that if
life be not extinct the extremity of the finger soon becomes
red, the depth of color increasing to dark red and violet,
while the skin above the ligature remains white, and it is
1873, and he says that this is easily understood, because if
there be any circulation of the blood the ligature prevents
the return of the venous blood, while the arteries still
continue to convey it to the capillaries, and he adds that a
test so simple can be applied without difficulty and seems
to be quite decisive, and Jesus said, "Take ye away the
stone. Martha, the sister of him that was dead, saith unto
him. Lord, by this time he stinketh: for he hath been dead
four days." And, then, to settle the old question of the exact
hour of the twenty-four at which a sick person is most
likely to give up and die, *Scientific American* asked Miss
Mary McFadden to study the records of deaths in New
York City for a whole year, and she found some remarkable
and unexpected results, the magazine says, noting that
doctors commonly believe that sick people are weakest in
the early hours of the morning and that death is more likely
in the darkest hour before dawn. It turns out, the magazine
says, that this is partly true, but there are some more
remarkable results; for example, sick people seem to stay

alive until after mealtime, not their mealtime, but the mealtime of the persons around them. And it is 1925, and Miss McFadden believes, the magazine says, that the interest and excitement aroused by this event urges a dying man to cling fast a little longer to his spark of life.

1. About 8 hours after death, a change takes place in the body.

2. The muscles gradually become stiff and rigid.

3. To this change is given the name, rigor mortis, or cadaveric spasm.

4. Beginning in the muscles of the lower jaw and the back of the neck, the stiffness spreads to the muscles of the chest, the upper limbs, and the trunk, the lower limbs being the last part affected.

5. Rigor disappears in the same order as it appeared, lasting as a rule about 4 or 5 days, depending on the cause of death, and the surrounding temperature.

6. As soon as death has been declared official, and friends have withdrawn, the nurse closes the eyes, keeping the lids in contact by pads of wet wool or lint.

7. The lower jaw is prevented from falling back by passing a bandage round the point of the chin and over the head.

8. A four-tailed bandage with a slit to receive the point of the chin may be used.

9. After rigor mortis is well established, the bandage may be removed.

10. Arms are crossed over the chest and the wrists tied.

8

11. Head and shoulders should be elevated. This aids in preventing discoloration of exposed portions of the body.

12. Next, the limbs are straightened, and within 1 hour the body should be laid out.

13. After washing, the orifices are plugged with cotton wool, the legs are tied together, any wound or wounds are dressed, the hair is brushed. Rings and earrings are removed (unless it is the special wish of the relatives that such be left), artificial dentures are inserted, and a clean nightdress is put on.

14. A clean sheet is now placed over the corpse, up to the level of the chin and the face is covered with a clean handkerchief.

15. When the patient is of the Hebrew faith, the above procedure is carried out, except for the following: the body is not washed, no pins may be used, the hair is not combed, the hands are not crossed, but are tied with arms at full length and the finger or toenails are not cut.

> — Adapted from Taber's *Cyclopedic Medical Dictionary*, revised sixth edition, 1955.

Boxcar Formation: Fragmentation of the columns of blood in retinal vessels are a sign of circulatory halt and confirm death.

d., signs of. The principal one is (a) cessation of the heart's action. Other indications are (b) opaqueness of the cornea; (c) the absence of reflexes; (d) manifestations of rigor mortis; (e) a mottled discoloration of the body, esp. over all parts where there is pressure. Many cases of death have been reported only to find after 24 hours that the person was not dead. For such reasons, more or less elaborate tests have sometimes been used to determine without doubt whether life is or is not extinct. The signs mentioned usually are sufficient to confirm one's opinion that death has taken place.

d., tests. (a) A drop of ether is instilled into the conjunctival sac of 1 eye, the other being used as a control. A reddening of the conjunctiva proves that life is present. (b) Sometimes the physician may pass a stylet through a small incision in the first intercostal spaces to the heart. Any movement of the heart will be communicated through the stylet. Removing the stylet may induce cardiac movement which may be augmented by artificial respiration. (c) A piece of litmus paper has been used under the eyelid, an acid reaction being shown by contact with the tears, the blood, or the organ in contact with the paper if death has taken place. (d) If a blister on the skin caused by application of a flame contains fluid, death is said to be only apparent, but if the blister fills with air and bursts with a crackling noise, leaving a dry skin, the person is dead. (e) Moisture appearing on the face of a mirror held over the mouth and nostrils is indicative of the fact that life is not extinct.

d., to determine how long since it occurred. (a) The leg is divided from the ankle to the knee into 3 parts. (b) Beginning with the kneepan as a 4th part, the limb to the thigh is further divided into 6 parts, or 10 in all for the entire limb. If Section 1 is colder than Section 2, the body is assumed to have been dead for 1 hour; if Section 2 is colder than Section 3, the body has been dead 2 hours, and so on. Experiments conducted in temperatures bet. 40° and 80° F. proved fairly accurate in over 100 examinations. In an emergency, the usual symptoms of death are often found to be unreliable. Attempts at revivication should continue to be made indefinitely. No harm can be done in attempting to resuscitate one who seems to be deceased. Successes are numerous.

> — Taber's *Cyclopedic Medical Dictionary*, revised sixth edition, 1955.

Death at the Cellular Level: These requirements pose certain problems of judgment regarding the definition of death which entail medical, legal, and ethical considerations. The problem is particularly complex because, in the final analysis, somatic death may be considered a relative state. The cells comprising the human organism do not die simultaneously but in a piecemeal process. Individual cells may outlive the functioning state of the organ they comprise, while individual organs, because of differing metabolic requirements, likewise vary in their ability to survive.

Our evolving views on the definition of life and death of the human organism are considerably influenced by knowledge gained in the tissue culture laboratory. It has been clearly demonstrated that individual cells, indeed fragments of whole tissue, removed from a recently deceased individual and explanted in a suitable medium, still possess the ability to grow in isolation, to form colonies and, under suitable conditions, to continue to maintain much of their original organization and normal function. Perhaps the best known example of a human cell line achieving near immortality is the so-called HeLa cell line, originally derived from a carcinoma of the cervix of one Helen Lane. This cell line is presently growing in research laboratories around the world, many years after the death of its progenitor. Similarly, certain animal cells have the recognized ability to remain viable after prolonged storage in the frozen state. This fact is attested to by the widespread presence today of bone marrow and vascular graft banks for human use.

> — *Ames/ Diagnostica*

11

CASE REPORT: A 32-year-old man was admitted to Newcastle General Hospital with multiple skull fractures and extensive brain damage. Fourteen hours after admission, on June 16, he stopped breathing. Artificial respiration was then begun by machine so that one of his kidneys could later be taken for transplantation to another man. After 24 hours of artificial respiration, a kidney was taken from the body on June 17. The respirator was turned off and there was no spontaneous breathing or circulation. NOTE: The reported comments by persons associated with this case are of interest. 1. The coroner stated that he thought the patient was alive when the kidney was removed, although there was no hope for him, but the coroner did not regard the doctors as having committed any offense. 2. A physician said that, in his opinion, when the patient ceased breathing on June 16 he had virtually died, but that from the legal point of view it would be correct to say that he died when the heart ceased beating and the circulation ceased to flow on June 17. In some reports, the physician is stated to have said that the patient was medically dead on June 16, and legally dead on June 17. 3. A neurologist said that, in his view, the man was dead before removal of the kidney. The brain damage was such that life was impossible, and the man was kept going by the machine to enable preparations to be made for the operation. 4. A pathologist stated that, in his view, the patient died from brain damage and removal of the kidney played no part in his death.

"After clinical death, the organism can be revived with special methods. By various cooling techniques, we have revived monkeys and dogs from 20 minutes to two hours after clinical death. Ladies and gentlemen, we are on the leading edge of a brand new branch of medicine, reanimatology."

43. And when he had thus spoken, he cried out with a loud voice, Lazarus, come forth.

"Our animals are maintained on a constant infusion of catecholamines, and we employ Levophed in a dose that is in excess of what is needed to stabilize blood pressure therapeutically. A couple of hours might elapse, with the animals kept going, before the dose becomes refractory. The heart will beat and all systems are go, so to speak, so long as catecholamines are instilled. And by varying the infusion rate, blood pressure, cardiac output and tissue perfusion can be maintained simply, or may be played with."

NEWS FROM NIH:
Man can live almost indefinitely with the aid of modern science. But is the person being kept alive by machines really living? Is science saving his life or prolonging his death? These questions lead to many ethical and theological discussions of the use of artificial methods to extend life. However, the problem is also being discussed on a purely scientific level as the medical world searches for a universally acceptable definition of death.

Traditionally, doctors have based the concept of death on cessation of heartbeat and respiration. However, the ability of modern equipment to maintain cardiopulmonary function artificially resulted in a challenge of this definition

13

and a redefinition of death based on the soundness of the central nervous system.

And Harvard says:
Our committee's first problem involved determination of the characteristics of a permanently nonfunctioning brain. The characteristics, the committee agreed, could be satisfactorily diagnosed by reference to these clinical signs:

1. Unreceptivity and Unresponsitivity. There is a total un-awareness to externally applied stimuli and inner need and complete unresponsiveness — our definition of coma. Even the most intensely painful stimuli evoke no vocal or other response, not even a groan, withdrawal of a limb or quickening of respiration.

2. No Movements or Breathing. Observations covering a period of at least one hour by physicians is adequate (sic) to satisfy the criteria of no spontaneous muscular movements or spontaneous respiration or response to stimuli such as pain, touch, sound or light. After the patient is on a mechanical respirator the total absence of spontaneous breathing may be established by turning off the respirator for three minutes and observing whether there is any effort on the part of the subject to breathe spontaneously. (The respirator may be turned off for this time provided that at the start of the trial period the patient's carbon dioxide tension is within normal range, and provided also that the patient has been breathing room air for at least 10 minutes prior to the trial.)

3. No Reflexes. Irreversible coma with abolition of central nervous system activity is evidenced in part by the absence of elicitable reflexes. The pupil will be fixed and

dilated and will not respond to a direct source of bright light. The establishment of a fixed, dilated pupil is so clear-cut in clinical practice, there should be no uncertainty as to its presence. Ocular movement (to head turning and to irrigation of the ears with ice water) and blinking are absent. There is no evidence of postural activity (decerebrate or other). Swallowing, yawning, vocalization are in abeyance. Corneal and pharyngeal reflexes are absent.

As a rule, the stretch or tendon reflexes cannot be elicited; i.e., tapping the tendons of the biceps, triceps and pronator muscles, quadriceps and gastrocnemius muscles with the reflex hammer elicits no contraction of the respective muscles. Plantar or noxious stimulation gives no response.

4. Flat Electroencephalogram. Confirmatory data may be provided by the flat or isoelectric EEG. We must assume that the electrodes have been properly applied, that the apparatus is functioning normally, and that the personnel in charge is competent. We consider it prudent to have one channel of the apparatus used for an electrocardiogram. This channel will monitor the electrocardiogram so that if it appears in the electroencephalographic leads because of high resistance it can be readily identified. It also establishes the presence of the active heart in the absence of the electroencephalogram. We recommend that another channel be used for a noncephalic lead. This will pick up space-borne or vibration-borne artifacts and identify them.

5. All of the above should be repeated at least 24 hours later with no change. The validity of such data as indications of irreversible cerebral damage depends on the exclusion

of two conditions: hypothermia (temperature below 90° F. [32.2° C.]) or central nervous system depressants, such as barbiturates.

And the University of Minnesota Hospitals adds:
1. No spontaneous movement.
2. No spontaneous respiration when tested for a period of 4 minutes at a time.
3. Absence of brain stem reflexes.
4. A status in which all of the findings above remain unchanged for at least 12 hours.
5. Brain death can be pronounced only if the pathological processes responsible for states 1 through 4 above are irreparable with presently available means.

And Kansas state law says:
1. Death occurs with the cessation of spontaneous respiration and cardiac function and hopelessness of attempts of resuscitation, *or*
2. Death occurs at the time of an absence of spontaneous brain function, and when, during reasonable attempts to maintain or restore circulatory or respiratory function in the absence of spontaneous brain function, further attempts at resuscitation appear to be hopeless.
3. Death is to be pronounced before artificial means of supporting respiratory and circulatory function are terminated and before any vital organ is removed for the purpose of transplantation.

To the Editor, *New England Journal of Medicine:*
. . . in view of the current long-established definition
of death that death denotes irreversible cessation of
functioning of the organism as a whole (not of the
whole organism, i.e., of the last cell of that organism),
the Harvard redefinition of death is not a redefinition in
any conceptual sense of establishing a different or new
end point but merely a redefinition in an empirical
sense. Thus, the Harvard redefinition cannot be used to
justify a new "conceptual approach" to ethics in medical care. Its immense importance lies in the fact that it
enables the physician to diagnose the death of a patient
whose entire brain is dead, yet whose heart is beating,
for the brain functions required to maintain the heart
action have been taken over by a machine.

Otto E. Guttentag, MD
University of California
School of Medicine

MR. ROSOFF: I am an attorney. I would like to suggest that
possibly we may be creating a problem in attempting to
find one definition of death which will satisfy a variety of
needs. For instance, there is a need for a legal definition
which occurs when we have to determine the time of
death, either in cases of homicide or in devolution of
property. We also need a medical definition which will
permit successful transplants. I think, therefore, if we
attempt to find one definition to satisfy all of these purposes it will satisfy none.

DR. VAN DUSEN: I am not advocating what I am now going
to suggest, but just mention it as an alternative possibil-

ity — that you need at least three major definitions which are authoritative for the three major professions that are represented here, namely medical, law, and ethics or, however you want to define it, religion. There will be different definitions, but surely they must cohere or we will be in a hopeless situation. If the medical profession thinks that the courts are going to hold to an utterly different definition of death than their own, they will be hopelessly handicapped and the same thing is true of the ministers.

NEWS RELEASE, HARVARD MEDICAL SCHOOL, AUGUST 5, 1968:
. . . The final determination of death through irreversible coma (brain death) can be made only by a physician who also must take responsibility for informing the family and all colleagues who have participated in major decisions concerning the patient, and all nurses.

At this point death is to be declared and then the respirator turned off. The decision to do this and the responsibility for it are to be taken by the physician-in-charge in consultation with one or more physicians who have been directly involved in the case. . . .

It was thought, by members of the *ad hoc* committee to examine the definition of brain death, that if new criteria for pronouncing death in an individual sustaining irreversible coma as a result of permanent brain damage were to be adopted by the medical profession, such could form the basis for change in the current legal concept of death.

"No statutory change in the law should be necessary," the report of the committee pointed out, "since the law treats this question essentially as one of fact to be determined by physicians. The only circumstance in which it would be necessary that legislation be offered in the various states to define 'death' by law would be in the event that great controversy were engendered surrounding the subject and physicians were unable to agree on the new medical criteria."

NEWS RELEASE, INSTITUTE OF SOCIETY, ETHICS AND THE LIFE SCIENCES, DECEMBER 27, 1972:

Who should establish the standards for determining whether or not a person has died: doctors, philosophers, judges, legislators?

What should these standards be and on what principles should they be based?

As controversy over these questions continues, various state legislatures are now considering statutes to "redefine" death; two states, Kansas and Maryland, have already passed such laws.

The approach taken by Kansas and Maryland is sharply criticized in an article in the latest issue of the *University of Pennsylvania Law Review*. However, the authors conclude that some legislation may be needed if confusion and conflict are to be avoided. The article sets forth principles for such legislation and offers an alternative model law. . . .

The use of artificial means of maintaining dying patients renders doubtful, in a growing number of cases, the significance of the traditional "vital signs" of pulse, heartbeat and respiration. As a result, physicians have turned to evaluating brain function in order to know when a person is dead.

A difficulty arises, however, because brain-centered

criteria used to determine death are incompatible with existing, judicially framed standards which define death as the total cessation of respiration and circulation.

Some commentators have argued that the formulation of standards for determining when a person is dead should be left entirely to the physician. The authors of this article reject such a position on a number of grounds:

1. The "definition of death" is not merely a matter for technical expertise.

2. The uncertainty of present law is unsettling for society and physicians alike.

3. There is potential for abuse and harm when uncertainty in the law produces doubt about the responsibility of the physician; and

4. Patients and their relatives are made uneasy by physicians apparently being free to shift around the meaning of death without societal guidance.

Among the principles suggested to guide legislation, the authors emphasized two. First, they believe that a statute should not establish a special "definition" for transplantation purposes, since death is a natural phenomenon which relates to a person and not to the use to which his organs may be put after his demise. Second, the authors caution that it is very necessary to keep separate the question "When is a person dead?" and the even more difficult problem of "When may or should treatment be stopped for a patient who is dying yet is alive?"

The proposed model statute bases the determination of death primarily on the traditional standard of irreversible cessation of spontaneous respiratory and circulatory functions. When, and only when, artificial means of support of these functions preclude the use of such a standard, the statute would authorize that death be determined on the basis of irreversible cessation of spontaneous brain function. Unlike the Kansas statute, this statute preserves the notion of death as a single phenomenon. It does not define two separate "kinds" of death, nor does it leave physicians without guidance as to when each definition is to be employed.

In the early twentieth century, a number of experiments aimed at proving that the soul left the body at a precise time were performed. Doctors claimed to have weighed, X-rayed, and photographed the soul. Among the scientists were five Massachusetts physicians described by the newspapers as being "of the highest professional standing." After working with patients in a sanatorium for some six years, they reported that when the soul fled the body it diminished the weight of the body by a measurable amount. They found this out, they said, by placing dying patients on a specially constructed platform balance sensitive to a weight of less than one-tenth of an ounce. With the patient on one platform of the scale and a counterweight on the opposite platform, the doctors waited for death to come. At that moment, they reported, as soon as the heart stopped beating, the platform opposite the one holding the patient "fell with startling suddenness, just as if something had been lifted quickly from the body." The simple use of silver dollars to balance the scale after the patient died established, the doctors said, that the human soul was a material thing that weighed from a half-ounce to an ounce.

William James of Harvard commented that the exact moment of death was so very vague as to be difficult to determine, adding that he would class the theory of the doctors "with those fantastic cranky ideas men get hold of sometimes."

In 1904, Professor Elmer Gates, director of a laboratory for psychology and "psychurgy" in Maryland, performed a series of experiments seeking to prove that living beings possessed auras, psychic emanations that contain the subtle essence of life. He coated a wall with rhodopsin, a photo-sensitive substance taken from the retina of a freshly killed animal. Professor Gates said that when he placed inorganic and inanimate substances between an ultraviolet light and the wall no shadow was cast. Living creatures, however, were opaque to the rays, he said, and they cast shadows as long as they retained life. Gates placed a live rat in a sealed glass tube held in the path of the rays and in front of the wall. While the rat was alive, said Gates, it cast a shadow. He killed it. At the same time, he reported, a shadow having precisely the same shape as the animal was seen to pass out through the glass tube and move upward on the sensitized wall. As it approached the top of the wall, the shadow grew dimmer, until it disappeared.

Dr. Patrick S. O'Donnell, a Chicago X-ray expert, con-tinued the aura experiments, and claimed to have witnessed "the flight of the vital spark" from a dying patient. He accomplished this, he said, by peering at his subject through a chemically coated glass screen. "Last night," he said, "I tried the experiment on a dying man. He was rapidly sinking. Suddenly the attending physician announced that the man was dead. The aura began to spread from the body and presently disappeared. Further observations of the corpse revealed no sign of the aura. We do not claim that the light is the soul or the spirit. In fact, no one seems to know what it is. In my opinion, it is some sort of radioactivity made visible by the use of the chemical screen. My experiments, however, seem to prove that it is the animating power or current of life of human beings."

44. And he that was dead came forth, bound hand and foot with graveclothes: and his face was bound with a napkin. Jesus said unto them, Loose him, and let him go.

TWO

A Problem
of Detachment

No physician, insofar as he is a physician, considers his own good in what he prescribes, but the good of his patient; for the true physician is also a ruler having the human body as a subject, and is not a money-maker.
— Plato, *The Republic*

"Talk to him and he's dying?"
"Yes."
"That's kind of mean. I mean, talking to a man and he's dying."
— Conversation with a nine-year-old

COMMONWEALTH OF MASSACHUSETTS

Case No. LME 11, 808

Suffolk, ss.

To Judge Charles I. Taylor, Roxbury District Court, Roxbury, Massachusetts:

You are hereby notified that on the 11th day of December, 1965, I received notice that there had been found, within said County, the dead body of a female infant whose name is _____, and who was supposed to have come to her death by violence. I make herewith a report of the examination thereof and of personal inquiry into the cause and manner of the death, and of the autopsy of said body, in conformity with the provisions of Chapter thirty-eight of the General Laws of Massachusetts. I certify that in my judgment the cause and manner of death could not be ascertained by view and personal inquiry, and that an autopsy was necessary for that purpose.

EXAMINATION: The examination was conducted in the City of Boston Mortuary, commencing at 11:00 A.M. Witnesses and technical assistants included Dr. Robert J. Segal, Dr. Richard T. Mason and Mr. David I. MacFarland.

EXTERNAL EXAMINATION: The body is that of a well-developed, well-nourished, female child weighing 23 pounds, 5 ounces, and measuring 31 inches in length. The hair is brown and the eyes are brown. The pupils are 5 mm. in diameter, round and equal. External examination of the body reveals an oval colostomy stoma in the right upper quadrant measuring 1¼ x ¾ inch. The margins of the colostomy stoma are well-fixed to the skin of the abdominal wall. There is a vertical 5¼-inch-long fresh abdominal incision to the left of the umbilicus running from below the costal margin to the level approximately 1 inch above the symphysis pubis. There is no evidence of healing of this incision. Numerous black sutures are in place. . . . Examination of the thoracic cavities reveals approximately 15 cc. of thin sero-sanguineous fluid in the left hemithorax and approximately 20 cc. of similar fluid in the right hemithorax.

Heart: The heart weighs 75 gm. There is approximately 3 to 4 cc. of clear yellow fluid in the pericardial cavity. . . .

Lungs: The lungs have a combined weight of 205 gm. The pleural surfaces are mottled pink-blue in color without fibrinous exudates or hemorrhages on the surface. The lungs are firm in consistency and retain their full shape. Multiple cross sections of the lungs reveal a mottled, pink-red-purple color, with foci of dark hemorrhagic areas. The lungs feel much more firm than normal to palpation. A moderate amount of frothy fluid can be expressed from the cut sections of the lungs. . . .

Liver: The liver weighs 410 gm. The gallbladder and external biliary tree are grossly unremarkable. The capsule of the liver is thin, gray, glistening and grossly unremarkable. . . .

Spleen: The spleen weighs 18 gm. The capsule of the spleen is reddish in color, smooth, glistening and somewhat wrinkled. . . .

Urinary Tract: The kidneys have a combined weight of 125 gm. The renal arteries, veins and ureters are all grossly unremarkable. . . .

MICROSCOPIC EXAMINATIONS: Numerous sections of all organs were prepared and examined. This examination included particularly extensive microscopic examination of the lungs. The pulmonary changes found were the only ones of real significance in this case. Basically the lesion found was consistent with a chemical injury and consisted of a vasculitis (pulmonary arteries and arterioles), severe perivascular edema, interstitial and pleural edema, and the presence in the alveoli of fluid with an obvious high protein content as well as thin edema fluid. The proteinaceous fluid resembling that found in hyaline membrane disease lined the walls of the alveoli, the central spaces left being filled with the thin edema fluid. There was in addition interstitial pneumonitis with widening of the septa with infiltrates of inflammatory cells. The damaged pulmonary arteries, usually small ones, show great swelling of the walls, damaged endothelial lining cells and rarely a fibrin thrombus in the lumens.

OPINION: It is my opinion that _____ came to her death as a result of: Pneumonitis, pulmonary vascular injury and pulmonary edema due to accidental intravenous administration of ether during surgical treatment of congenital disease of colon. Accident. Boston, Massachusetts.

> Michael A. Luongo, MD
> Medical Examiner
> Suffolk County, Northern Division

CITY OF BOSTON
POLICE DEPARTMENT
Bureau of Field Operations

January 12, 1966

FROM: Lieutenant Detective John J. Donovan
TO: Deputy Superintendent Edward W. Mannix
SUBJECT: Investigation in re: Death of _____, 15 months old, at the _____ Hospital, December 11, 1965.

Sir:

About 3:00 P.M., Saturday, December 11, 1965, Lieutenant Detective John J. Donovan of the Homicide Unit received a telephone call from Dr. Michael A. Luongo . . . requesting Lieutenant Donovan to conduct an investigation into the circumstances surrounding the death of _____. Dr. Luongo stated that he had been notified of the child's death by a member of the hospital staff at 4:30 A.M., December 11, 1965. . . .

About 9:30 A.M., December 13, 1965, Lieutenant Donovan and Patrolman Joseph Daly with Stenographer George Indingaro went to the hospital where the director, Dr. _____, reaffirmed a decision for complete cooperation. . . .

The hospital records indicated that _____, a fifteen-month-old female, was suffering from a congenital disease of the distal colon known as Hirschsprung's Disease. . . . On July 13, 1965, an operation known as a right transverse colostomy was performed on the child to enable the child to have a bowel movement without the stool having to pass through the abnormal colon. . . . She was readmitted to the hospital December 3, 1965, for surgery to remove the dilated distal colon. . . .

Before the beginning of the intended operation, a minor surgical procedure known as a cut-down procedure was carried out by Dr. _____. This consisted of the insertion of an intravenous catheter into a vein in the child's right arm in preparation for intravenous administration of fluids and blood transfusions should they be necessary during the course of the operation. Directly after the insertion of the catheter, Dr. _____ flushed out the catheter with a syringe containing about two cc. of fluid which he thought was saline solution. He immediately noticed that the blood in the plastic catheter was not mixing with the saline solution as it usually does. The blood and saline solution usually mix evenly so that the solution is a pink color. In this case it seemed the two solutions remained separate and appeared more of an emulsion. Dr. _____ asked Miss _____, the circulating nurse, what solution was in the medicine jar from which he filled the syringe. She answered that it was ether. The fact that it was ether rather than saline solution that had been injected into the child's vein was immediately confirmed.

Dr. _____ and Dr. _____ were called into the operating room and a general conference of surgeons and anesthetists took place, and a decision was reached to proceed with the operation because the child showed no unusual reaction to the ether injection and it was felt the amount of ether injected would not be detrimental to the child or make the operation more difficult. The doctors proceeded with the operation.

About thirty minutes after the operation commenced, Dr. ———, the anesthetist, reported a drop in the child's blood pressure. The operation was stopped and blood was administered intravenously. This did not improve the blood pressure and it was decided to terminate the operation. The abdomen was closed and the child was taken to the recovery room. The child's color was mottled and her respirations were shallow and she experienced a gradual fall in blood pressure. It was at this point that the doctors felt the injection of ether was the cause of her difficulty. . . . Every therapeutic method known to modern medicine was used in an effort to save her life. . . .

In this particular operation, the circulating nurse was Miss ———, 27 years old, single, of ——— Ave., Boston. She is a native of the Republic of Panama. She speaks fair English. She was graduated from the ——— Hospital School of Nursing, Panama City, in 1962, after a three-year course in nursing. . . . In June of 1965, she came to the ——— Hospital to work, and underwent an orientation period covering the entire hospital after which she spent a two-month orientation period in the operating room. During this orientation period in the operating room, she worked under the direct supervision of an experienced nurse. For about three months prior to December 8, 1965, Miss ——— had been acting as either circulating nurse or scrub nurse without direct supervision. However, there would always be a head nurse on duty supervising the nurses in all the operating rooms on the floor.

Miss _____ stated to Lieutenant Detective Donovan that on the morning of December 8, 1965, she was in the operating room before the child arrived and before the doctors came into the operating room. She was going about her duties as circulating nurse. She saw the doctors in a room adjoining the operating room where they were scrubbing for the operation. She went to the door of the room and asked the doctors if they were going to use a cut-down tray. One of the doctors said that they were. She went to a small table whereupon the cut-down tray was set. The child had arrived in the operating room by this time. Miss _____ started to prepare the cut-down tray when Dr. _____ asked her to get stirrups to be used to hold the child's legs in place. She left the operating room to get the stirrups and was gone a couple of minutes and when she returned, Dr. _____ had completed setting up the cut-down tray which included three small medicine jars about the size of a whiskey glass. The circulating nurse usually has these jars filled with the solutions to be used in the cut-down procedure. One of these jars is filled with alcohol which is pink in color, one is filled with iodine which is brown in color, and the third is filled with saline solution which is colorless. Miss _____ stated that she did not have time to fill the jars with the solutions before Dr. _____ asked her to get the stirrups. When she returned from getting the stirrups, Dr. _____ asked her to get the "prep solutions." She went to the cabinet in the operating room and got alcohol, iodine and ether that were in their original containers and poured the solutions into the medicine jars on the cut-down tray. She stated to Lieutenant

Detective Donovan that she did not see Dr. _____ fill the syringe with ether and inject it into the catheter. If she had, she stated, she would have cautioned the doctor that he was using ether. She stated she thought the ether was going to be used to prepare the skin on the arm in preparation for the cut-down incision.

Miss _____ stated that she had previously been circulating nurse at operations where a cut-down procedure was used on about three occasions and on those occasions the solutions that she set out were alcohol, iodine and saline. However, the prep solutions for an orthopedic operation generally used at the hospital are alcohol, iodine and ether. The last day Miss _____ worked prior to December 8, 1965, was Friday, December 3, 1965. On that day she circulated at three operations. The last two operations were orthopedic operations and the prep solutions she set out for these two orthopedic operations were alcohol, iodine and ether. . . .

THE COMMONWEALTH OF MASSACHUSETTS
MEDICAL EXAMINER FOR SUFFOLK COUNTY
Office of the Northern Division
Boston, Massachusetts 02118

Judge Charles I. Taylor
Roxbury District Court
88 Roxbury Street
Roxbury, Massachusetts

Dear Judge Taylor:
The report of the autopsy performed December 11, 1965, on the body of _____ who died in the _____ Hospital in Boston on the same day is enclosed. An

extensive inquiry was made into the circumstances surrounding this death by Lt. John Donovan, homicide unit, Boston Police Department. He has prepared a 72-page typewritten account of his interviews of all the individuals involved (physicians and nurses). . . .

The child lived about 60 hours and expired 3:16 A.M. on December 11, 1965.

An autopsy was performed by me on December 11, 1965. The findings indicate that death was caused by the ether injection. The delay in reporting the facts to the Court was necessitated by the fact that I had not had previous experience with such a pathological problem. Nor had any other physician in this area. I therefore performed a series of experiments using animals (rabbits), concluded only today. The results of these experiments proved to me and my associates quite conclusively that the postmortem findings in the child were the result of ether administration.

As a physician and medical examiner, I was unable to find any evidence of recklessness on anyone's part, nor was there evidence that any law regulating hospital work had been violated. The unfortunate accident was as simple as described. . . .

If other information is required at this time by the Court, I shall be happy to furnish it. Lt. Donovan has available the typed interviews of the doctors and nurses.

I respectfully suggest, realizing that the matter lies solely with the Court, that a judicial inquiry would not uncover further useful information regarding the cause and manner of death.

Sincerely,
Michael A. Luongo, MD

COMMONWEALTH OF MASSACHUSETTS
Municipal Court of the Roxbury District
January 19, 1966

Relative to the death of _____

In conformity with the provisions of Chapter 38 of the General Laws of Massachusetts, I have received from the Medical Examiner for Suffolk County, office of the Northern Division, Doctor Michael A. Luongo, a notification of his inquiry into the cause and circumstances of the death of one _____, together with a copy of his report of the autopsy performed December 11, 1965, on the body of _____ who died in the _____ Hospital on the same day.

I have also received from Lieutenant Detective John J. Donovan a report of his investigation.

A copy of all the above reports is included in my decision.

The Medical Examiner states in his report that he was unable to find any evidence of recklessness on anyone's part, nor was there evidence that any law regulating hospital work had been violated.

The investigation by both Doctor Luongo and Lieutenant Donovan does not reveal sufficient evidence which could be classified as "wilful, wanton and reckless misconduct," necessary to make any of the hospital staff criminally culpable. Consequently, I find that any further judicial inquiry is not necessary.

To prevent repetition of such tragic incidents, it is my suggestion that the public health authorities should put in force much stricter regulations pertaining to preoperating procedures to apply to all hospitals and doctors, particularly a regulation which would require all receptacles containing prep solutions to be distinctly labeled and another regulation requiring the operating surgeon to personally ascertain the contents of these receptacles and not to rely solely upon others.

Charles I. Taylor
Justice

PRESS ADVISORY

An error was made by an individual — not a doctor — in the operating room of this hospital on December 8, resulting in the death on December 11, of _____, age 15 months.

The error was immediately recognized by the surgeons and a total of 30 team members worked around the clock in shifts in a concerted effort to save the child's life.

She did show temporary improvement but died from pulmonary insufficiency.

The parents were advised of this matter and were most understanding.

The hospital has conducted its own investigation and steps have been taken to insure that an incident of this sort cannot happen again.

There has been disciplinary action against the individual responsible. The individual has been relieved of all responsibilities as a result of the accident.

The hospital is unable to adequately express its deep regrets.

> I profess both to learn and to teach anatomy, not from books but from dissections; not from positions of philosophers but from the fabric of nature.
> — William Harvey

> The human body is a watch, a large watch constructed with skill and ingenuity.
> — from *L'Homme Machine*,
> by Julien Offroy de La Mettrie

First day in class. Introductory lecture by Dr. S. who doesn't at all look like someone Burke and Hare would have done business with, a pleasant man not without a sense of humor who opens with a story about medical students fleeing en masse from the anatomy laboratory when they recognized a cadaver as a popular hooker. He delivers the punch line with appropriate dramatic pause: "She had a very large . . . clientele."

There are 103 of us, 100 men and 3 women. All but me will be physicians one day and this course, gross anatomy, which will add significantly to their mechanical expertise, is to be their first professional experience with a dead human being. Their laughter at his little joke seems exaggerated, but it is difficult to tell whether they are masking uneasiness, as I am, by playing the insensitive role tradition dictates or whether, because of their prior exposure to the detailed study of lab animals, they are truly desensitized in matters of death and well on their way to becoming good doctors of machinery.

My participation in the course, as a medical journalist, had been permitted for background purposes, to plug an educational gap. There were, however, other and more personal motivations. There was a gnawing need to shake off the fear and revulsion the dead had planted in me. As a beginning reporter I had seen death, but always it was violent and revolting and at a distance. The charred remains of the victims of a jetliner crash strewn about an Illinois cornfield like burned and broken jackstraws. The bloated body of a child, drowned under the ice on which he had played. The severed head of a drunken driver who tried to beat a train to a New Hampshire crossing in the middle of the night. A gangland victim, the side of his head blown out, bloody and brain-scattered, by a shotgun blast fired at close range. The young woman impaled, face up and arms outstretched, on the spikes of an iron gate beneath the window from which she had leaped. The contorted face of a lineman shocked to death on his high-wire job. Museum images of Bosch and Dürer and Holbein, the horrible Dance of Death theme, cavorting demons and skeletons leading unfortunates to the infernal regions. The childhood dread of coffins and candles and draperies of black, of muffled drums and the creaking gates of a cemetery, and the chilling words of the Mass of the Dead. Bottomless pit. Sharp flames. Torments of hell. Day of wrath. Mouth of the lion.

Did you ever think, when the hearse goes by, that some fine day you are going to die? They'll put you in a wooden shirt and cover you over with gravel and dirt. The worms crawl in, the worms crawl out, they're in your ears and out your snout. Boo hoo, boo hoo, boo hoo hoo hoo.

I had seen death and smelled it, and always I had turned away, and I had never touched it. My grandfather lying in an ornate casket, his face painted and covered with a fine muslin cloth, the hint of a smile he hardly ever smiled fixed in place for years to come, smiling underground when he had no reason to, and I could not touch him as my mother had done, or kiss his white forehead after my mother, and I thought now that somehow a course in anatomy might help me face and touch death without fear and help me understand, just as the babies I saw being born and the patients I watched undergo surgery were fulfilling experiences, helping me know a little more about birth and suffering and how close to the edge man treads in the striving for his ultimate goal, and that of all living things, survival. No textbook, no lecture series, no beautifully executed anatomic drawings, I was convinced, could substitute for the specimen that had to be observed, touched and dissected before any logical conclusions could be drawn.

The medical student, says Dr. S., has to acquaint himself with some 10,000 special terms, and gross anatomy is responsible for about 8,000 of them. He discusses the early development of the science. The difficulty making progress at first because of ancient taboos against desecration of the human body. Egyptian mummy-makers who contributed a good deal to the future knowledge of anatomy. Used to pack the bodies in salt, immerse them in honey, and coat them with wax. They got better at it later on. They'd extract the brains, open the body by incising the left flank, and remove the viscera except the heart. Double up the corpse, jam it into a jar filled with a salt solution where it would remain for several days. Dr. S. confesses the process reminds him of an old New England recipe for corning beef where you take a piece of brisket, weight it down in a crock full of water, salt, saltpeter, saleratus, and brown sugar, and in a month it's ready.

After the epidermis and fat were dissolved, the body would be taken from the jar, worked over, straightened out, and dried. The cavities and skull were packed with herbs and myrrh, and the whole thing smeared with a paste of resin and fat and wrapped in bandages. None of this, says Dr. S., will be found in Gray's or Grant's, but he thinks it should be thrown in in case the dropouts decide on embalming.

Then it was on to Aristotle, the father of anatomy, whose conclusions were drawn from studies of lower animals and probably not from actual dissection. Warming up, Dr. S. tells us about Herophilus of Chalcedon, who, in 300 B.C., worked his way into the brain and recognized it as the seat of intellect, of Erasistratus, who had a theory that the whole body was made of tubes, and another Greek, Galen, who took apes and hogs apart and wrote an inaccurate but convincing anatomy book. Da Vinci did thirty dissections until the pope made him stop. But it was Andreas Vesalius, a Belgian, who was responsible for modern descriptive anatomy. In 1543, he published the first comprehensive analysis of the human body based on detailed observation. Vesalius stole his cadavers when he had to, employed a naked attendant when he needed a live subject for his "pubic, ah, public demonstrations," proved that Galen "knew an ape's ass from its elbow and nothing more," managed to stay out of the clutches of the Inquisition although someone started a nasty rumor that he got religion "after some thumb-screwing by the Church," and went on a pilgrimage to Jerusalem, all because he supposedly opened a woman's chest to determine the cause of death and found the heart still beating. Dr. S. says that even though Vesalius confused nerves and ligaments, he was, let there be no mistake about it, the first anatomist to quarrel with the existence of pores in the interventricular septum.

He is into the resurrectionists, who snatched bodies for medical schools before laws made it legal. Contrary to popular opinion, he says brightly, and what we may have seen in the movies, they didn't raise the coffin. They simply dug down by the head, broke a hole into the front end of the box, yanked the body out through the hole with a hook sunk under the chin "which raised hell with the thyroid cartilage, not to mention the depressor anguli oris," replaced the dirt, and rearranged the stone and flowers on top. Other

ways to get bodies. In Massachusetts, in 1784, the Act of
Dueling law. The point was to discourage dueling, but it
also allowed the bodies of slain duelists to be turned over to
the anatomists. Sometimes they'd charge the winner with
murder, hang him, and let the schools have at him. Dr. S.
mentions someone named Cunningham, "Old Cunny," they
called him, who was a notorious snatcher of the 1800s. He
used to dress his stolen cadavers in old clothes, sit them up
on the buggy seat with him, and admonish them loudly
for drunken behavior. Once, he tried to ship a body long
distance over the rails, but the express company opened the
box and sent it back to Cunny. Medical students used to
put him on, and to get back at them he once snatched the
body of a smallpox victim and had it sent to the school.
He was delighted when a number of students contracted
the disease. His widow had the last laugh. She sold his body
to the Medical College of Ohio for $15. William Burke,
Dr. S. informs us, got up to £14 a body. Then he quotes a
Dr. Donald Forman of Northwestern University Medical
School, who says that the approximate value of all chemicals
in the average adult human body is $3.50. Dr. Forman says
this represents a 257 percent increase over the same
chemicals' estimated Depression-era value of $.98 in 1936.

The Medical College of Ohio again, which figures
because Old Cunny was from Cincinnati. Before he was
President, Dr. S. says, Benjamin Harrison went to the
college to look for the stolen body of a friend. Instead, he
found the body of his father, U.S. Senator John Scott
Harrison. The public furor that went up helped stimulate
anatomy acts that allowed universities to have unclaimed
bodies from asylums and almshouses.

Today, Dr. S. emphasizes, medical schools do not buy

bodies, and it is now possible to donate all or parts of one's body to schools and hospitals under the Uniform Anatomical Gift Act. Fifty percent of the bodies at this school have been donated, he says proudly; the rest come from state institutions. There is, however, a shortage of anatomic material. Dr. S. blames the funeral directors' lobby for stressing the therapeutic value of funerals and invoking visions of Nazi experiments on humans, and the relative affluence that enables virtually everyone with a friend or insurance policy to be buried. In the Depression, enough unclaimed bodies turned up in the city morgues to supply the needs of the medical schools. Dr. S. characterizes the donation of a body as a noble gift because dissection is the only way future physicians can gain the basic information essential to the diagnosis and treatment of disease, and he sees it as a way to beat the high cost of dying. While the nearest of kin must bear all the expenses of cremation or private burial, he explains, the remains may be buried without expense to the donor or to his estate in cemeteries owned by the medical schools. What is gained, he asks, when a body is placed in a casket, buried in the ground, and allowed to disintegrate? Better that the dead should teach the living. There are no religious prohibitions, he says, save that the dissection be carried out with scientific objectivity and that the remains be respectfully interred and not disposed of as ordinary refuse.

An informal survey has revealed that the vast majority of physicians do not practice what they preach to their patients about the need for donating bodies and organs for research and transplantation.

Their reticence to do so, some suggest, is inappropriate

43

at a time when both the number of bodies donated for anatomical study and organs for grafting are in critically short supply.

The survey disclosed that few doctors are members of hospital organ banks, organizations formed to promote the procurement, preservation, and distribution of tissues and organs for transplantation. Few doctors have willed their bodies to medical schools and of those who are interested in performing this unique service to mankind, most are more willing to donate organs than the whole body

"It's the old story," commented Professor William J. Curran of Harvard's Department of Legal Medicine. "The physician is usually the last one to get a cancer checkup. My impression is that many doctors would be willing to donate their organs rather than their bodies and I think a lot of this stems back to their days in anatomy class. There's a lot of denial in the medical community, you know."

Dr. S. tells us that for centuries dissection was a dangerous procedure, but that we shouldn't worry about contracting any kind of disease or infection because modern embalming techniques have wiped out any problems. Several gallons of formaldehyde, glycerol, borax, and dye are injected into the arteries. The common sites of injection are the armpits, the neck, and the groin. The solution spreads through the vascular system and reaches the tissues, and the blood displaced by it is drained off by opening a vein at the place of injection. The abdominal wall is incised and gases are allowed to escape and fluids aspirated. Hollow organs are perforated, as is the diaphragm, and in the case of cadavers for dissection latex is pumped into the arteries, puffing them out for easy identification and handling.

Dr. S. has one last thing to say, and that is that we not ask the identity of the cadavers. They are owed their anonymity, he says. They are paupers and professors, and it makes not a bit of difference whether we know who they were. He urges us to approach the investigation of the dead with dignity and reverence. He says he is not telling us this out of any belief that the body is the repository of the immortal soul, for that is a personal thing. Respect, he says, is owed rather on sound moral-humanistic grounds. He dismisses us to the laboratory, and there is a disquieting overtone to his words as he tells us that for a generation which has been crying out for relevance here it is, at last.

I am aware of the gross lab before I get inside. The door-knobs are greasy to the touch, and there is a penetrating, pungent odor of preservative in the hall. In the room, the bodies. There are twenty-five or thirty of them, most of them white and old, with gray tufts of pubic hair that draw gazes like a magnet because we are all crotch-fixated from Eden, and the hair is on dead people, and death and sex preoccupy Americans more than anything else. So here it is, combined, in this room full of dead, helpless, pulseless, defenseless, breathless, maybe victorious people, all lying naked and stiff and wet and glistening on hard, black tables, their heads and hands swathed in bundles of cloth to prevent drying. That, says Dr. M., who has taken over this phase of instruction, is because we won't get into the hand until late March, and the face not until sometime in April, which is just as well because they didn't seem as dead masked as they were. There are skeletons hanging in corners of the huge, high-ceilinged room, bright lights overhead, deep sinks, wheeled, plastic-lined baskets near each table; buckets hanging from the tables, hacksaws,

wooden mallets, bone forceps, scalpels, squirt bottles filled
with preservative, rolls of paper towel on wooden tables,
blackboards against windows whose lower halves are
painted black on the street and campus side, and this is
just as well, too. Outside, it is crystal cold, and the hard
sunlight that streams through the tops of the windows does
not warm but is enveloped by the controlled chill of the
room and neutralized. Winter's dormancy victorious.

Standing on a high stool among bodies that would not
rest in peace, Dr. M. says we are to go at it region by
region. Abdomen, thorax, upper limb, vertebral column
and vertebrae, head and neck, perineum and pelvis, lower
limb, and forget the sugar, spice, and everything nice
because we'll know soon enough, if we didn't already, that
Avicebron was right when he said that man was a carcass
fouled and trodden. He says we will work four students to
a body. Two will dissect one area, two another, and then
all swap information at the end of the day. There will be an
hour lecture each lab day, followed by six hours in the lab,
with review lectures once a week. He talks about the
architectural plan of the body, the intricate piece of
machinery, the engineering marvel, the highest product of
the evolutionary process. He says it will take us about 150
hours to break it all down. A crash course in demolition. He
says he shouldn't have to go into that the body is a large
unit made up of lesser ones, that cells form tissues, tissues
organs, and organs and other parts make systems, and that
these, it goes without saying, are the skeletal, muscular,
digestive, circulatory, respiratory, integumentary, nervous,
urinary, reproductive, and endocrine.

He says we shouldn't look for any more because anatomy
is anatomy, although Neanderthal man is strikingly different from Homo sapiens, as we all know, with an average

brain size of 1,450 cubic centimeters as against modern
man's 1,350, but then there is — he is sure we are all
familiar with this — the middle Acheulian hand-ax culture,
not significantly divergent from modern man in anatomical
features. He dashes through, with proper apologies for
taking us over such familiar ground, human topography
and map reading and planes and cavities, superior, inferior,
anterior, posterior, quadrants, cranial, medial, caudal, proxi-
mal, midsagittal, frontal, transverse, the dorsal and ventral
separated by the diaphragm. He advises us to approach our
work as geologists seeking to establish a stratigraphic
framework, and that just as Department of the Interior
surveyors probe large masses of sedimentary rocks beneath
the Atlantic Coastal Plain and Shelf to assess the petroleum
possibilities of this unexplored province, so, too, should we
probe these, and he sweeps a hand out, who will teach us
in silence, who reach back to the Australopithecines of the
early Pleistocene — not for petroleum, of course, he wants
to make it clear.

*Some medical students, psychiatrists say, are overly con-
cerned about their own health and well-being, an attitude
that may be linked to a fear of death.*

*"The average medical student in this country comes from
a family in the middle or upper middle class," Dr. Charles
H. Goodrich, a community medicine specialist at Mount
Sinai Hospital, told the First Euthanasia Conference of the
Euthanasia Educational Fund. "He has probably lived a
sheltered life in regard to death, questions of death, certain
physical representations of death, and frequently he enters
the medical school with the idealistic notion that what he
wants to do is help people. And the first thing he is presented with is a cadaver, a dead body. Now, that should be*

47

the beginning of his education about death. Yet I don't know of any medical school with the exception of isolated experiments which has on any concerted basis tried to deal with this first contact with death. Those of you who have seen a cadaver that has been in cold storage for months will understand that this student not only unlearns any feelings he may have about death, but represses them rapidly. He usually assigns the cadaver a nickname to permit him to deal with it as a thing rather than as a person. His repressed feelings come out as a kind of gallows humor usual among medical students. This inadequate training for death is then reinforced: in the second year, the student has his first encounter with the autopsy, where the patient has so recently died that it's hard to deny he was a person. The only help in terms of his feelings is being taught to concentrate his attention upon the organs rather than the person. By the time he gets to his clinical training, when for the third time he sees the human body being assaulted by the knife on the surgical table, it is not surprising that he is detached from it as having anything to do with human life or death. The best we can say is that we have tried to train him in something called detached concern."

The students are young and exceptionally bright. It is boasted that they are the best. The men wear their hair long, with beards and moustaches, and dress in old jeans, war surplus coveralls, sweatshirts, pajama tops, boots, and loafers without socks. A few have on white lab coats with red fists stenciled on the back. One wears a black rubber apron with a pair of rubber gloves in the pocket. The woman are in baggy dungarees and men's shirts, and the three of them have their foreheads ringed with Indian bands. A new breed of doctors in the making, more socially conscious, it is said, more interested in staffing storefront clinics and fighting the university's emphasis on research, being against the AMA and not interested in taking care of some debutante's crabs or charging $35 just to wrap an Ace bandage around a kid's sprained wrist. A far cry from those who passed through here in years gone by — or are they, will they be when it is over, when the ass-busting days and nights in labs, classrooms, dorms, and hospital wards are but distasteful memories? When their dues are paid, will they succumb to the lures of lucrative solo practice and forget their drum-thumping for health care as a right for everyone regardless of ability to pay, or will they have no choice as the increasing sophistication and demands of a consumer no longer awed by the godlike presence of The Doctor redefine his role, deemphasize his professionalism, and force him to be more responsive to the needs of society?

We are assigned to our cadavers, I and my partners to a short, slight female with shriveled breasts and milk-white skin and crinkly gray hair caught in the folds of the head wrapping. As I look at her lying in state, without the security of a coffin or clothing or the vault of a cathedral, unstimulating in her dead, aged nudity, examined curiously now but soon to be brought to a second end, her cloth-covered head like a white beehive propped upon a wooden block, her legs together, arms stiffly down by her sides, her mind mute and blind, her body drained, I ask myself, because man is unconsciously convinced of his own immortality, where she has gone. Does she continue to exist, not as a woman but in some other organic or inorganic form? If her soul is standing by and knows what we are about to do, is it saddened that its old home is to be torn down, or is it uncaring because its new dwelling place is

49

bright and beautiful? Or is there no one standing here but
students and instructors, and she as well as her body is truly
dead. I ask one of my partners what he thinks she would
say were she watching us and he answers directly, "She'd
probably say, man, I've still got it. Everyone's still trying
to get into me."

Dr. M. distributes scalpels, probes, forceps, small scissors,
and sheets outlining the lesson plan for the next few months.
Two members of each team are to begin with the surface
anatomy of the thorax, the pectoral region, and the thoracic
and upper abdominal walls. The other two are to start on
the surface anatomy of the thigh, skin the lower extremity,
and begin the femoral sheath. He picks up a small plastic
squirt bottle from the head of one table, points it at the
cadaver and squeezes out a stream of preservative, playing
it over the body as though he is at an outdoor barbecue
squirting lighter fluid over charcoal. He tells us we should
reflect only that skin over the area to be studied because
skin, the largest organ in the human body, he reminds us,
affords the best protection against drying of the parts
beneath. We are to see that our charges do not dry out, and
a few squirts from the bottle every so often, he demon-
strates again, will keep everything nice and moist. When
we are done for the afternoon, he says, we should give the
remains a good dousing, lay paper towels over the underlying parts, and if we've left skin flaps attached along one
border so that they can be folded back over what is beneath, why then we could close up shop, so to speak, with a
clear conscience.

We open our anatomy atlases, prop them against the
cadavers' heads, and listen intently as Dr. M. advises us
that before we do any cutting we get the lay of the land
and, with apologies to the ladies, this means that in the

pectoral region we are to first palpate the chests of the cadavers as though we are palpating the chests of our girlfriends, identify the bony points, the prominent medial ends of the clavicle, the sternum, the sternal angle marking the junction of the manubrium and corpus sterni, the position of the nipple which usually corresponds to the fourth intercostal space, four inches or so from the sternum, in the female atop a rounded mound made up of superficial fascia containing the mammary gland, and us *Playboy* readers ought to know what that is, all right. We lay our hands on the flattened chest, my partner as gingerly as I, it is pleasing to note, and it is the same as when some Japanese doctors in Tokyo whispered among themselves and chuckled and got me to go with them to a bath, and I knew they were standing outside the door wondering whether I would go through with it while I stripped naked and let a girl bathe and then massage me with her hands and feet while she kept looking into my eyes with an expressionless face.

We begin, loudly at first, shouting questions at Dr. M. or the roving instructors, slicing into leathery skin. Wondering who she is, what killed her, who had loved her, I do a superficial dissection of the pectoral region, making a chest flap, tracing around the nipple so it will stay perched on the fascia beneath when the flap is pulled back, cutting through the deeper fascia to expose the pectoralis major, muscle that looks like flank steak, chunks of fat layering the area like the soft salt pork in baked beans, and it is like cutting through linoleum. Stopping to turn the pages of the atlas and peer inside, matching the color plates to the body and suddenly realizing, with some dismay, that the neatly mapped textbook is as near to the real thing as a Vargas nude is to the model.

Dr. M. advises us not to be discouraged, that Mother
Nature hasn't read the textbook, in fact hasn't taken the
course, and that people don't always have everything in the
right place and even if they did we probably wouldn't find
it all because there are just some things that cannot be seen
in a fixed body, only in a fresh one. Cutting, I ask silently
does this hurt? and if it does I am sorry. How frustrating it
must be if her consciousness remains intact and she knows
what we are about and can do nothing. Like a stroke victim
who cannot move or speak but who understands and sees.
Like being accused falsely and no one will hear you. Death
checkmates. Had she died before she could apologize? Or
someone to her? Had she been fulfilled? Had she died
before her body died? Had she never won by winning and
now had won by losing? When the circus performer has
defied death and beat it on the high wire, the spotlight that
has held him for the crowd is extinguished and quickly
beamed on again to capture another act. Her act, too, is
ended and yet the light still holds her. How can she rest in
peace?

It goes slowly. Cutting and probing, tissue by tissue,
hands chilled as when trying to work partially thawed
hamburger from the freezer into a meatloaf, the medicinal
stench of formaldehyde rising up and smarting the eyes;
reflecting the skin, checking the underlying fascia, picking
it away tediously, trying not to harm the structures
embedded in it, dropping bits and pieces of tissue into the
buckets. Organs and muscles go into the plastic-lined
barrel, as I wonder which bucket gets the lumps of red
latex that pop from every severed artery, stopping for a
look and a probe at the male cadaver on the next table, they
looking at ours, identifying each muscle, each vein, each
nerve and artery, tempted to forget what cannot be found

because after all, we tell each other, parading knowledge of a sort, there are like 60,000 miles of blood vessels in this lady, along with 600 muscles, 2 million sweat glands, 35 million gastric glands, and 12 billion nerve cells in the brain alone to worry about when we get there, and hey not to mention 200 bones and joints, 6 billion fibers, and 72 feet of nerves in a square inch of the skin we have knifed into, but brought to our senses by Dr. M., who keeps showing up at each table to tell us not to be careless because the more thoroughly we clean an area the easier it will be later on when we are in deeper.

It is over for the day, and we have invaded her privacy. Laid open to some depth, her chest and leg in tatters, she is a poorly dressed scarecrow, a nameless, faceless instructor stretched stiffly on this slab, shamelessly exposing herself, sharing her deepest secrets with total strangers, allowing us to see what neither she nor any of her loved ones could ever have seen. I think of a jingle about Victorians and how they would react if they could see her. "They asked no social questions, they probed no hidden shame, they never talked obstetrics when the little stranger came." She and all the others are methodically moistened with the squirt bottles, paper towel is layered on, the skin flaps carefully rearranged but not fitting anymore. We cover them with huge sheets of cellophane, then wrap them in purple cloth. It is as though we have undone someone's handiwork, have second thoughts and are trying to restore the finish we have marred, or, knowing that we cannot, are trying to hide what we have put asunder so callously.

Later, on the subway going home, the smell of formaldehyde sticking to my nostrils, I feel strangely exhilarated, and somewhat shaken, as if I have just cheated on my wife for the first time. Smug or guilty, I cannot tell

53

which. I look into bored faces, trying to arrest a pair of
eyes, wanting to shout out, hey, if only you knew what I've
been doing you wouldn't look so damned dull. At home, it
grows dark and I thumb through the anatomy book. Brute
memory. Jargon. Fifth costal cartilage, serratus anterior,
rectus sheath, tendinous intersection; origin of the obliquus
internus, fleshy from the outer half of Pouppart's ligament,
anterior two-thirds of the middle lip of the iliac crest and
posterior lamella of the lumbar fascia; its insertion, crest,
and pectineal line of os pubis with transversalis muscle —
forming the conjoined tendon, part of the posterior
boundary of the external abdominal ring — cartilages of
the three lower ribs, and by an aponeurosis, which splits
for its upper three-fourths to rectus muscle, into linea
alba. . . . Deep into it until snapped to by yellow smudges
on the slick, white pages and I think of her again as her
and not it, cuts and wounds swathed in bandages, never to
heal. I wonder how it would be if I went back to the school
at this late hour, let myself into the lab and stood alone in
that room, and I know I could never.

The course wears on. Revulsion sublimated in the work
and patois but suddenly resurfacing. Like the pain that lies
dully beneath the morphine until the drug wears off. A
student waves a scalpel while I lean on the swathed head
with my elbows, in calculated cool, listening to his com-
mentary on the Super Bowl. "Put down that knife, son,"
says Dr. M., ducking. "You're among friends."

The stench is familiar now, and I am more comfortable.
It is like the apprehension that nags when a new job is
begun and new friends are to be made, and in two weeks or
less it is as though you've always done it, always known
them.

Lower abdominal wall and inguinal canal, introduction

to the arm, forearm, and hand. Finish femoral sheath, canal, triangle, and adductors.

"What's the matter, can't find the fascial midline?" asks Dr. M., approaching a table where four harried students are attacking an obese cadaver. "Forget it. Just dig that stuff out or you'll be here next semester, too. I don't want any of that 'See these hands, they saved your life' crap. Get in there. Go. You're not surgeons yet, you're high-class butchers. Don't pat yourself too hard. If that guy down at the corner market could have gotten up the dough he might have made it into a classy place like this."

We pull her arms out from her sides with effort, and I listen, jaws clenched, for the creak, but there is none. We shove boards under the shoulders and stretch the arms out on them and tie them at the wrists to the board. Dr. M. drones. Identify and clean the cephalic vein. It's in the present area of dissection in the groove between the upper border of the pectoralis major and the deltoid. Watch it. It disappears from view behind the clavicle in the delto-pectoral triangle. I got it, I got it, someone shouts. Globs of fat, like chicken fat, removed with fingers that feel for the deltoid branch of the thoraco-acrominal artery, which, Dr. M. reminds us, accompanies the cephalic laterally, supplying the anterior border of the deltoid. Veins and nerves stringy, buried in fat and muscle and fascia, a pulpy computer with its case removed to expose the maze of wire.

Back and dorsal shoulder, and we turn her on her face and she is rickety and slippery. Hip joint, gluteal region and hamstrings. Hands groping inside, the sartorius muscle reminds me of a chunk of dark turkey drumstick, and Dr. M. tells us of the woman who telephoned to ask for the dental plate of her sister whose body had been donated to the school, and of the students who, at the close of a day's dissecting, inserted a severed penis into the vagina of a coed's cadaver, covered her up, and the next morning, when the girl uncovered the body, how she was only momentarily shaken and delivered a great putdown, "Looks like one of you guys really left here in a hurry last night." Do you help your patients, doctor, the old man, the old woman, because they cannot help themselves, or do you do it because you are trained to do it? Do you get angry at patients for being sick?

A researcher from the university was discussing his recent project. He waved a hand to the projectionist and said, "And now, slide, this funny little group with congestive heart failure."

He was interrupted by a question from the floor.

"Doctor, were the prisoners you used in the study cooperative?"

"Oh yes," he replied. "Very. They loved it, actually. They got paid, you know, and they could use the money to buy candy and gum."

Lateral neck, pleura, superior mediastinum, and pericardium. A student across the room frees the sternum, ties a string to an end and raises the breastbone by pulling the string through an overhead light. "Hey, man, that's engineering," says another. Introduction to the cervical fascia. Outline triangles of the neck. Posterior triangle. Interesting area. Thyroid gland. "If you go in," says Dr. M., "it's going to be lost to you. Don't skin it too much or you'll dehydrate and you've got to come back to it later. Look for the external jugular. It's an invaluable landmark." Someone finds it first and says so, and someone else says, hey, give that man a box of balls. An exasperating dissection filled with lots of fat, and fibrous nerves and connective tissue look alike. Dense, but with diligent picking, says Dr. M., we'll get through. "But don't be discouraged. We'll be in the heart after vacation."

We attend a surgical film. It is about surgical approaches to the hip joint and is produced by the Veterans' Administration. There are cheers and a few hisses when the narrator tells us that a team from the University of California Medical School is involved. There is laughter when he says, "Before we go on with the operation let's look closely at these parts in our drawing." Laughter again when he tells us to notice that the patient is lying in the prone position.

In the lab a student says, "She couldn't have done much necking," as he struggles to bend the neck to get at lateral dissection. Hard work, no give. Students leaning on foreheads and faces of cadavers as they discuss the next move. Heads uncovered, and ours looks like the face had done isometrics before it died. She is old, nutcracker face, chin turned up to meet downturned and flattened nose. I do not know her. We move her again and her ripped skin flaps heavily. A student wants to take home a piece of bone for a keepsake and a girl admonishes him, "These people appreciate being buried with all their parts." Later, she cuts herself with a scalpel and someone tells her to watch out, she'll get cadaveritis.

Vacation, and back to an exam. "The following questions are offered to help you assess your progress and intended to help you relate your knowledge to function and to clinical application, and to give you some familiarity with the kinds of information sought in state and national board examinations for medical licensure. Give the course, branches, and function of a typical thoracic nerve. The attachments, innervation, blood supply, and actions of the pectoralis major. Describe a possible route of collateral circulation from the subclavian artery to the vessels of the leg if the aorta is congenitally constricted or narrowed by disease. List the coverings and contents of the spermatic cord. If you are seated and cross right leg over the left leg, what muscles would be principally involved in executing this movement?"

In the lab, I look at the heart, brownish-red and hard, for the first time, nestled in the chest cavity. Sections of ribs, with muscle adhering, broken off, like spare ribs. Lecture by Dr. L., a crowd-pleaser who calls students "kids" and the heart "headquarters." He stops by our table, chides me for being too meticulous. He removes the scalpel blade and blunts away at the juicy fat on the heart surface. "You haven't got the time," he says. "This really is like masturbating, you know."

The heart is out, and holding it in my hand it is cold, and I think of hard-hearted Hannah the vamp of Savannah and heart of my heart and Valentine cards and love, courage and the strength of kings and lions, and someone sings softly, "I left my heart in Philip Blaiberg." I look closer at this stilled engine that has pumped tons of life in its lifetime and I think of the Living Theatre and its obsession with nudity, its actors who rip off their clothes and scream of honesty and this is the way it is and I say no it isn't. This is it, this heart, this cadaver torn open for all to see, recesses that have been hidden all through life; but then, as I hold the heart and squint at it I have my doubts about even this piece of truth, because it may be filled with latex.

Dr. M. is in high gear, telling us, come off it, Denton, the name of the game isn't surgery, it's systematic destruction. Get your hands in, you're the worms of Job. You're not going to be sued by that one so don't be dainty. It's too bad you have to learn all this stuff, isn't it? Should have all been chiropractors, learned it in six months. Bright kids like you would learn it in two. You've got a textbook body there, boy, open it up. Come on, lady, look at it. It's not pornographic on the inside. Remember, the lab cadaver is going out of style some day. Be a historical oddity, so get in there before it's too late, enjoy your necromania.

The National Institutes of Health has awarded a contract to the University of Colorado Medical Center to develop and evaluate an innovative course in gross anatomy.

The pilot project highlights student participation in the presentation of course material as well as the study and use of audiovisual techniques. It differs from traditional instruction in gross anatomy in that each student will study in depth and dissect only one of the four major regions of the cadaver. Pairs of students, using audiovisual methods, will present some aspects of the dissection to the entire class. In addition, fewer hours will be involved, and both beginning and advanced medical students will be intermixed in the class.

"If the method is successful," a spokesman said, "it could affect favorably undergraduate, graduate, and continuing physician education. Schools will be able to train more students in gross anatomy in less time, with the same or less faculty, and with closer contact between teacher and pupil."

We finish the heart, which has been dissected open, washed in the sink of its fibrin and sludgy blood, simple intricacy. Gallows humor picking up, out of necessity to offset the grim work, or something deep-cached, inadmissible. "Here, catch," says a student, lobbing a heart across the room. "How about a transplant?" asks another. Someone

else says, "Cough," inserting a finger up under an
esophagus. A girl walks into the lab and approaches one of
the students. Unruffled in this place of split-open and frayed
cadavers, she discusses something in a low voice, and I am
angry because she is oblivious in this privileged preserve,
because she has come into this house of carnal knowledge
with that same air of detachment that teenage girls assume
so well at a dance. Screw her.

"Let's juice her up," says someone loudly, squirting preservative. It sloshes on his partner's feet and he yells, "Hey,
man, what are you trying to do, preserve my balls?" The
slosher says, "No, just want to keep 'em cool." How
melancholy at a funeral, how light-hearted here, and I
wonder which is real, or are both displays a fraud?

Lungs and posterior mediastinum. Slice through the
ligamentum arteriosum, through the cartilaginous trachea
a few inches above where it bifurcates. Questions fired from
the roving instructors. What nerves supply the larynx?
Show me the manubrium of the sternum, boy. The right
bronchus begins opposite which thoracic disk? Wrong. Free
the pulmonary veins from the what? What is it that you're
going to separate from the thoracic wall? It's like unhook-
ing the hoses before removing the motor, and the lungs are
out and lying between the knees of our subject, spongy, the
bronchi twiggy roots. We try to inflate them with a bicycle
pump but have no luck. Study them. Interlobar fissures.
Groove for the first rib. Dissection of the hili. Is there an
eparterial bronchus in the right lung? Did she smoke? Yes.
Right.

Radiology lecture. "When you look at the chest radiologi-
cally you are basically looking at arteries," says Dr. T. He
tells us that a skilled radiologist can tell whether the
X-rayed subject is a blond or brunette. Slide. Skeleton.

Chest. "Here's a brunette who wears braids. The coiled hair in pigtails massed along the shoulders is dense enough to stop the rays." He says, "I'm not orally fixated, but all sorts of interesting clinical conditions can be observed in the boobs. Okay. Who likes boobs? Who likes blonds? Is this a man or woman? Right. The areola shadow. Terrific. You can take your boards next week. Okay, now a rapid tour over the bronchial tree. Note that the right diaphragm is slightly higher than the left. This, slide, happens to be a publisher of some magazine. *Time* or *Life*. I don't recall who, but he had emphysema. You'll see this is supernormal, which is what the editor of one of those magazines should be, I suppose."

Finish posterior mediastinum, begin ventral shoulder and axilla. Amputate at mid-thigh, popliteal fossa, anterior and lateral leg and dorsum of foot. To the arm and elbow, hand, plantar foot. It is beginning to grate, like Ravel's "Bolero." Our lady is an only to us. Like the only in only 20 kilotons, not a full-scale thermonuclear explosion. Or only 1,279 deaths from malnutrition. Or the overall death rate for the 300 cases was 0.33%, there being only one death. She is 65% oxygen, 18% carbon, 10% hydrogen, 3% nitrogen, 1.5% calcium, 1% phosphorus, and 1.5% other. Or she was, and if that was all then it makes no sense.

> Resolved, That the depredation of morals consequent upon the disinterment of bodies and the annihilation of the bitter feelings and sentiments that usually follow a long familiarity with the horrid dissection room, renders it no doubtful question whether medical colleges are not productive of more mischief than benefit to the country.
>
> — Citizens' Resolution,
> Painesville, Ohio, 1845

To the dorsal forearm and hand, the joints of the lower extremity, and she is a mess, limbs severed and sawed. Some clown has positioned a loose leg between her thighs, the toes pointed toward her head. I feel a light touch on my shoulder and turn to see a white, bony hand dangling bits of skin and stringy veins and nerves, clutching at me, and I swat at it in panic knocking it to the floor, and someone says, hey, cut the shit, and everyone laughs then grimaces as a student raises a disconnected leg with its curled toenails and yellowed sole, holds it in front of his mouth and screws up his face in a fiendish expression, making as though to take a bite. Near the windows a girl in baggy PJs holds high an amputated hand, its middle finger rigid, extended, the others folded down, and someone yells right on, Freda, and someone else says you mean right up, and another remarks yeah, up hers, and someone says the fist would fit better, to which is added how do you know? and Freda says fuck you, and everyone cheers.

Against the hacksaws' rasp it is the Bruins and the Rangers, getting shitfaced, balling, the party at Mammy-Jammer's, Ralph Nader looking for volunteers for six weeks, 100,000 doctors have quit smoking, beer. And there's the little mother right in there you extensor pollicis brevis you, and someone singing, come to me my melanoma baby, reciting mnemonics to identify the carpal bones, Never Lower Tilly's Pants, Mother Might Come Home. Did you hear the one about the doctor examining the teenage girl? He puts the stethoscope on her chest and says, big breaths, and she says, yeth thir and I'm only thirteen. How was that belly dancer show? Abdominal. Hello, Doctor? I'm terribly embarrassed but did I leave my panties in your examining room? No. Oh, come to think of it, maybe it was at the dentist's. This guy runs into a doctor's crowded waiting room and he's yelling, Doc, Doc, my cock, my cock. Just a minute, sir, says the nurse, aghast. Please use a more delicate term. Okay, says the guy, my finger, my finger. That's better, she says. What's wrong with it? I can't piss through it, he screams. Hey, there's this guy lying in a sack at the hospital and he's really pissed about all the tests and crap. . . .

An argument breaks out at the next table over who should have the patella, extricated with difficulty, for a keychain or a charm bracelet. "Send it to Joe Namath," says someone, grumbling, as he fights his way through bands of cartilage and fiber and tissue to get at a knee joint. "Look what happened to the fat ballet dancer," says another, pushing a severed foot against the table so that the toes bend into a grotesque position. "I don't think I'm going to be anything when I grow up," says a girl, ruefully. "I should have majored in arts and letters."

Dr. M. grabs up a wrist from a table and tells us that plenty of tendons cross it, it's a busy street. Look, see the beautiful tendinous arch here. Here's the hamate, and the hamate has a hook on it. See? Three muscles form the boundary of the snuffbox. See? This isn't just some stuff hung on a cadaver. It's hung on your shoulders. Get in there. Do some plumbing or carpentry or whatever your trade is. What do you tell students about the hand? Nothing. You scare them, that's what you do. There are only three specialists alive I'd trust to operate on my hands, and none of them are in this city. Warning. If we've anything left of the hand when we're through dissecting then we haven't done it. Look. See the hook of the hamate. See the pisiform. It's beautiful.

We are into the peritoneum and abdominal topography. Mobilize the intestines. Begin abdominal circulation. The stomach, portal system, spleen. The inner sanctum. Liver, biliary tract, pancreas and duodenum. Spermatic cord and testis. Identify the ejaculatory duct, cut into the mons pubis, identify the clitoris, the twigs of posterior labial veins. Slice open a penis that looks like a cold, blackened frankfurt, and who'd want to screw after all this. Dr. T. lectures on liver trauma, which is rising. "This one, slide, is from an accident right on our own expressway. This fellow, slide, did well enough to go on to jail."

We remove the large intestine and take it to the sink, fix it to a spigot and turn on the water. It bulges, bursts, and sprays us. "What's the matter, didn't you ever stuff sausages before?" asks Dr. M. One student has draped a length of bowel around his neck. "Welcome to the Aloha Restaurant," he says, bowing. Gallbladder slit open, green inside, it has two small stones. Liver removed, cold calves'. "Best thing to do," says Dr. M., "is to get a pound or two at the market and dissect that at home for practice." Ours is overly large and heavy and slices cleanly with a scalpel. Stomach opened. Chalky material inside, ridges prominent, like tripe. Intestines like Christmas tree tinsel, limp, once full and fat. A student with a lump of red latex hidden in his hand walks over to a friend, coughs into his hand and startles him with mock blood. We find an amber-colored, semihard piece of something stuck into a kidney and no one can identify it. "Hey, guys," says someone, "Dr. S. is walking around and he's got a book that gives the cause of death of all the cadavers, and he's asking questions." Dr. S. asks us and we tell him atherosclerosis. He shakes his head, disgusted. "You're going to make great allergists," he says, and walks away. A student activist suggests putting a cadaver on every committee, and someone else feels it is such a nice day we ought to take the bodies out on the lawn where the secretaries are sunning themselves only a few feet away and finish out there where it is spring. Resurrection time. In here there is none, at least none that we can see, only Dr. M. saying, "Get your face into that anus. Get your finger into that rectum or you'll put your foot in it. Get it in there if you're going to get anything out of this course. One finger in the rectum, two in the vagina, and remember you're not making a social call." Into the hardened vagina and beyond with knife and fingers probing, seeking more than what that old gang of mine, if they could see me now, used to sing, when much to her surprise her belly began to rise and out of her cunt came an Indian runt with his ass between his eyes. I unravel her sex, a grand tour, passing again through the mysterious and forbidden gateway I had traveled through once years before, before memory, and many times since, remembered, in an opposite direction, on different missions. We are tracing farther inward but we find nothing but what we are supposed to find and often not even that. I am disappointed. Dr. M. says, "Why anatomy? Ask it. Well, it's like this. It's nice to know what you're doing. Some goddamned idiot will suture a medial nerve to a tendon and it's good-bye Broadway, hello Skowhegan. That's all there is."

Lecture by Dr. S. "The professional anatomist is not merely someone who dissects cadavers. His field of interest is a broad one that involves the scrutiny of the structure of organisms at a number of levels of magnification. In the basic research laboratories he uses an electron microscope to study, in detail, subcellular organelles and macromolecules, going deeper than his knife can take him. His sophisticated equipment has a resolution of between 5 to 10 Angstrom units and the magnification is around 250,000 times. This deep-seeking is essential if we are to understand how

various systems funtion and mesh, how normal and pathological processes occur in cells and organs."

She is a heap, the hint of a human form. Only the neck
and head are left, a broken plaster bust, the rest crammed
into buckets and bags. Ruins of the dead. Our bodies lull
us into a false sense of security. They're but passing
travelers on a one-way trip from here to there, wherever
that might be.

"We might as well face it," says Dr. T. "We're going to
have to do the muscles of facial expression." We hiss. In
the lab, we expose the depressor anguli oris ("When it
contracts, you get a grin"), the buccinator ("Dizzy Gillespie
has a fantastic bux"), the masseter ("When you clench your
jaw"). Her features are now rubble, and with this last bit of
her individuality ruined she looks like every other cadaver
in the room. In the lecture hall, Dr. T. concludes with four
slides of a pretty girl's smile, a pleasant ending, but at the
same time it cannot hide, after what we have seen, what lies
beneath that lovely face, behind that blemish-free skin and
capped white teeth, a grinning skull no different from
what we have left in the lab. It is like the plush nightclub
when all the lights are on and the cleaning ladies are at
work, and what shows are the snags in the rug, the nicks in
the furniture, the paint streaks on the walls. It is being
where the dirty dishes are stacked in a fancy restaurant, or
sitting next to the waitresses' station where their complaints
and mocking remarks about the customers are overheard. In
one sense, I am pleased with this view of reality that makes
all men brothers. In another, I am sorry I have seen it. For it
leaves me with a sense of loss. A sexual chase ended. The
bright promise of a lunar landing no more. Anticipation that
is more exciting than the act, and it can never again be the
same, to enjoy the morbid thrill I have associated with

closeness to the dead human body, the ultimate in expectation.

Scalp, removal of the brain, cranial and spinal meninges. Orbit. Ear. Parasagittal section of skull, nose, and parasinal sinuses. Larynx, trachea, and esophagus. "You can look for it but you won't find the back of the mind," says Dr. M., "even though you're supposed to be putting all this stuff there."

We dissect the eyelids and there is nothing inside, so we study the cavities and the diagrams in the atlas. Two of us hold the head on a block while one saws the top of the scalp. Bone dust and the smell of a woodshop. The top is pried off and we stand ready to catch the brain should it fall out. It does not, but droops liquidly. It is soft and pulpy, badly preserved, and we dump it into the bucket, this most magnificent achievement of biological evolution, a computer turned to jelly. The inside of the skull is smooth, mother-of-pearl. A student holds up his half head by the backbone and remarks it would be great in a torchlight parade to the stadium. At another table someone has a firmer brain, and he skins off a portion of the cerebellum and asks, "How do you like it, rare?"

It is over at last, and I know nothing more of death, only bones and bodies, the symbols of death, and about all I have done is join an exclusive club that will never forget these long days, that has overcome a built-in aversion to corpses by simply treating them as machinery. There is no understanding of death in the laboratory, though its form is there. That may come when we stand on the brink of the grave or it may not, but that is not important. What is more material is the dying, the relentless process by which we pass into extinction, often alone and helpless and despairing. The laboratory is rewarding for I have seen my inner physical self in the mirror of a cadaver. It has stamped out a fear. But it has not taught me nor these physicians-to-be anything about dying and may even have prevented many from ever learning about it. For the anatomy lab tends to deflect from humankind's ideal which is empathy. It would have been better if the cadavers we had dissected had been identified, if we had been told something about their past lives, their work, their illnesses, if we had had access to Dr. S.'s book detailing the causes of death. Then they would have been human beings, and the hardening process that goes on in the gross lab would not be transferred as easily to living people and to patients later on. Tempered and distorted by his experience, and somewhat arrogant now that he has reduced what once lived to a pile of offal, the fledgling physician often will treat his patients in the same cold, businesslike way he treated his cadaver. He will regard death and dying merely as inevitable and he will avoid the subject because it focuses on his inability to guarantee immortality. When he does face it he often will equate it with the symbolic death in the laboratory or the morgue, and that is not pleasant to contemplate, or he will subject his dying patient to long and costly medical and mechanical procedures to prolong his life, sometimes needlessly.

Some, however, will hold a dying person's hand one day. They will talk openly about death to people who are dying and to relatives of the dying and they will learn that what the person whose time has come fears most is dying alone. They will understand that if they do not speak candidly to those who are leaving life, if they do not individualize their relationships, the despondency that comes with dying is magnified.

There is much that can be done to help a person to live until he dies. The concern should be more with how one dies, not with the fact that he has.

We were listening to a psychiatrist as he talked about the symbolism behind some child's drawings that had been projected on the screen.
"Forgive me for taking you through some rather boring artwork," he said, "but, really, the child didn't have you in mind when he did them, you know."

SURVEY

Dear Fellow Surgeon:
Much attention is being paid these days to the patient's right to die with dignity, to euthanasia, to whether a patient should be told he is dying, and to physicians' attitudes toward death and dying.
We would appreciate your responses to the questions below:
1. Has being a physician/surgeon had any effect on your attitude toward death and dying? What has facing death in your practice done to or for you?

A. After thirty-five years, I have become inured to death.

A. Maybe I'm more humane.

A. No one wants to die, not even me. I would be just as depressed as anyone else if I found out that I had a terminal illness. And I know that I'd rather die than be a paralyzed, bedridden patient.

A. No, but being a Christian has given me a special attitude.

A. I really couldn't say.

A. Yes, I'm more like Ted Williams, and I always swing for the fences when I'm faced with a bad one. This is one surgeon who doesn't like to strike out.

A. Yes. I worry more now than ever that I might die from an elective procedure.

A. Hell, no.

A. What attitude? The other day my own path report came back indicating a malignancy. I'm afraid.

A. Yes. It makes me realize how short life is, and how useless we doctors are.

A. Yes. That death may be a better alternative sometimes than dying.

A. Increases my sense of awe, wonder, and curiosity, and I'm not as afraid as I was when I was young.

A. It has made me colder.

A. No. In forty years of a busy practice I have never been able to completely divorce myself emotionally from my patients or their loved ones. Facing the patient's death and trying to explain it to his survivors is still an ordeal which I dread. This, despite the fact that I believe I have gotten fairly proficient at it.

A. Yes. I don't have the false hopes of the layman.

A. It has made me more conservative. I now realize that the more I operate, the more comers I take on, that my chances of killing someone on the table are better.

A. I know that I am a gateway to eternal damnation or eternal happiness.

A. Being a surgeon does not make me more fearful of dying, but it has made me more cognizant of the closeness of death; each day, when I operate, so many things can go wrong, so many times so close to death, a matter of so many missing heartbeats — so many things, unexpected — and this makes me think of death every single time a patient is lying on that table, and this is good.

A. Yes, I've developed a percentage outlook in risk-taking.

A. I believe I am very close to God's secrets.

A. No, unless the fact that it doesn't come any easier as the years go by can be considered an acquired attitude.

A. It certainly has. I have become more pious. I spend more time with relatives and with my patients.

A. Yes. Philosophical.

A. Yes. I've been the beneficiary of the wisdom of the survivors.

A. Yes. It has given me the means of fighting death by actions, physical actions, thus involving me in the process of my patient's dying in a way that a nonsurgeon cannot experience. I hate that famous picture of the helpless doctor at the dying child's bed. I truly hate that picture!

A. Yes. I've become more of a perfectionist, and that is the difference between life and death.

A. I've seen too much of it, and that's not good, baby.

A. Yes. Am in horror of lingering death.

A. Yes. I'm better able to predict when my own is coming.

A. I worry about some damned fool killing me with the wrong medication.

A. Yes. I go to all the wakes now, knowing that I'll be there for myself someday.

A. If I answered this question someone might get the impression I've seen a lot of death and that, therefore, I had killed my patients.

A. I suppose the answer to this is yes. I believe it would be best stated as a physician, not as a surgeon. Death, to me, is just as mysterious as life, but I do know that being a physician has made me appreciate all the good that death accomplishes, although this attitude maybe has come more by maturity than by profession.

A. Working with the dying is a strong experience for me, as contrasted to churchgoing, which is an abstract sort of experience.

A. Ask the geriatrician. He's the real pro.

A. Yes. I have seen so many good people die, that I can now readily accept capital punishment.

A. Yes. Being a surgeon has made me hope that I'll have a quick MI and then be cremated.

A. That's a question for lawyers and theologians.

"She was my cousin, and she was seventeen, and she was dying of leukemia. They didn't tell her, ever, but still she knew she was dying. She was in the hospital for the last year of her life, and she knew later on that she was dying, but we all knew it long before her. At first, she was very brave about it; then a couple of months after that she got very frightened of death. And in the last weeks, she didn't want to talk at all because she was very sick, at least that's what I think. She didn't want to talk about death or anything for that matter. And when she did it would be something like, I hope my mother gets insurance when I die. She just started to think about herself as a problem and in the very end was so ill that I didn't want to go in and see her, and I didn't go in, because she was like a shell of herself. The leukemia went through her body. In the end, I wouldn't go in. I didn't want to see her that way and I don't think she wanted anyone to see her that way. She said just her mother could come in. So she died like right after that. It was so hard. I mean, you couldn't talk about the future to her. You could talk about things but the underlying theme of death was still there, and I mean, you couldn't talk about that, it's so gross. You couldn't talk about next year at school, or the summertime, or what are you going to do when you get out because she wasn't going to get out, so there was really nothing you could talk about. I could have talked about things I'd done but then it was, like, I can do those things but you can't, you know? And I didn't want to tell her about all the times I went skiing and all that because she couldn't. . . . She had a boyfriend and he stopped coming to see her, of course, and she was pretty upset at that, I think, even though she knew it was better that way. He was at the funeral, and he seemed pretty upset there. They had a closed casket at the wake, and that was a good thing . . ."

— A teenager

Kathy Riordan, 23

She is an EEG technician in a Chicago hospital, five years out of high school, no college, a former secretary in a women's wear factory, with a year of on-the-job training in a small hospital in Ohio. Her white mini-uniform is excruciatingly tight, and she displays an unlimited expanse of white-leotarded thigh as she sits, dragging deeply on a cigarette and waiting for her next patient. "That was boring," she says of her secretarial job. "That was very depressing work. So I looked for something more challenging, like work in a hospital, and a friend of mine told me about this sort of work, and I just took a shot at it, and I've been doing it for two years. It's okay, and some of the patients you can have some fun with, but you have to play that by ear because some of them may be really out of it with, you know, question of brain tumor, and some aren't too coherent. Others are okay, though, and you can jive them a little." She laughs. "As long as no one dies on me, I like it okay. Knock on wood, that's never happened. I like it okay, but two years, you know, that's enough for me on any job, and I'm going to move to London, I think, get a job doing this over there."

She handles six to seven patients a day, each EEG test taking about forty minutes to an hour to complete.

"Have you ever had a brain wave test before, Mr. Davidson?"

"Pardon?"

"I asked you if you ever had a brain test, a brain wave test, you know, an electroencephalograph test?"

"Well, they did a brain scan this morning, and . . ."

"Okay, this . . ."

". . . and they took skull pictures."

"Okay, this is a little bit different."

"But I don't recall ever having this sort of thing done. Boy, oh boy, that's some hunk of machinery you got over there."

The testing room is small and soundproofed, green walls, a single window, a black, soft simulated-leather couch, and a shiny console with a nameplate: GRASS MODEL 6 ELECTRO-ENCEPHALOGRAPH. *An electrode board to the left of the couch:* LEFT HEMISPHERE–RIGHT HEMISPHERE, *wire leads, colored red, green, yellow, black.*

"Okay, I'm just going to use this special paste in this little tube, and I'm going to paste some of these little electrodes on your scalp. It doesn't hurt at all. It's real easy."

"All right, I've had so many things going on and being done to me today that this won't make any difference. See this mess here on my shirtfront, this blood . . ."

"Okay, just lie back here now, bend your head back, that's right, against this couch . . ."

"Well, after the girl downstairs drew some blood from the arm, you know, she went and slipped or something and it just flew all over my shirtfront here . . ."

"That's right, just lie back there now, and relax . . ."

"And I'll have to go back to Gary like this now, with this blood on my shirt, and that's a pretty . . ."

"Okay, now."

"No, I don't think I ever had this test done before, but you know I've had so darn many things, skull pictures and brain scans and God knows what else, so many things that I just can't remember them all."

"Oh, you had a brain scan?"

"Yes. This morning, and I got the works, too, everything they could think of. But I guess if they can tell me what's . . ."

"Uh-huh."

"And all I came in for was that I have this awful pain in my right leg. . . . I had that pain in my leg, and now it's in the head, too, and I don't . . ."

She dots his head with little squirts of paste from the tube, and presses the metal tips of the colored wires into the puttylike globs. As she completes the job, he begins to resemble a gorgon.

". . . know what it is, and I don't think they do, either, you know."

"Hmm."

"And that's been going on for months now. But you know, I wonder if it maybe is that medicine I'm taking, maybe I'm taking too much of the drugs that they've given me for my heart condition, you know? I'm taking some kind of quinidine sulfate, I think it is, and I take a couple of those every eight hours or so, and I take six tranquilizers, too, every day . . ."

"Uh-huh."

"That's a lot of drugs every day of your life, you know, and I've come to the conclusion that every time I use one of these quinidines it causes these terrific, painful, pulsating throbbings right down in the feet, mostly in one of the feet, my left isn't so bad, but the right. . . . And it gets so bad that I can hardly walk sometimes, and I cannot figure what to do about it. I was in another hospital, in Indiana, for a couple of weeks a few months ago, and they gave me all kinds of myelogram tests and so on, but they kept me on the same medication."

"I see. Still on the same medication."

"Still taking it, yes. But they may be going to cut down on that, I don't know, at least I think they should. That may be too many."

"Uh-huh."

She has finished applying the electrodes. She steps to the window and draws the shade.

"And the headaches. Those have gotten . . ."

"Now the rest of the test will be . . ."

"You know, it just seems that every time I put one of those pills, one of those big white pills into my mouth my right leg begins to pain something fierce, and I never had that before, not until I started taking that stuff several years ago when they diagnosed me as a right bundle branch block, that's the heart condition they use the stuff for, and ever since that time I've been getting this horrible pain . . ."

"Now the rest of this test will be real easy. I just want you to lie back and you won't feel anything at all. Just like you're going to rest in a hammock. Just lie back and close your eyes and I'll tell you when to open them . . ."

"And right now, at this very moment, the right foot is killing me, and my head is starting up a little, too. . . . You know, I had an idea they were going to give me the works up here, so just before I came over I went to my barber and I told him to give me a crewcut, you know, just in case you people wanted to get at this skull of mine, and he cut it real short, didn't he? I told him, give those folks over in Chicago a break, so they can work on me easy . . ."

"That was very nice of you."

"You know, I haven't been here in Chicago for a number of years. My wife is gone, and I'm retired from my job. . . . I was a fireman on the main line of mid-America, you know that one, don't you?"

"No sir, I can't say that I do."

"The main line of mid-America . . . Illinois Central. But things have changed since I started out, since I started firing, and today, you realize, they hardly do anything, the firemen, on the diesels. We really had to work. . . . Didn't even have stokers, you know, had to shovel ourselves and that was tough work. But I've never minded. . . . Even when I was a wiper . . ."

"Okay, now just relax while I move this couch a little . . ."

"I was going to ask you if it's going to take very long, and if it is would you mind if I loosened my tie a little, and maybe if I take off my shoes. Me and my feet, they hurt me so that if I can just slip out of them it might help a bit. It's amazing how . . ."

"Sure, that'll be real fine. Okay?"

". . . painful these damned things have become. If I were firing today I'd never make it."

"Okay. I'll be right back, now. I just have to go and wash my hands. . . . Okay, now. Just keep your eyes closed and stay real still."

"Keep my eyes closed?"

"Until I tell you to open them."

She sits at the console and begins flipping switches. The machine hums and a series of pens begin writing his mag-

78

nified brain waves in a squiggly hand on a moving strip of paper. Every so often, she taps her class ring on the side of the console to keep her patient alert, and she rubber-stamps a drawing of the top of a head onto the paper record. Occasionally, she glances at her charge, and she makes notes on the moving paper that folds his history neatly in a tray at one end of the console: ALL TO P_2 . . . AWAKE . . . G-5 . . .

"Open your eyes . . . now close them."

She reaches inside her dress and adjusts her bra strap.

"Open your eyes . . . now close them."

She clears her throat and writes: AWAKE . . . E/C.

"Open your eyes . . . now close them."

She fixes a red tab to the folded record and scratches her ass.

"Open . . . now close."

She draws a line across the moving strip, makes an adjustment on the machine, and sighs.

"Open your eyes . . . now close them."
"Okay, now. I want you to stay real still and breathe in and out through your mouth, and I'll tell you when to stop, okay? But try and keep your head real still while you're doing it, okay? Close your eyes . . . no, a little bit faster . . . in and out . . . in and out. . . . Like this. . . . See?

Like this. . . . No . . . a little bit faster. Like this. Got it? Close your eyes. . . . Breathe . . ."

"Oh . . . wowee . . ."

"Close your eyes and try to do it a little faster, okay?"

"Oooh . . ."

"Not quite so deep, but try and do it a little faster, okay?"

"Ohhh. . . . My feet . . . my feet just kill me when I do that."

"Your feet hurt when you breathe deeply like that?"

"Lord, yes."

"Okay, just a little bit more."

"Sore . . . sore . . . sore . . . oooh."

She writes on the strip: PT. FEET HURT WHEN BREATHES.

"Your feet feel okay now?"

"Lord, no. They never do. . . . They're just . . . pulsating. . . . It's like trying to jam my foot into a shoe that's two sizes too small."

"Okay, just lie real still and close your eyes, now. Just breathe normally."

"Oh, boy."

"Okay. Now you can open your eyes for a minute. Now, this light is going to flash different colors off and on in your eyes, okay? I'll just set this right here. Now, I just want you to close your eyes again."

"Close my eyes?"

"Yes. And I'll tell you when to open them, okay? This'll just take about two minutes, okay?"

"Yes."

"You're not light sensitive, are you?"

"Gee, I don't know."

"Okay, now. Open them, now. . . . Now close them. . . .
Open. Close. Open. Close. Open, close, open, close."

"Open?"

"No."

"Close?"

"No. . . . Now open them. Now close them, okay?"

"Keep them closed, right?"

"Uh-huh, that's real good."

*She shuts off the light, lets up the shade, and flicks on the
room lights.*

"Well, that'll do it. How'd you like that?"

"Are we finished?"

"Uh-huh."

"Yessir, that is quite some hunk of apparatus you got over
there. Must cost an arm and a half."

"Uh-huh. Now I just have to take these things off your
head, okay? Sort of like getting your hair done, isn't it?"

"I'll just have to get my shoes on and I'll be on my way,
I guess. If it weren't for this damnable pain in my lower
extremities I wouldn't be such a . . . testy old guy. But,
oh God, this is just something. . . . And I never had this
before."

"Okay, just a second or two more. . . . I'll just wash
some of this paste out."

"It's just all day long, too. You know, from the moment I
get out of bed in the morning. But what's strange is that I
get up and get dressed and go out and take a walk, you
know, and after the first few blocks it just sort of subsides.
And if I go on a long walk, why it just goes away entirely.
And as I said, it just seizes me when I'm not walking, and

it just grips at my leg, climbs right up that leg, you know. It's a real mystery . . ."

"Your hair will be a little bit sticky, but it'll come right out when you wash it, okay?"

"Oh, don't worry about that, miss."

"Now, there. You've got a new hairdo."

"Say, miss. Do they have a boys' room on this floor?"

"Yup, sure do."

"I, uh, well, they had me doing all kinds of tricks that required me to drink huge glasses of water, and bring specimens in to them, and I had to keep drinking and drinking and drinking all that water in order to be able to come up with the specimens every hour, you know."

"Didn't get rid of it all, huh?"

"Didn't get rid of it all, no. Oh, say, that's good enough, I'll just run a comb through it when I get out, just so I don't scare the gals at the reception desk downstairs, you know. Hair's cut so short, though, maybe ought to just run a washcloth through it."

"Okay? See, you even got a free head massage with it. Right?"

"Yes. That's right. Say, you ought to make a little on the side, my God."

"Right."

"Yessir, that really is a hunk of apparatus you've got over there."

"You like that, huh?"

"Yessir. Say, what do you call your job, miss?"

"EEG technician. Brain wave technician."

"B . . . B . . . technician?"

"No. EEG. It stands for electroencephalograph. You know, like electrocardiograph?"

"Yes."

"Well, this is an electroencephalograph."

"Technician?"

"Uh-huh."

"Well, young lady, you've got a real unique career for a young lady."

"Well, thank you."

LaJean Jandro, 36

She was a nurse's aide in what is kindly known as a nursing home, south of Boston. The nursing staff at the home is large, but as in other such institutions throughout the country, trained nurses are a scarcity, and aides comprise the bulk of the care-giving staff.

Listen, I stayed with it two years, around that, and like I've had it, you know? It was freaking me out, and I wasn't any good for the patients either. Like, whenever a call light'd flash up I'd find myself . . . something'd be telling me not to, you know, move it so fast if it was lighting for a . . . [She starts to say "crock."] a terminal. I don't know. I guess after a while you get to feeling you want to get away from the losers, and that's what it's all about, isn't it? I mean, it's life that's what's important, not death. Death is . . . it's just it, that's all, the end, baby, and there's no pill that's going to stop that one, am I right? Listen, I know that sounds kind of bad, and I don't mean. . . . Like, I'm not one of these defeatists who doesn't believe in anything and like that, but let's face it, just like it's not everybody who dies in a hospital or a place like this goes out smiling, with Mom and Dad and the kids crying around the bed, like in the books, or like that real hard-ass under the sheets at the end with her man in *Love Story*. . . . That's too . . . stereotyped, I guess you'd call it. Maybe some do, but I've never seen that happen too often.

If you want it straight, most of them go out pretty shitty, that's how. They're old in there, you know, and they can't hack it anymore without the medication. Most of them have got some kind of chronic brain thing as well as the physical things that come with just being old. And they aren't just lying there, a lot of them, peaceful and so forth. Most of them are sick, throwing up, incontinent, and when they die it's rough to watch for the most part. Oh, some of them just gasp and give it up, but not all of them like that. Some cry at the end. I'll tell you, like I said, I'd had it.

It's really depressing, and it got so bad there for a while that I couldn't even talk to my kids without getting uptight, like the supper table was a free-for-all, and I know it was me, so I said screw it and I quit. I'm a lot better now, there's no hassle on the job, and the doctor I work for now's a good guy with a quiet practice, and it's right here near the house, only fifteen, twenty minutes away. I was lucky to get in; he told me I was the first aide he'd ever hired to run his office for him.

Yes, I have heard of that lady doctor, Kübler-Ross, and about talking directly to dying patients about their illness and their problems, and maybe that's a good thing, but only if they want to. But I get the feeling that a lot of these doctors and psychiatrists and nurses are doing most of the talking. I just don't know if every dying patient really wants to be bothered that much by people asking them all kinds of things, and worse, telling them things about their condition and so forth. That's cruel, I really do feel that. All I'm saying is that maybe it's a good thing, all of that counseling, but it's not for me, I'm just not built for it, that's all. At the nursing home I was at, they brought in a bunch of these death people once . . . the nurse who ran the place was always going off to some out-of-town seminar and she ran into some of these people someplace . . . and they got us together in a room and started to tell us all about the four or five stages dying patients go through and how we have to start facing up to it all or we'd become depersonalized, or the patients would, and we'd never look at the patients as anything but some disease and like that sort of stuff, and that we'd have to start caring, really caring, and stop denying death and avoiding it, you know. And then they asked us to write a paper about our feelings on the wards with terminals, like what it had done to us, how we saw our roles as nurses and aides and so forth, whether we talked to the patients, right? And why? So they could publish it all someplace, I suppose, help some pussy-striper get her master's over to Simmons. Anyway, we listened to it all, and some of them wrote up their thoughts, but I couldn't be bothered, and they left. I think they were kind of pissed at me and a couple of others, though. [Laughs.] But, I don't know, I feel you ought to let this stuff lay, let those people die in peace. Just leave them alone. I don't mean leave them *alone*, you know, like in a room, but leave them alone, like don't bug them. Like I say, I don't know if dying people want to be bothered like that. I would think, too, it is depressing for them to talk about the end. People are not. . . . Death is something. . . . Well, they just don't want to accept it for themselves, that's all. People, listen, people keep on smoking even though that warning is on the pack, they don't wear seatbelts, you know? They do all these life-threatening things. No. People don't want to accept it for themselves. You just can't talk to most patients about it. Some would just fall apart, wouldn't be able to carry on and function properly to carry out what's required of them the last few months or so. Even if they want to know you wouldn't tell them all the time. You'd put them off, instead. That's the way I think you do something for the patient's benefit. You can bug some of them too much and you'll harm them. No one wants to hear they're going to die. I suppose in some instances it's going to help, but in more it's going to be disastrous, a disaster. You tell a patient he's got cancer, say, and he's going to die, and he immediately has visions of pain and suffering and he goes out and he kills himself, then how are you going to feel? [Laughs.]

And, look, I don't think you're going to reach all those people anyway. I just love the way some of these pros, who never seen the inside of a hospital ward, figure they can work it all out right. Those people lying there, when they're really sick, are just naturally pissed at you because you're walking around healthy and young, and . . . It's like when you're growing up with kids who don't have any more money than you do, and then your family makes it pretty good and you still have your old friends and you feel sort of funny talking to them about all the things you've got now and they don't have. . . . You're going to walk into a lot of walls, let me tell you, you just won't reach them, and some of them, like, they can get pretty nasty, too, like I'll bet if they could they'd say up yours, and they'd give you the finger as soon as you walk out the door. Probably not that bad [laughs] but I've seen some pretty rough ones, dying as well as curable. They're really pissed because they're in that sack, and they think you've got it knocked, and you feel sometimes like saying, hey, bug off, I didn't put you there. And they're what you call behavior problems. . . .

86

If they've had like brain damage, senility, cancer and like that, they try to take out the urinary tubes, or yank out the IVs and they try to climb out of bed. And so you got to try to protect this patient from harming himself and that becomes a full-time job, you become a wrestler [laughs], so who's got the time to take care of the emotional problems?

I mean, I know it's no bed of roses, and I hope to God I don't ever end up like that, in a place like that where I worked. I want to go like whammo, zap. [She snaps her fingers.] But I guess they can't help it. . . .

It can be pretty grim, particularly for some who've never worked in a home . . . even for those who have. I wouldn't go back. Screw that noise. They're just warehouses, most of them anyway, is what they are, where they go off to die. And it's about all you can do to keep them comfortable, let alone talk to them about their condition and all that. And we were busy as hell, too, don't forget that, like sixty patients and maybe two nurses on a shift, and who the Christ ever saw the doctor, he'd drop by every so often to . . . when someone would start to go down, or to sign a death certificate, but we'd do that ourselves every so often, and we weren't supposed to . . . I don't mean me but some of the nurses . . . but you couldn't leave the patient just lying around if the doctors weren't right there . . .

I have to say honestly I haven't ever gotten a thing out of it, I just don't see how you can go except down, and the feeling like I had to get out because I'm not doing anybody any good, myself included.

And let's be honest. What's dying but dying? A smile on someone's face? Like that joke about the old guy who wants to be electrocuted for rape at a hundred and three. People just don't go out like that, at least not the ones I've seen. If a person accepts his death . . . and I don't think anyone can ever accept that . . . but if someone does I suppose that's okay, but in the end of it all what the hell difference does it make? He's going to accept it only for a while and then he whacks out anyway. And then, dead. I mean, like he can get shot to death by some nut on the street, some guy he doesn't even know can shoot him and kill him right in front of his house, or he can choke to death on a hunk of sirloin in some fancy restaurant, and he's still dead, right? So what difference does it make whether he accepts it? Does that change what happens in the end? I don't really think — unless all this study has shown otherwise — that the person who talks about it is better off than those who don't. If you concentrate on it, like I say, you're going to end up with a person who's very depressed, and dead finally. . . . I'd be damned if I'd want to run over and over it again and again, that I'm dying, I'm dying, you know . . .

I really don't think I'd want to know if I were drying anyway. I mean, living is . . . living is thinking and walking and all that, and I'd find it hard to think that I'd be going to lose it all. I don't think I could take it, just like I couldn't take seeing those people who knew they were dying, the ones that did in that home. If I ever wish anything it's that I won't have to die there, no way. I think I'd take the gas pipe first . . .

Would you believe I'm even scared to get a Pap smear? And I been around hospitals and doctors, for God's sake. But what if they found something? But I know a lot of people are like that. My mother wouldn't ever go to a doctor for a checkup, never ever went. She used to say the same thing, what for, what if they find something, and they'll find something, she'd say, because if they didn't they wouldn't be doing their job. Sometimes I wish they wouldn't keep publishing all those danger signals for cancer and diabetes, all that, lumps, persistent coughs, unexplained weight loss, watch what time you go to the john, thirsty, you know, increased urination, tired all the time. . . . For God's sake, you can't make a move and it's a symptom. No way. I think hope is important, and I wouldn't want to know. I'd rather die hoping than despondent. I would, really. I mean, like I said, what difference does it make after the person is gone? At least if you stretch it a little, the truth, I think that's better . . . I'd rather zap out grabbing at some straw.

So, you don't tell them outright, you play a little game with them, you give them a little bit of hope, and that's being more kind to a dying patient than sitting there asking them how does it feel, like some TV newsman sticking a microphone at some earthquake disaster survivor and asking him, say, how was it? What did you feel like when it happened? You can't tell me he wants to hear that. Maybe he would if he was a masochist or someone like that, some people are like that, they want to talk about it, they'll talk about anything, like how great their kids are when they're really little bastards, how many times they make it a week with their husbands, about their sex problems. I can't see that. I never talk about my kids to anyone, and the last thing in the world I'd talk about to anyone is my sex habits, for God's sake. So the dying patient . . . maybe he's like that, too. He's saying, bug off, will you? And if someone knows they're dying, I would rather believe that they're looking for someone to tell them that it isn't so, that they're not, rather than telling them it is. Then they can't play the game that they want to play, neither them or their survivors. That's a plus, the game, you know. With the game everyone functions. All of them. Everyone is playing. They do it and they enjoy it so why take that away? Like I think it was

Eisenhower they asked one time, they asked him who wants to be ninety years old? And Ike said, the guy who's eighty-nine. That's human nature, right? Survival is the name of the game. Sure, a suicide gives up and accepts death, and I had a cousin who did that, he just gave up, but I don't believe a dying patient ever does because he doesn't want to die, not unless the pain is so horrible that he wants it over. Take away his pain, though, and he's going to stop wishing he was dead.

You just never accept it, not unless you're like I say, a suicide, and even that, don't they leave notes as a way of asking for help, or supposedly take . . . like some women will try pills because it's not so sure as a gun and they're just hoping that someone will run in at the last minute and rescue them before it's too late. . . . Why the hell should anyone accept death anyway? We know it's going to come, sure, but when you say accept . . . accept means to me like you're looking forward to it. I think if I knew I was going to die I'd be madder than hell, besides being scared, and I also know that I'd stay mad and I don't know if I'd ever come around to accepting my dying. You know what would really piss me? If I found out tomorrow that I was going to die in a month. It would piss me that I've got some things to do, a lot of things, like go to Japan and live for a while there, I've always wanted to do that, and like my husband and I are divorced and I just have a good time, I mean there's lots of things I want to do and see. So I could never accept it at this point in my life, and I don't know if I could ever accept it later on in life either. Even if I had everything that I wanted, I'd find some other things that I hadn't done and that I'd want to do and I'd think about them. [Laughs.] I used to hear nurses, and priests, too, say things like if you've lived a full life you won't mind your death so much. Hey, why are so many nurses like priests anyway? Must be the work. [Laughs.] Well, I say that's foolish. I know guys and women who did everything they wanted to do before they were married, you know, and you'd think they'd be ready to settle down because they'd got it all out of their systems, right? You know, lived a full life? So what happens? They still . . . they still ball around, even today. Even after they're married. You'd think, you believed that idea, that because you've done it all you lose the feeling. What crap that is. You just want more of what you enjoyed doing, not less because you've experienced it. I can think of a person who led one helluva life, went everywhere before he was married, must of had everything he wanted. Then he got married. And you'd think that maybe that would be it for him? This guy was always faithful to his wife afterward, I mean he never cheated. But oh damn did he want to, I could tell. And he was pissed because he couldn't, because he was married, so there's a case of someone who had a full life and wasn't fulfilled. I used to hear some girls say, goddammit, I never had any experience, or things like that, I wish I knew which side of the street the rapists were working, I'd leave the door open just a hair, things like that. [Laughs.] I remember one story about a bunch of Catholic women at a sodality meeting and they were listening to the priest talk about sin and whether you're responsible for certain actions. Well, he told them that fornication, even fornication, wasn't really a sin if you were, like, drunk, because you weren't in your right senses. And this one old broad giggles and looks at the priest and she says, oh father, *now* you tell us. So if she was told right then that she was going to die in a week, what do you think she'd go right out and do? [Laughs.] Right. Get herself shitfaced and laid. . . . A woman told me just yesterday that she doesn't travel anymore because she's afraid of flying and because her husband is dead she doesn't go anymore. So, I suppose you could say she's resigned to that, and that she's accepted that she can't, or won't, go anymore. But I don't believe she ever has, really, because in the next breath she tells you, God, did I love to travel, even when she didn't fly. So, even though you might think she's accepted the fact that she had a good life traveling and all that, she really hasn't, and she'd like to keep on. . . . And I think she's very depressed over it. So, no, I don't think anyone ever really accepts death, and I don't care how many books get written, and how many psychologists and nurses and conventions they hold. People are always going to be afraid of death, right? They're always going to dread it, and they're always going to wish they didn't have it to bug them, they're always going to wish they could live, and the fuller the life, I'll even say that, the fuller the life the harder it is to let go, not easier. So don't give me any of that full life stuff. Maybe if you lived a lousy life without any fulfillment it would be easier to let it go, I don't know, this gets pretty heavy, doesn't it? I read this great interview the other day with James Caan, you know that gorgeous hunk who was Sonny in *The Godfather?* He said something like he rides in rodeos on weekends, and that if he can't screw around and have fun the hell with it all. He says he loves life and that he sees people committing suicide all around him and that he wants to live to be nine million. And to me that's a lot of sense. Who the hell wants to keep talking about death all the time? You come this way once, right? And like that ad on TV for the beer says, grab all the gusto you can get because you only come around one time.

No. I think the best thing to do with dying patients is to make them as comfortable as you can, run a game on them if you have to. Everyone likes games, don't they? I mean, like we play them all the time. They're a great defense. It's like when I put my glasses on, I put them on and I feel like I'm sitting behind something, like a shield or something, and I figure that no one can see me, I mean that they can't see what I'm really thinking or what I'm really like. Reminds me of that joke I heard when I was in the service, about the bunch of WACs who are standing nude and this medic comes walking by with a stethoscope, saying, OK girls, close your eyes, I'm coming through. Maybe we ought to give all terminals glasses [laughs] with rosy lenses. I read someplace that they use LSD in some hospitals in England to keep dying cancer patients high. I think that's great, I really do, and I never use the stuff myself, believe me. I think there's nothing wrong with going out as easy as possible and if it makes them happy in an unhappy time to be drunk or high, then fine. You've got to make them comfortable, if you can, and that's the best way to do it, and like I said it just wasn't for me to do, I couldn't handle it too well, but that's me. . . .

Office of Public Information
Columbia University
New York, New York

FOR USE UPON RECEIPT

The clergy is not sufficiently trained or involved in the care of dying patients and their families, say two Columbia University experts on the care of the dying.

The charge will be made by the Reverend Robert B. Reeves, Jr., chaplain of The Presbyterian Hospital at the Columbia-Presbyterian Medical Center, and Dr. Austin H.

Kutscher, president of the Foundation of Thanatology at Columbia, at an all-day symposium on "Ministry to the Dying Patient and the Bereaved" Saturday at Riverside Church.

Mr. Reeves and Dr. Kutscher say clergymen are either poorly trained or not trained at all in divinity schools to deal with the dying person. The Columbia experts also charge that in hospitals, clergymen are too often excluded from the professional team that cares for the terminally ill.

Mr. Reeves and Dr. Kutscher will recommend that hospitals incorporate into their medical records chaplains' notes on the general condition and emotional status of patients. "Few hospitals now allow such evaluations to enter patient charts," says Dr. Kutscher, adding: "Frequently the chaplain is the only person who really knows what is on the patient's mind. The patient reveals to his physicians only restricted portions of his concerns — whether emotional or medical. When he needs comfort, he is more likely to confide his anxieties to a clergyman if he has been able to establish a relationship with one. A clergyman can be helpful in a general way, even when a patient has rejected specific religious practice. It is high time that ministers routinely become part of the team of physician–nurse–social worker attending the dying patient and his family."

PSYCHIATRIST: What about our hospital chaplains?

PATIENT: Well, you know, you don't see too much of the priests or the ministers when you're in the hospital . . . at least I haven't.

PSYCHIATRIST: Think that would be helpful?

PATIENT: I don't know. I think it would be up to the patients, really, themselves. Maybe it would be helpful, for instance, if the chaplains had like a bulletin board and they could notify the patients when they'd be available to see them at their bed or talk to them someplace. That might be helpful. But as far as a chaplain visiting every single patient every day, I don't know as there's too much to be gained by that. So many people wouldn't have that much to say to a chaplain. And some people'd just as soon make a little visit.

PSYCHIATRIST: Visit?

PATIENT: Yes. You know, to a chapel or something. I think having a chapel is nice. Sometime just a place to go and be alone with yourself.

PSYCHIATRIST: Are you a religious person?

PATIENT: Well, if you mean do I go to church and believe in God . . . I go to church every so often when I'm able, and I even take Communion on days when my stomach is good, even though I don't go to confession anymore. I can't see that business of listing things like a shopping list anymore. I believe in my conscience, and I don't have any more trouble telling right from wrong anymore, like I did when I was young. Besides, I just don't feel right about taking advice from a very young priest who I don't really think knows anything about life or my personal troubles. When I was a kid maybe I would, and I did. It was like worshiping baseball players. When I was older and they were younger I didn't pay much attention to them anymore. I remember my grandmother used to listen to everything the priest said, even used to ask him who she should vote for. But that's all changed now, I believe. Used to be that the priest was the only educated man on the block, now the kids know more than he does. My grandmother used to listen to younger priests, but she was uneducated and she respected they went to college and all that.

PSYCHIATRIST: What about God?

PATIENT: Well, you know, I've always believed in something. . . . Maybe it's more like nature, though. Like I used to like to walk alone on a lake and think about how somebody must have put it all together. But that's why I like to make a visit now and then, to a chapel. You can think and not be interrupted by some sermon about sin and hell. I think the last time I really sat through a mass was in 1966, before I started getting sick, and it was down at St. Margaret's on the South Shore. They used to hand out these church bulletins before you got into church, listing the times of the daily masses and the prayers, and telling you about the month's mind low mass for so and so at such and such a time, and they'd mention the banns of marriage for somebody. And the pastor there was a real jerk if I might say so, always complaining about people coming in late and so on. I remember one of them bulletins listed all the sins, like missing mass on Sundays and holy days of obligation was a mortal sin, and missing parts of the mass was a venial sin, and hearing mass and being distracted was a mortal sin and missing a main part, like the offertory or the consecration, was a mortal sin. Oh, yes, and then it said something about the proper reception of Holy Communion. . . . The pastor, he didn't like unsightly confusion during the distribution of Communion. . . . And the bulletin said that we were to file down one aisle and up another and fill in the whole rail, not just parts of it, and all that. And it'd tell you about the annual collections for . . . The Grand Collection, they used to call it . . . to be taken up at all the masses after the distribution of Holy Communion, and this would take the place of the monthly collection. A sacrifice of a day's pay, he used to call it. Then there was the special collections, like for the Negro and Indian missions and for the archdiocesan charities, and they'd remind us to be generous . . . and that's what it would say, that His Eminence, the Cardinal, was asking us to be generous. . . . Church has got really . . . I don't know. That bulletin was always full of stuff like that, and I never could see it had much to do with what was going on in the world and like . . . like the times I wanted to be alone with myself, maybe even after mass was over I'd stay around and think a little. I wish I could have saved some of those bulletins, you wouldn't believe them. . . . Annual luncheons and bridge parties of the Phila . . . Philomantha Club or something . . . CYO basketball games, all the sports stuff.

I guess I pray now and then, like at times when I need help and I suppose that means I believe in God. But there's no formula. Insofar as priests and confessions are concerned, I don't see as they . . . I can't go that way anymore. Last time I went to confession was years ago, and that was a pretty awful time, I don't think I'll ever forget it, and I guess it was a turning point, you might say, for me. My husband and me had lost just about everything in this fire at the house, and there wasn't enough insurance and so on, and even his job was being abolished . . . that was before the fire, and it was a real mess for us, I didn't think we'd ever get out of it. We had two kids and we figured no more, so we practiced birth control, and when I went to confession that last time I told the priest that we were doing that, and he called me a whore, he actually said I was no more than a whore and that I should try to control myself. That was it for me . . . no. The last thing in the world I want right now is a visit from a priest. Maybe some people would, but not me. And I don't think I've got much time left . . . but even at that it wouldn't do much for me the way I generally feel about them.

PSYCHIATRIST: How do you feel about them?

PATIENT: Well, like I said, I don't think many of them know what's going on, they're out of it, you know? I think if they were in this world and not out of it they'd be more helpful. If one came in here now he'd probably try to either cheer me up, and like I know I haven't got too much left to go, and the last thing I need right now is people coming in here to cheer me up. I don't need that. Or he'd probably read me off, tell me I got to accept it all as God's will, like the last time in confession. God's will, he told me it was then, too. Well, maybe it is, but that doesn't mean I have to like it, and like I'm strange sometimes, I guess, but when I get mad every so often I just don't want people trying to get me to stop being mad. How can you not be mad when you are, Doctor? It's like when my husband and me used to have a fight, he could turn it off if he knew someone was coming to the house, like some actor who figures the show must go on or that clown in the opera who cries behind the laugh mask. We'd have a roaring fight, and if someone was coming to the house he'd make as if nothing had happened, and I just couldn't do that and it would show when the people came in, and it would hang on for the night, too. No. A priest in here now probably would not let me be mad. He'd have his collar on and his prayerbook . . . and really he'd upset me, he really would. I don't think I could take cheering up now, Doctor, I really don't. First of all I don't think I could . . . I know I couldn't . . . and I don't want to, really. Why should I?

PSYCHIATRIST: Are you mad now?

PATIENT: I suppose I am, Doctor. The whole thing is so . . . hard to believe. It's so goddamn hard to believe. Excuse my language, Doctor, but I've . . . never really wanted to swear more than I do now, and I guess that means I'm mad, doesn't it?

PSYCHIATRIST: Are you mad at anyone in particular?

PATIENT: That's a hard question. No. No. I don't think so. Just mad at the whole thing, that's all. No one to blame, and I suppose that's just the way it is, but I don't like it that way. I hate it. And I suppose if a priest came in here now I'd be mad as hell at him.

PSYCHIATRIST: Are you mad, do you think, at God?

PATIENT: I guess not. . . . I don't think that God is something you can get mad at, because it's not like a person that I know. If God was a person who really did this to me, really did it, then I would be mad at him. . . . But I'm not. I don't know if there is somebody who . . . put it all together . . . or whether it just fell that way, and if it did just fall like that then it's pretty lousy. I'm only forty-seven, right? And I just think it's a pretty rotten deal at this stage in life, and I guess I'm mad because I don't really . . . can't really know why it had to happen now, at this time. I don't know why I keep talking about those church bulletins, but I feel like taking that . . . those

99

women who typed those things up and ramming the typewriters down their throats, I really do.

PSYCHIATRIST: The pastor?

PATIENT: That one. That goddamned jerk. Him too.

Preparation for the Last Sacraments

A small table covered with a white cloth (pure linen if possible), upon which must be placed the following:

1. Crucifix.
2. Two candlesticks with wax candles.
3. A vessel containing fresh water.
4. Six balls of cotton.
5. Crumbled bread or salt.

The Priest should be met at the door with a lighted candle and reverently accompanied to the dying person's room.

After the sick person has made his or her confession, those present may enter the room again and assist the Priest by saying the responses and praying silently while he administers Holy Communion.

Form of Confession

Say first: "Bless me, Father, for I have sinned. It is (state the time) since my last confession and these are my sins." Then, confess sins. Do not use words "several times" or "quite often" or similar expressions. Be specific about the number of times each offense was committed. At the end, add: "For these and all the sins of my past life, especially (here mention, in general, sins against charity, obedience, purity and anger) I am heartily sorry." Then make a perfect act of contrition based on perfect love of God.

PRAYER: Oh most loving and gracious Lord Jesus Christ, only hope for the salvation of my soul. Grant to me true contrition of soul, so that day and night I may by penance make satisfaction of my many sins. Savior of the world, Oh good Jesus, who didst give thyself to the death of the Cross to save sinners; have pity on me, and give me the light to know my sins, true sorrow for them, and a firm purpose of never committing them again. I implore thee, Gracious Virgin Mary, Immaculate Mother of Jesus, to obtain for me by thy powerful intercession these graces from thy Divine Son.

INSTRUCTION: Immediately after death, your soul will stand before Christ to be judged by Him individually. In this judgment you will be examined in regard to your entire life; on faith and the words of God which you have heard; on the Commandments of God and your obligations according to your state in life; on prayer and your use of the Sacraments. The sentence will be irrevocable and just. He, who will be found without sin and adorned with divine grace, will be admitted immediately into Paradise. He, who is found with venial sin, or has some penance to fulfill, will be sent into Purgatory. He, who is found to have only one mortal sin or more, will be condemned to hell. There will be no more time, no mercy. The damned will say: "We were fools!" The Saints will say: "Blessed penance and labor! The trial was brief, our reward, instead, will be eternal!"

EXAMINATION OF CONSCIENCE: Have you willfully doubted or denied your holy religion? Have you taken part in services other than those of your religion? Have you consulted fortune-tellers? Have you read forbidden books? Have you taken pleasure in that? Have you despaired of God's mercy? Have you been angry? Have you neglected to worship God? Have you taken the name of the Lord in vain? Have you made false, unlawful or unnecessary oaths? Have you missed Mass on Sundays or Holy Days of Obligation? Have you done unnecessary servile work on these days, or caused others to do so? Have you neglected your parents? Have you been disobedient? Have you displayed anger toward them? Have you fulfilled your obligations toward your children? Have you been violent toward another, or caused violence without just cause? Have you been jealous of others? Have you drunk to excess? Have you taken pleasure in impure thoughts? Have you committed impure actions? Have you gone to places of amusement that you knew would lead you into sin? Have you stayed away from other occasions of sin? Have you failed to observe Church regulations with reference to the Sacrament of Matrimony? Have you stolen anything? Or defrauded others, or cheated in weights and prices? Have you made restitution for past sins of this nature? Have you now any ill-gotten goods? Have you injured (without just cause) the name or reputation of another? Have you restored his good name when you have by untruth harmed it? Have you fasted on the days appointed, and abstained from meat on the days of abstinence? Have you made your Easter duty faithfully? Have you contributed to the support of your Church?

Communion of the Sick and Dying

The Priest enters the room and says:
   V. Peace unto this house.
   R. And to all who dwell herein.

He places the Blessed Sacrament on the corporal spread upon a table and genuflects. All present kneel. The Priest then sprinkles all with holy water, saying:

Ant. Thou shalt sprinkle me with hyssop, O Lord, and I shall be cleansed: Thou shalt wash me, and I shall be made whiter than snow.

Ps. Have mercy on me, O God, according to Thy great mercy.

V. Glory be.

Ant. Thou shalt sprinkle me, etc.

V. Our help is in the name of the Lord.

R. Who hath made heaven and earth.

V. O Lord, hear my prayer.

R. And let my cry come unto Thee.

V. The Lord be with you.

R. And with thy spirit.

Let us pray. Hear us, O holy Lord, almighty Father, eternal God; and vouchsafe to send Thy holy angel from heaven, to guard, foster, protect, visit, and defend all that are assembled in this house. Through Christ our Lord, Amen.

The Confiteor is recited by the sick person, or by someone in his name. Then the Priest says:

May almighty God have mercy on you, and bring you to life everlasting, Amen.

May the almighty and merciful Lord grant you pardon, absolution, and forgiveness of all your sins, Amen.

The Priest genuflects and says:

Behold the Lamb of God, Who taketh away the sins of the world.

O Lord, I am not worthy that Thou shouldst enter under my roof, but say only the word and my soul shall be healed.

Then the dying person, together with the Priest, says the

same words at least once in a low voice. The Priest gives the Holy Eucharist to the sick person, saying:

Receive, brother (or sister), the Viaticum of our Lord Jesus Christ that He may preserve thee from the malignant enemy, and bring thee to life everlasting.

Postcommunion: We beseech Thy clemency, almighty God, that by virtue of this sacrament Thou wouldst deign to strengthen us, Thy servants, with Thy grace, so that at the hour of our death the enemy may not prevail against us, but that we may deserve to be accompanied by Thy angels in our passage to eternal life. Through our Lord, etc. S. Amen.

> Are you the widow Jones?
> My name is Jones, but I ain't no widow.
> Yeah? Wait'll you see what they're bringin' upstairs.
>
> — *Anon.*

Earl Marchand, 42

A general assignment reporter, he works nights for the Boston Herald American.

I remember a story Joe McLean, who worked the lobster shift here, told me about a Charlestown truck driver who was killed after midnight. Around 2 A.M., Joe went to the wife's home to get handout picture stuff, and she came to the door. And the doorbell and Joe and so on aroused her bunch of kids, six or seven of them, from toddlers up. The woman was in her thirties, and Joe wasn't banging her with the news right off that her husband was dead, he was being diplomatic, but she quite quickly caught on. She threw her hands up in the air, and she said, Jesus Christ, what am I going to do with all these fucking kids?

For myself, I don't know how many experiences like that I've had over the years. . . . Not that many, I guess, considering the length of time I've been at this, maybe a couple dozen times or so. . . . Talking to families who've lost kids. . . . And I've managed to duck out on others. It's no fun, talking to close relatives of people who die violently or suddenly . . .

What I do is try to get it over with without wasting any time thinking about the assignment. When the editor gives me a story, I get on the phone fast, or I go out to the house, fast, and I start talking. As I say, I don't like to think much about the job to be done, but I do try to put myself in the right mood. I try to empathize. Feel like they do. With empathy the tone of voice and choice of words tune with the sadness of the event. This way you don't jar the survivors any worse, hopefully, than they already have been. And, also hopefully, you don't get tossed out of the house or cut off the phone until you get what you want, and that's, of course, information and pictures. Yes, you can't help but feel you're maybe selfish when you butt into some family's death, and your purpose is self-serving, a good story, that's the objective, a good story about death and sorrow and all that that the public likes . . .

There's not much you can do for the ones who are grieving. . . . Offer some hollow words of sympathy, like, I'm very sorry about your tragedy, I know there's no words that can really help at a time like this, like that. Then you shake your head a little, and you look down on the floor. Sometimes it seems appropriate to mumble something about helping in some vague way, or you stutter something about the newspaper helping in some way that you don't say how, maybe you just drop a hint about a fund, or something like that. . . . Then you slip into some soft questions, like, did Billy go to school near here? Things like that. If they answer this okay, you slide into some others. Does he have any brothers or sisters? If the conversation goes along well, and nobody tells you to stop or tells you to screw, you can go into the picture angle. You might say, looking at a picture that might be on a table or somewhere, you might say, is this a picture of your son? Then you might stare at it, maybe shake your head, and you look down. If you can pull it off without sounding too phony, you might mention that the deceased is handsome, or pretty, you know, before you bring on the photographer. . . . Could we get a picture of this picture, it'll only take a minute. . . . Or, could we borrow this for a while?

But with all that empathy it's still a little difficult for me to keep from feeling a bit phony, you know. These are people you don't know, so naturally you don't reach the depths of sadness they are feeling. . . .

On all these assignments I feel uncomfortable, and even a little embarrassed. And when I leave the house I feel really relieved. I discard the empathy . . . the gloom goes away, but then back in the city room when I sit down to write the story, I try to pick up that empathy again.

There are a lot of stories around about reporters running into angry relatives of untimely death victims. I haven't ever run into anybody so angry they threw me out, but I've been refused cooperation a few times . . . and that's part of the whole thing. Usually, the relatives tolerate you . . . and some of that is out of normal politeness, and at a time like this, naturally, they really couldn't care less about newspaper stories. That's generally true . . .

In most instances I've found that the women are crying
. . . most of the men don't, at least not in front of reporters.
Now I'm talking about the people I've met right after a
death, say, within a few hours or an hour. Days later, the
women won't cry until they've been talking for a while
about their kid.

One time, and this was a little over a week ago, two
brothers, seven and six years old, drowned in the Charles,
and they had fallen off a makeshift raft. When I went to the
parents' home the shades were down and no one answered
the knock. A couple minutes later a neighbor came out of a
house and she asked what I wanted, and I identified myself.
She said, they're in the house, in my house, but she's in a
bad way. She asked me to come back tomorrow. I told her
we had to have the story that evening, and I got in something about like how the story would include a warning to
other kids about playing on rafts and things, or on thin ice.
She agreed to try to talk the parents into talking with me.
She told me to come back in half an hour, and I did. She
brought the father to the door, and he was a young man in
his twenties, and they had two other children besides the
dead boys. They had two girls. . . . We shook hands, and
I explained frankly what we were after, and this was after
I gave some weak sympathy. Something like, I'm terribly
sorry about the loss of your sons. My experience has been
that generally close relatives of the dead, especially mothers
and fathers of young children, aren't very talkative to reporters as a rule. This was no exception. He was, in fact, one
of the quietest and hardest-to-get-to parents I've ever come
across. We already had a pretty good story, and basically I
was trying for pictures of the brothers. It went something
like this as I recall it. . . . I told him, I know there's nothing I can do to help you, your loss is something that can't be

brought back, like that . . . I said it softly, but realizing I couldn't bring myself down to the level of his sorrow . . . I told him, we'll be running a story on this tomorrow, and we're going to warn other youngsters. If I had said that we were going to warn parents, as should have been the case here because the kids should have been in school and the parents knew it, they knew they were lax . . . if I had said that, it would have been a serious mistake and I would have been cut off fast. I told him there was nothing we could do to help him, but maybe we could help other youngsters avoid a tragedy like this. . . . And I was wondering, I told him, if a photographer could come in and take a picture of a picture of the kids, and that it'd only take a minute and we wouldn't have to take the picture away from him that way.

Well, he wouldn't buy it, and he said that he didn't have any pictures of his boys anyway. But he invited me into the kitchen where his wife was standing, smoking a cigarette, and she was a thin woman, dark-haired, in her twenties. I offered her the same weak sympathy, and then no one said anything for a long time, and she had been crying and her cheeks were still wet. I said something again, like, I'm sorry, and then I waited a second, and figured I'd try for the picture again, and she just stared at me as if I were a ghoul. Her eyes were wide, and she just said no, just said no, in a strange way I couldn't begin to describe. Then she shook her head, and sat down at the kitchen table and started sobbing. . . . Well, in a situation like this, where two kids had just died, you hate to use the word embarrassing to describe anyone's emotions. But more than any other feeling, my mood at that time was just that, embarrassment. Here I was, intruding on what had to be the most tragic moment of their lives, and what for? The real objective, of course, was to get a story that was . . . entertainment. More than anything else, a death story like that one is an entertainment story, let's face it. The people who need to be informed about it, the people who *really* need to be informed about it, could have been informed by word of mouth, from the relatives. That's all they are, these stories, a grim form of entertainment for media readers and watchers. So the newsman's job is to make the entertainment good . . . plenty of detail, plenty of pathos.

A lot of people, of course, want to be left alone in their misery. But I remember a couple of years ago, it was up on the North Shore, a boy five years old and his sister, about three or so, fell into a ditch in their backyard and drowned. I was at the house, knocking on the door an hour or so later, with a photographer, and unlike the couple I just mentioned this couple had a gang of relatives and neighbors in with them, and we didn't expect to get past the front door. But the father invited us in, quite cordially, I thought, under the circumstances, and he was talkative as hell. We sat at the kitchen table and he gave us the whole story about his kids, what they were like and so on, matter-of-factly, while his wife was crying herself out in the living room. He had a good set of pictures and Paul took shots of them, and then Paul suggested that the mother and father pose holding a large, framed picture of the children. The father said something like, well, she's in a bad way . . . but he agreed to stand holding the picture, and while he was posing, she came screaming in, yelling, no, no don't let him take a picture of you, don't . . .

As I say, getting in the right frame of mind usually helps out on these stories, but there was one time I might have empathized too much, and there was this fourteen-year-old from Milton who had been invited on a free plane ride, and the pilot was a relative or someone he knew. Some other kids went up, too, and the plane crashed, killing everybody. I got the assignment, and thought a lot about all the sorrow the family must be feeling, got myself in the right mood, and then I phoned the house, where the fourteen-year-old kid lived. That was about three hours or so after the crash. The person who answered the phone put me on with the mother, a German-born woman who had married an American serviceman over there, and in my lowest voice I offered my sympathies. I even stumbled and stammered a little, you know, trying to get some of that sadness and empathy into it, trying to show her she wasn't alone. . . . And she said, this comes very hard to you, doesn't it? She asked me how long I had been a reporter, which I didn't particularly like, but I told her for a good many years, and that death stories always came hard to me. . . . And she was so candid about her feelings and her voice was firm and unemotional. She said, he had a good life, he died doing what he liked to do most, there is life and there is death, it is very natural, and you can't cry over death. . . . She said things like that . . .

Sometimes you get your foot into a sticky one, like a few years ago we got this report of a seventeen-year-old Newton girl who had died from an overdose of drugs. A few days after the kid's death, I called her mother and I said something like this. Hello, Mrs. Cohen? This is Earl Marchand of the *Herald American,* and I'm awfully sorry about the death of your daughter, the tragedy in your family, and like that. Then I pulled a beaut. I told her I was interested in doing a story about her daughter, and I knew there wasn't much we could do, and all that again, but maybe this story would help warn other young people about the dangers of drugs.

. . . Well, she really got pissed and she said, wait a minute, wait a minute, where are you getting your information from? She said there had been no autopsy report, that the cops hadn't said so, that it was drugs, and that the kid might have died from a virus. . . . I didn't know whether she was telling me the truth, whether she just didn't know her kid was on dope, or whether my editor had given me a bum steer. . . . I stumbled along anyway, and I told her I still wanted to do the story if that was all right with her, about the untimely death of a young girl and so on, and after a minute or two she really shocked me when she said, okay, come on over. And I've run into that sort of thing several times, parents who really want to have stories written about their dead children. Maybe that gives them a little something solid to hold onto once they've lost the kids, a bit of immortality maybe, not quite that, I suppose, but something. . . . But that's good if they feel that way, because then the story serves a little more than pure entertainment purposes . . .

This point, that a story in good old black and white confirms that a person has lived and done something in this world, can be used best by people whose loved ones have died maybe days before. I don't think that idea works in people whose kids, say, have just died hours before; they're still too shook to think about preserving the deceased in a newspaper story.

But often you don't have to tell the survivors that a newspaper *story* is the objective. . . . One easy way to get stuff is what we've all used, the obit thing. You call up the relatives of someone who has just died and you just ask about funeral arrangements, whether they're complete, where and when and so on. . . . For some reason, they'll talk when you do that because people don't seem to resent a straight obit in the paper, they think that's natural . . .

People talk to you for a lot of reasons, I suppose. There was this mother and father of a sixteen-year-old boy who had died after an OD of heroin, and I had gone through the usual routine about warning other kids and so on, and the parents really leveled with me about a week after the kid died, leveled in the sense that they *talked* to me. They told me he was a good student, a good kid, had never got into any trouble, a model youngster and all that. . . . It took them a couple of hours to tell me all this, and I think they had always wanted their son to accomplish something in life and when he died he couldn't, and that they were using what was left of him, sort of his memory, to do that for him . . . to accomplish something for him . . .

It goes different ways and for different reasons. A few months ago I went to talk to the parents of an eleven-year-old girl who had been killed in Woburn at a neighbor's house while she was visiting a girlfriend and her brother. One of the things I remember was that she died in the kitchen after eating a pizza. And the girlfriend's brother had apparently accidentally killed the kid, a rifle he was showing her went off. What was different about this one was that I didn't call the parents, they called the paper. And this was about a week after the kid died. They were really mad about the boy and the boy's family and so on, and they believed strongly that the kid had murdered their daughter, they felt they hadn't got any satisfaction from the cops, and they said the kid that had done it was a mental case. This was a tough one to write, and a tough one to sit through because the mother kept breaking down and crying in the middle of it all. . . . So I wrote the story, but kept out their bitterness.

(By the American Hospital Association)

1. The patient has the right to considerate and respectful care.

2. The patient has the right to obtain from his physician complete current information concerning his diagnosis, treatment, and prognosis in terms the patient can reasonably be expected to understand.

3. The patient has the right to receive from his physician information necessary to give informed consent prior to the start of any procedure and/or treatment.

4. The patient has the right to refuse treatment to the extent permitted by law, and to be informed of the medical consequences of his action.

5. The patient has the right to every consideration of his privacy concerning his own medical care program.

6. The patient has the right to expect that all communications and records pertaining to his care should be treated as confidential.

7. The patient has the right to expect that within its capacity a hospital must make reasonable response to the request of a patient for services.

8. The patient has the right to obtain information as to any relationship of his hospital to other health care and educational institutions insofar as his care is concerned.

9. The patient has the right to be advised if the hospital proposes to engage in or perform human experimentation affecting his care or treatment.

10. The patient has the right to expect reasonable continuity of care.

11. The patient has the right to examine and receive an explanation of his bill regardless of source of payment.

12. The patient has the right to know what hospital rules and regulations apply to his conduct as a patient.

Billie Wardhouse, 48

A nurse's office in a Boston hospital. He is tired, and has just left his daughter's bedside.

Well, I'm afraid I'm not a very good talker, and I'm not a college graduate or anything like 'at, now. I was raised on a farm and I moved to Biloxi when I was a child, and I'm a hardware dealer by trade, been a hardware man for thirty years, working for P. B. Young. And I flew down to Mississippi from here last night, I mean yesterday, and I came back last night. Mostly because I wanted to talk to the folks down to the hospital there, and to Dr. Marlowe. I didn't get to see him, but I talked to his secretary to see if we could get Zoe Lee entered in the hospital there.

See, the problem seems to be that no hospital seems to want to take someone who's real sick, who's dyin', because for that you got to have fifty to a hundred thousand dollars, you got to be a person that money's no problem to. Well, they said they would take her, finally, but I have to put up a thousand dollars' deposit, they tell me, and that's just to get her in there, has nothin' to do with the transportation from here, you know.

The reason they won't take her is that, in other words, no one knows how long she'll be in this condition, on a respirator, and they worry about who'll pay. Course, we can carry her home paralyzed like she is, but a respirator we cain't, see. She's got trach tubes down there . . .

She's born with scoliosis, but it was in the lower part of her spine, and 'course twenty, thirty years ago they didn't have the facilities, and back then they just said wait. Well, a coupla years ago she started weakenin' down. She worked for almost six years, but you know in the mornin' she'd be holdin' onto the walls she was so weak. She'd just be scootin' along the walls. So we carried her to a doctor that we'd been goin' to, and he said, after they interviewed her in the hospital, after the neurosurgeon and the orthopedic surgeon looked at her, and X-rayed her and everything, that there was a bone that was growin' against the spine, the cervical spine, in the interior part of it, which is I guess the way you'd put it. And no one in the United States, they thought, could take her except this Dr. James Hoffe up in Boston. And she was sufferin'. Well, we did make an appointment, and we waited two months, and then we come up here and saw him. And he agreed that it was the bone, uh, a vertebra, growin' on the cervical spine, and that he had to remove it. See, she was able to walk when she come here, and we took her on American Airlines. That was in . . . oh, around October 25 and around October 27 she entered the hospital here.

She's just twenty-three, you know, and this problem started up . . . well, we noticed her goin' downhill a couple years ago. Course, when you live with someone ever' day you don't notice it as much as someone would, like a physician, or someone who would see her ever' six months or like 'at . . .

Well, first thing he done was a . . . a posterior fusion, on her cervical spine, and that night he brought her back to the recovery room, and they kept her there a long time. And

then he noticed that . . . in some way I don't understand
the fluid was not flowin' through her spine. So, he said, well
I got to take her back to surgery, so he did, he carried her
back and opened her up again, and loosened her bones or
somethin' like 'at in her posterior fusion. Well, he got that
straightened out and she seemed to get all right. Then ten
days later she still hadn't . . . Well, she paralyzed. And
went on her respirator. Well, they said, we got to get the
bone out. So they, I don't think I can pronounce it. . . .
Anyway, they did what means splittin' you open, and he
did an anterior fusion, or somethin', while he was in there
and he removed the bone by chippin' it. He couldn't cut
any, he had to chip it out, I understand. Anyhow, now she's
recovered from two major operations, as far as surgery goes.
You walk in and look at her layin' in the bed and she looks
good, but course she's paralyzed from the neck down and
on this respirator which she has been on for a week or so,
the way I figure it.

And that's the problem. We talked to several doctors. And
they *has* been people that's been on these respirators for
four months, six months, and if her movements was to come
back she could get off it. But Dr. Hoffe says they's no one
he knew that can set any time limit on it, or as to whether
she'll recover or not. The odds are against her recoverin'
because a trach tube tends to ruin your windpipe, and it's
been in there a long time. But, she's fairin' pretty good,
breathin' on the machine, and that's workin' pretty good too.

And she's . . . she knows it all. She's aware of her situation. Course, she cain't talk because of the trach tube, but
I read her lips and spell out words and everythin'. I know
she's never given up that she won't get well. I mean, how
she holds up, I don't know. . . . The only way she can
attract attention is to smack her mouth and you can't hear

116

that very far. They's also been several times that this trach tube has popped up. The air would have a blowback and she'd just throw it up. Fortunately, we'd been there. One time, I had to put the tube back myself, because one girl was turnin' her, a nurse was turnin' her, and maybe I shouldn't say this, one nurse was turnin' her, and it's not her fault, I'm not sayin' anythin' about anyone, but anyway the trach tube pulled out. Completely. Well, the nurse had to do somethin' with the machine, and what else was I to do but put it back. I mean, I had no experience with trach tubes, but I did it and I could have killed her then. I could have.

Well, that's the reason we have stayed close to her. She cain't talk, she cain't move, and the only way she can talk is with her eyes. She closes her eyes and it means yes, and she leaves 'em open and it means no. And she can move her mouth. Dr. Hoffe says it's the worst case he's ever seen, or that he's ever had here in this hospital. The worst one he's ever had.

It's just an odd bone growth, that's all. As maturity come on. They must have grown curved and pushed against her spine. And then the paralysis . . . takin' that bone out didn't help it. Well, no one knows what caused her to be paralyzed. The doctor hasn't explained it to me yet. Maybe they just don't know.

And she wants to go home. That's the reason I went down home. Between National Guard and congressmen, callin' people in this state. . . . People here, people there. They been promisin' us to try to get a plane but we haven't had no luck there. And she wants to go home. She knows she won't go to her house, but to the hospital at home where she can see her friends.

One of the doctors here in orthopedics is in the Air Force

Reserve or somethin' like 'at, and he'd been tryin' too, but he couldn't get the Air Force to take Zoe Lee. Then Dr. Hoffe tried callin' Washington to see if they could get a Air National Guard. Well, they first promised us a plane, everythin' was fine, and we was relieved, but then they called back and said sorry we can't furnish you a plane for this sort of thing . . .

And the commercial airlines say they cain't do it because the government won't let them, someone as sick as her. They'll get fined, they say, a hundred thousand dollars fine, I understand, if they was to take her on board like 'at. Now, this is hearsay, but I'm told that they'd have to pay this fine. Like, I could take her that way if they'd go for it, we could take out a coupla seats and lay her down and a doctor and a nurse could go along, too. But the government won't let 'em, is the way I understand it. You know, she needs that respirator to go with her, and a anesthetist, if we are to get her home. So, we'll have to charter a Lear jet to get her there, and it's got to have the doctor and a nurse accompanyin' her to make it as safe as possible. They's some risk to it, you know. And what it is is I haven't got the money. And then there's the special voltage that's necessary for the equipment that's got to go with her, and like 'at. . . . Well, my sister has a little savin's that she's offered to donate because she thinks so much of Zoe Lee, and she's our only child and the only girl in the family, so she says, well I'll donate the plane, 'cause all we want to do is get her home. It's gonna cost, I don't know what I'll have to pay the doctors, but the plane is gonna cost somewhere around three thousand dollars.

Well, I know it's hard on her, but it's been hard on us. I mean a hundred and somethin' days up here, livin' out of a suitcase and runnin' from the hotel to the hospital here has about finished my wife and I off, too. Plus, like one of the respiratory doctors told me the other day, if we had somethin' to look forward to in the future, maybe it'd pay us to stay up here. But no one knows. It may be six months, and you know what six months here will cost us . . .

I do hope that hospital will take her. They's no way she can stay at our home, for she has to be suctioned and the respirator has to be taken care of, and that takes college work, you know. So, she's just got to go to a hospital. She realizes all that and she just wants to get back where she can see some of her friends and to, like I say . . . well, she hasn't give up. Like I say, she looks good. She come in with a smile and she still got a smile. She cries sometimes. But she has held up amazingly well. More than I probably coulda done, I know. Well, I know I couldn't have. I don't know really how she does it. And, you know, she's always been small all her life, seventy-five to a hundred pounds all her life, eighty pounds, and she's kinda short . . . don't look like much of a fighter, you know.

She's kept us goin', and we believe that. And if some of them people in Washington was to come down here just one day and walk up and down them halls out there, see them kids out there, on the cancer floor where they all are, I believe they'd go back to Washington and they'd have a plane set aside for people that needs it to go home. If they was a chance, you know, that she could be saved by some special treatment or such, why she'd probably be able to get someone to pay for her to go to that special treatment or hospital no matter where.

You know, I read all the time in the papers about some kid down in South America or places like 'at gettin' free planes from the State Department or somethin', or a fund is raised by some club or organization, and they fly the kids anywhere if they figure they can get 'em some treatment or medicine that'll save 'em. Well, seems to me that when they know you just want to go home to . . . die, or are goin' to need some long-time help to stay alive, well, they just don't buy that news. But if they was a magic vaccine or a serum someplace that might save a kid's life, well, hell, they'd come tearin' down the road to get some of it, and nowhere would be too far 'cause they figure they got a winner. But like I say, we haven't given up hope, though. I hate to say it, but the money is what stands in the way. When they find out you got a seriously ill patient you've got to show 'em you can pay 'em 'fore you goin' to get into the hospital. Else they just goin' to let you lay out on the sidewalk and die, and I hate to say that.

You know, like I said, we haven't got much, didn't have much when we got here. I mean, I got a house, and. . . . But it takes time to sell a house. See, it isn't completely paid for, but I got some equity in it. And I told 'em down in Mississippi that if I cain't get back I cain't sell the house with me here and the house down there. I'll spend everthing I got so far as that goes, on her, house and anythin' I got durin' this life. Yes, it's cleaned us out, more than cleaned us. And the hospital here has been nice about that, though. Said they don't want us to sell the house.

But if I cain't get her in there at home then I'll just have to stay on here and get a cheap place to live, but it'd be a real blow to her if I had to tell her that. But we're hopin' to get her in, and I don't think they would have promised like 'at yesterday and then back out. I wouldn't think they would do that.

They should be willin' to take us back. I mean, they told us to come up here in the first place. It don't make hardly any sense. Just to say, now, we sent you up there, so just you stay up there. And you know, I haven't worked any since she was in the hospital down there, and my wife has been laid off her job, and they said they couldn't extend her leave of absence. It's hard to hold up under somethin' like 'at, but you know, the main thing has been her and tryin' to get her supported, give her support, 'cause she cain't help the position she's in, and maybe the doctor couldn't, either.

My wife is takin' it good, but she's really runnin' herself down and that's another reason I'm pushin' to get Zoe Lee back home. My wife is losin' a lot of weight. And, you know, another thing I cain't understand. They been good to us here at this hospital, and the hospital owns the hotel over there where we're stayin' but it's managed by some big corporation. Why, why, will you tell me, don't they . . . that's the only thing I want to know . . . why don't they give at least the parents a break on the livin' expenses. I mean . . . we been here . . . we're here to get treatment, and it looks like they could cut down a little bit on the room bills. And I say they could still make money. They get twenty-three dollars a day now, and I may be wrong but they could, I believe, make money on fifteen dollars a day . . .

THREE

A Matter
of Dignity

To live is to function.
        — Justice Holmes

    I was in the lounge at the hospital, and I was the emergency physician for the day, and I heard this Code 99, emergency rah rah rah and all that, so I rushed, and they're all up there traching this guy and giving him oxygen and cardiac massage and all that jazz, and I saw it was a real old guy, so I said, Christ, he looks a hundred, and this nurse laughs and says, would you believe he is? So I said, so let the poor guy go, but they didn't. His problem was old age, and I don't know what the hell they were trying to do or save . . .
        — An emergency room physician

    I pray you take no more trouble about me. Let me go off quietly. I cannot last long.
        — George Washington,
          to his physician

Harry S. Truman

© New York Times News Service

KANSAS CITY, MO., DEC. 7 — FORMER PRESIDENT HARRY S. TRUMAN RALLIED SOMEWHAT TODAY IN HIS FIGHT AGAINST A LUNG INFECTION, BUT DOCTORS KEPT HIM ON THE CRITICAL LIST BECAUSE OF A WEAKENED HEART.

MR. TRUMAN, WHO IS 88 YEARS OLD, WAS RESPONDING TO ANTIBIOTICS, AND CONGESTION IN HIS CHEST WAS SAID TO BE DIMINISHING. HIS BLOOD PRESSURE, TEMPERATURE AND OTHER PHYSIOLOGICAL INDICATORS ALSO WERE BEGINNING TO MOVE BACK TOWARD NORMAL.

MRS. CLIFTON DANIEL OF NEW YORK, HIS DAUGHTER, VISITED HIM EARLY IN THE DAY AND TOLD NEWSMEN LATER:

"HE WAS WIDE AWAKE AND SMILED AND SHOOK HIS HEAD. IT'S THE DIFFERENCE BETWEEN NIGHT AND DAY, HE'S SO MUCH BETTER TODAY. THE WAY HE LOOKS AND RESPONDS TELLS ME ENOUGH."

I swear by Apollo, the physician, by Aesculapius, by Hygieia, Panacea, and all the gods and goddesses, that according to my ability and judgment I will keep this oath and stipulation. I will look upon him who shall have taught me this art even as one of my parents. I will share my substance with him, and I will supply his necessities if he be in need. I will regard his offspring even as my own brethren, and I will teach them this art, if they would learn it, without fee or covenant. I will impart this art by precept, by lecture, and by every mode of teaching, not only to my own sons but to the sons of him who has taught me, and to disciples bound by covenant and oath, according to the law of medicine. The regimen I adopt shall be for the benefit of my patients according to my ability and judgment, and not for their hurt or for any wrong. I will give no deadly drug to any, though it be asked of me, nor will I counsel such, and especially I will not aid a woman to procure abortion. With purity and holiness will I pass my life and practice my art. I will not cut a person who is suffering with stone, but will leave this to be done by those who are practitioners of such work. Whatsoever house I enter, there will I go for the benefit of the sick, refraining from all wrongdoing or corruption, and especially from any act of seduction, of male or female, of bond or free. Whatsoever things I see or hear concerning the life of men, in my attendance, on the sick or even apart therefrom, which ought not to be noised abroad, I will keep silent thereon, counting such things to be as sacred secrets. While I continue to keep this oath inviolate, may it be granted to me to enjoy life and the practice of my art, respected always by all men; but should I break through and violate this oath, may the reverse be my lot.

KANSAS CITY (AP), DEC. 11 — FORMER PRESIDENT HARRY S. TRUMAN WAS REMOVED FROM THE CRITICAL LIST YESTERDAY AND TOLD A NURSE HE WAS FEELING BETTER, BUT HIS HEART DEVELOPED MORE FREQUENT ABNORMALITIES IN RHYTHM DURING THE EVENING.

KANSAS CITY (UPI), DEC. 13 — FORMER PRESIDENT HARRY S. TRUMAN'S WEAKENED HEART GREW STRONGER WEDNESDAY AND "HE IS HOLDING HIS OWN," HIS DOCTOR SAID.

THE FORMER CHIEF EXECUTIVE'S TEMPERATURE ROSE EARLY WEDNESDAY TO 101. HIS PULSE QUICKENED, BUT DOCTORS WERE NOT ALARMED.

"HIS HEART CONDITION IS FAIRLY STRONG NOW," SAID RESEARCH HOSPITAL SPOKESMAN JOHN DREVES.

"PRESIDENT TRUMAN RESPONDED TO VERBAL STIMULI BUT DID NOT TALK DURING THE NIGHT," SAID DR. WALLACE H. GRAHAM, WHO HAS BEEN TRUMAN'S PERSONAL PHYSICIAN SINCE WORLD WAR II. "HE IS HOLDING HIS OWN. HE HAD A QUIET NIGHT."

ALTHOUGH DOCTORS SAID TRUMAN'S RECOVERY IS UNCERTAIN, THE PEOPLE IN HIS NATIVE NORTHWESTERN MISSOURI HAVE FAITH THAT THEIR NO. 1 CITIZEN WILL RECOVER.

"HE'S A RUGGED GUY WHO'S HANGING IN THERE, AND HE'S GOING TO MAKE IT," DR. ELBERT C. COLE, PREACHER OF THE CENTRAL UNITED METHODIST CHURCH IN KANSAS CITY, SAID.

TRUMAN WAS BEING FED THROUGH A TUBE IN HIS NOSE AND RECEIVED OXYGEN THROUGH A FACE MASK. TINY PLASTIC HOSES ATTACHED TO HIS ARMS SHUTTLED INTO HIS BLOODSTREAM MEDICINES TO KEEP HIS BODY CHEMISTRY BALANCED. . . .

"THE MAN SAID HE'S GOING TO LIVE TO BE 90," SAID
WILLIAM R. WYCKOFF, 54, KANSAS CITY, KAN., INSURANCE
MAN. "IF HE SAID HE'S GOING TO LIVE TO BE 90, I EXPECT
HIM TO DO JUST THAT. HE'S THAT KIND OF GUY."

First MD: As a surgeon, I believe in prolonging a patient's life with everything I have at my disposal. When I have exhausted all the tools, knowledge, medicine and so on that I have, I am satisfied that at least I have done all that I knew how to do. I well remember a kindly old lady I operated for cancer of the colon.

Following the surgery, metastasis appeared and radical groin resections were done, and after this, other evidence of spread arose, and X-ray therapy was given, and chemotherapy administered. I was able to carry the patient along fairly comfortably for about one year, and she entered the hospital in shock, and an infusion was started to which stimulants were added. This went on for two days, and while I was on the floor one day, the nurse said that the infusion had come out and asked if I would come in and start it. I was getting ready to give her the infusion and she looked at me in the most pitiful way and said, "Doctor, why don't you let me die in peace?" I immediately put the needle down, patted her on the head and told her, "All right, that's just what I'll do." I ordered all infusions stopped and discontinued all the orders except something for pain. This was about 10 A.M. At approximately 3 P.M., the nurse in charge of the floor called me at my clinic to tell me that the patient had not died but had suddenly become much improved and was walking in the hall. I felt like telling the nurse that, what the hell, was she on dope or something? But since I had known her for many years I finally believed her. It was the truth. Within the next day or so, I discharged the patient home to remain for one or two months in fairly good health. She returned to the hospital and died quietly, and this is one of the reasons I try not to be God.

KANSAS CITY (UPI), DEC. 15 — THE CONDITION OF FORMER PRESIDENT HARRY S. TRUMAN WEAKENED TO "VERY SERIOUS" YESTERDAY.

HIS DOCTORS SAID HIS VITAL SIGNS WERE STABLE, BUT MR. TRUMAN WAS UNABLE TO SPEAK, HIS LUNGS FILLED WITH FLUID AND HIS KIDNEYS WERE IMPAIRED. DOCTORS ADMINISTERED MEDICATION TO STIMULATE HIS HEART, RELAX HIS MUSCLES AND FIGHT INFECTION.

And everyone interviews the world's longest living heart transplant, Louis B. Russell, Jr., forty-seven, who, on his 1,461st day with the heart of a seventeen-year-old beating in his chest, observes: "I'll go whenever He gets ready to take me." But in the meantime, he says, he's using every day to do what he can to help people and to make this world a little bit better place to live. And everyone interviews the centenarians who are asked to give their recipes for long life. They do. The Russian who worked up until his death at age 160 as a watchman on a farm, riding his donkey over five miles of mountain slopes to his job every day, fathered his last child at age 130 and had a blood pressure of a man in his thirties, and he says it was Allah and the Soviet power that kept him going, or maybe it was his children and good nature, or pure water and no alcohol and no smoking. Another says it was a free life and no diet; another who wore plain clothes, ate plain food, retired

early and rose with the sun. Another who followed an oc-
cupation that kept the body and the mind occupied, and
another who drank three pints of whiskey and six glasses of
beer a day and smoked a strong pipe tobacco, and that one
was 105. Or there is one who eschews worry and who talks
only of cheerful things and laughs often, and another who
consumes large quantities of hot tea, a mixture of potatoes
and fat and sweet oil and herring, and another who blames
short lives on daily bathing, pie and cake, and another who
eats rare steak three times a day, and another who exists
solely on fatback, collards, turnips, and cabbage, and they
say funny things, too, like, "You take my brother, he never
took care of himself and he only lived to be ninety-five," or,
"I always go with the prettiest girls I can find," or, "I picked
my grandparents very carefully," and philosophical things
like, "The closer you come to age one hundred the more
careful you are to reach it," or, "I just lived, that's all," or,
what doesn't get in the papers, "How the fuck do I know?
I'm just a lucky sonofabitch, that's all."

And a Harvard team tests an artificial blood in monkeys
and the monkeys live, and scientists seek the answer to why
body parts wear out and they send messages to one another
via their journals in the genetic code, all of it incomprehen-
sible to the elderly they study, and they keep a chicken's
heart alive for thirty-five years by feeding it new chicken
embryo cells, and they know that very old cells contain the
information in their DNA to generate replacement parts of
all kinds, and that the aging process might be controlled by
transplanting DNA from a young person to an old person,
or by breaking down cross-linked molecules in cells, or by
tampering with the biologic clock, slowing it down, post-
poning most of the deteriorative changes that affect individuals, and they suggest that substances which chemists add

to cereal and rubber tires to prevent them from spoiling may be the key to prolongation of human life, and they experiment with these chemicals and find that they can increase the life spans of mice by 40 percent, and they study microscopic animals like the rotifer which lives in fresh and salt water and goes through a whole life cycle in twenty days, and they change this creature's water temperature and his nutrition and thus regulate his aging rate, and they are heartened. They take spleen cells from mice and inject them into other mice and extend their life spans by a third, or they reason they might remove disease-fighting cells from a youth and deep-freeze them and inject them back later in life, raising the body's capacity to battle infection, or they freeze a sex cell from a dead person and they try to reproduce that person, and they study woodchucks, ground squirrels, and dormice who, during hibernation, have their bodies reduced to near the freezing point and who have very slow heartbeats and respiration, and they know that bats who hibernate regularly live longer than those which hibernate occasionally, and they envy the sea tortoise and the Irkutsk bacteria which lived for 600 million years.

And they freeze cats' brains and thaw them out and find that they register electroencephalograms, and they say things like, "Death is a disease, a serious one, generally fatal but not necessarily incurable," and that the average life span will be doubled and tripled, even quadrupled, that we might be Methuselahs, that we may be deep-frozen, too, like the cells, and kept that way until the time when they find a cure for the disease that killed us, and we will be thawed out, treated for the disease and brought back to life, just like it happens on the late show, only it won't be in some crackpot scientist's lightning-pierced lab or in some ground-fogged graveyard by the light of the moon; it will be clean and nice and sweet victory over that grim old equalizer, and on our license plates and bumper stickers we will put "The Last Enemy That Shall Be Destroyed Is Death — 1 COR. 15:26," and our children will hang wall posters of Benjamin Franklin with his words, "All diseases may by sure means be prevented or cured, not excepting that of old age, and our lives lengthened at pleasure even beyond the antediluvian standard."

And their journals will seduce them and sell them with glistening, glossy, color-splashed ads drawn and painted and written and photographed for a legion of medicine-makers and equipment-fabricators by hip and beautiful people in blue-carpeted and walnut-paneled studios far removed from the choking, moaning, vomit-sodden and blood-spattered world of the sick and the dying, and they are the reincarnation of the snake-oil salesman who could cure it all, fight it off, with but a single swig from his little green dollar-a-bottle, feeding the myth of the Doctor-as-God, the healer, the death-fighter, the oath-taker, the good guy Marcus Welby, "The Bold Ones," "Temperatures Rising," "Police Surgeon," "Emergency," "Young Dr. Kildare," "Medical Center." Boy Scouts in white. Track records like Perry Mason. And the message is the same. You can. You will. You must. Repair, rejuvenate, revive, resuscitate. There is Dalmane ("for the elderly patient who can't sleep"), and Robitussin and a chugging steam engine ("Clear the tract with the Robitussin Line"), and Vioform-Hydrocortisone and a reclining blond in a crocheted bikini ("Bikinis and plain topical steriods both may be inadequate . . . for more complete coverage. . . ."), and Hydergine and a grandmotherly type dialing a phone in a blue haze ("less confused in her thinking"), and Cyclospasmol and a neat old man playing croquet ("Help keep their 'collaterals' open for the good years ahead"), and Ovral and a languid beauty peering through foliage ("Can a woman who's unhappy with one contraceptive find happiness with another?") and Butisol ("It's over 30. Trust it."), and Tofranil and a guy in funky clothes watering an alarm clock ("Should old depressives be forgot?"), and Fiorinal and a handcuffed head ("Headcuffed by tension headache"), and Ritalin and a classroom ("Here is a child who seems to get very little out of school. He can't sit still. He doesn't take directions well. He's easily frustrated, excitable, often aggressive. And he's got a very short attention span."), and Antivert and a blurred lady pushing a blurred shopping cart in a blurred market ("Round and round she goes and where she stops . . ."), and Veetids and a bottle and a plastic spoon atop a wedding cake with a loving knot overhead ("Joined together"), and Premarin and a bitchy-looking broad in black ("Therapy for all stages of estrogen deficiency"), and Minocin and a thermometer ("We'll race anyone from 104° to 98.6°"), and Butazolidin and a nice old lady in front of a chorus line ("Sally's back in sew biz after an arthritic flare-up"), and Hydropres and a harried teacher in a montage of a switchblade, a newspaper with a STUDENTS STRIKE head, and a principal, and a blackboard eraser, a note, a PTA button, pencil and chalk ("When life's pressures build up blood pressure in the hypertensive patient"), and Dulcolax and a patient in green pajamas hanging from a chandelier over his bed and a toothy nurse clutching a tubed bag ("A Dulcolax suppository can do anything an enema can, except scare people"), and Lomotil and a cartooned sweating bride and groom ("When diarrhea wrings the wedding belle"), and Ser-Ap-Es and a stockbroker in front of the big board ("He has a system that wins"), and Macrodantin and a microscopic view of a bacteria-filled urinary tract ("The fight against stream pollution"), and Milpath and a woman in the shape of a wooden chair ("GI problems making her a fixure in your office?"), and "Listen, physicians, and you shall hear, Of the nasal congestion of Paul Revere. 'Twas the eighteenth of April in seventy-five, And poor Paul Revere felt barely alive. . . . The wise doctor knew the ride had to be made, So he went to his desk drawer and pulled out Ornade."

Hear the amplified voice of technology promising the security of the backup laboratory. Expensive brochures that tout cinescintigraphy systems and isn't it fortunate that our ability to employ engineering successfully in medical applications came at a time of rising demand for improved health care, and press kits with drawings of a 200-pound calf kept alive on a nuclear-powered heart, on St. Valentine's Day. Automatic superspeed refrigerated centrifuge, automatic gamma sample counter, efficient constant temperature circulator, high performance special purpose biomedical recorder, precision-operated tissue sectioner, double focusing mass spectrometer, high resolution liquid chromatograph, completely safe ultrasonic cell disrupter, point-to-point electron microscope, compact and self-contained microprojection system. A three-stage alarm compensates for intermittent breathing patterns while providing an early warning for apnea meets modern medical safety standards. Blood urea nitrogen can be done fast, easy. Refractometer, photometer, monochromator, viscometer.

And nestled comfortably amid their lively sponsors, the CASE REPORT, X ray, table, figure, reference, method, comment, conclusion, summary, bibliography, chart, graph, and bare and spare and dry as sand, proclaiming that resection of the polyp after manual reduction of the intussusception resulted in prompt recovery, and that the convalescence was uneventful and she was discharged from the hospital on the seventh postoperative day, and at the time of this report J. T. is no longer psychotic and is employed in a factory in the area where his employer is pleased with his diligence and ability, and since 1910 there has been a marked reduction in communicable disease death rates in the United States, and in 2,000 patients operated for gallbladder lithiasis we have encountered neither mortality nor important complications. And when the CASE REPORTS die the authors are as laymen grieving, we who say passed away and with the angels, and the doctors say an eighty-year-old man with vomiting secondary to acute calculous cholecystitis developed hematemesis and succumbed with bilateral pneumonitis, or the patient's postoperative course was complicated by fever, hypotension and renal insufficiency and she expired three days after surgery on the twenty-fourth hospital day, or the patient jerked, blood pressure, respiration, and pulse — zero, or CO_2 built up gradually to the point of further depressing the respiratory centers and a fatal course was run, or following the experiment the rabbits were sacrificed.

A tradition of service to the living. There when you need us. Cremation — The Dignified Solution. Bring us to your side. Two decades now since you took flight, your face today is just as bright. With love, on this your second birthday in God's cradle of love. Rest peacefully, darling. And it was so awful I thought I'd die and a fate worse than death and O grave, where is thy sting?

There's plenty of good news around. When are you guys going to report that for a change? Hope, pillar of strength, it springs eternal. FOUND: FOUNTAIN OF YOUTH IN PILL. URINE CA TEST PROMISING. TB VACCINE MAY HALT CANCER, TUMORS.

NOW: KNIFELESS BRAIN SURGERY. OPERABLE LESIONS FOUND IN STROKE PATIENTS. NEW SENSORY AID FOR THE BLIND. ARTHRITIS SOLUTION HELD NEAR. ARTIFICIAL EAR IN OFFING.

KANSAS CITY (AP), DEC. 16 — HARRY S. TRUMAN'S KIDNEYS CONTINUED TO WEAKEN FRIDAY AND THE 88-YEAR-OLD FORMER PRESIDENT REMAINED IN SERIOUS CONDITION.

RESEARCH HOSPITAL SAID TRUMAN SLEPT ONLY IN SHORT INTERVALS DURING THE NIGHT AND HIS KIDNEY OUTPUT CONTINUED TO DECREASE DESPITE MEDICATION.

TRUMAN WAS HOSPITALIZED 10 DAYS AGO FOR LUNG CONGESTION AND BRONCHITIS, BUT A WEAKENED HEART AND FAILING KIDNEYS HAVE BECOME MAJOR OBSTACLES IN HIS FIGHT TO STAY ALIVE.

First MD: You know, it's been my experience that most patients want to live, and they'll tell you that. Doctor, they'll say, please help me, don't let me die, I'm not afraid of dying but I'm not ready yet. Or, look Doctor, haven't you got something in that black bag that'll do black magic on me? And sometimes we do have, we've all seen unusual improvement in hopeless cases, just look at chemotherapy and bypass procedures for inoperable abdominal carcinomas causing obstruction, and not to mention the transplants. Further studies may bring us more in the way of treatment for those in extremis. Or moribundus ad latum. Furthermore, I'm only a man who does not have the right to give up on any patient. You prolong with all you've got. We've all been trained to heal and ease pain and prolong life. Is there anything wrong with that? All this talk lately advocating letting the patient go, making their own decisions and so on, you'd think we were the ones in the wrong, for Chris-sake. My conscience would persecute me the rest of my life with the idea that perhaps I had actually killed someone if I didn't do everything I could to save his life. I sleep better.

KANSAS CITY (UPI), DEC. 18 — FORMER PRESIDENT HARRY S. TRUMAN, CLINGING PRECARIOUSLY TO LIFE IN THE 13TH DAY OF AN ILLNESS THAT THREATENED IMPAIRMENT OF HIS KIDNEYS, LUNGS, AND HEART, WAS "IN VERY SERIOUS CONDITION" YESTERDAY.

HOWEVER, HIS PHYSICIAN INDICATED IN A STATEMENT THAT THE 88-YEAR-OLD TRUMAN'S VITAL SIGNS REMAINED RELATIVELY STABLE.

AT 9 A.M. EST HIS BLOOD PRESSURE WAS 108 OVER 40, TEMPERATURE 98.2 DEGREES, PULSE 72, AND RESPIRATION 24.

"IN EVALUATING ANY ONE SYSTEM IN A WEAK INDIVIDUAL OF 88 YEARS," SAID DR. WALLACE GRAHAM, "PHYSICIANS MUST REALIZE THAT JUST ONE SYSTEM CANNOT BE TREATED AS A SEPARATE ENTITY SINCE WE MUST EVALUATE AND TREAT THE ENTIRE INDIVIDUAL. A PERFECT EQUILIBRIUM MUST BE KEPT AND FREQUENTLY ADJUSTED. MR. TRUMAN HAS THE ADVANTAGE OF EVERY FACET OF MEDICAL SCIENCE FOR SUPPORTIVE AND THERAPEUTIC TREATMENT."

KANSAS CITY (AP), DEC. 19 — FORMER PRESIDENT HARRY S. TRUMAN REMAINED IN VERY SERIOUS CONDITION BUT A HOSPITAL SPOKESMAN SAID HE SEEMED MORE ALERT AFTER A RESTFUL NIGHT.

JOHN DREVES, THE HOSPITAL SPOKESMAN, SAID TRUMAN
"FOLLOWS PEOPLE'S MOVEMENTS WITH HIS EYES BUT HAS
NOT SPOKEN TO THEM."

TRUMAN ALSO HAS DIFFICULTY IN ABSORBING THE PRO-
TEIN FROM HIS LIQUID TUBE FEEDING. NEWSMEN ASKED
IF THIS PROBLEM, COUPLED WITH THE REDUCED AMOUNT
OF PROTEIN HE IS BEING GIVEN, WOULD RESULT IN INADE-
QUATE NOURISHMENT.

"IT'S ALL RELATED," SAID DREVES. "THE HARDENING OF
THE ARTERIES DIMINISHES THE BLOOD SUPPLY AND
WEAKENS THE HEART. THE KIDNEYS NEED 30 PERCENT OF
THE BODY'S BLOOD TO KEEP THEM WORKING AND WHEN
THEY DON'T GET IT THEY ARE DAMAGED."

First MD: Let me be honest. Every so often, maybe when
laparotomy shows multiple metastasis, I wish I had the guts
to drop my knife onto the aorta and let the patient go in his
sleep. But I'm not God. It's my duty and my privilege to
keep him alive. I have to, that's all. If he's suffering, perhaps
that's God's will, too. I recall something Pius XII said, that
if some dying patients accept suffering as a means of expia-
tion and a source of merit, and they abandon themselves to
His will, the doctor should not force anesthesia on them.
And if they don't accept suffering, all I can do is relieve
that with medication. But I've got to watch what I give him
in that weakened state. I can't . . . I am not allowed to
kill him, and I don't want to. If he asks for death he's asking me to aid in a suicide, and if I do it on my own, I'm a
murderer, simple as that . . .

God has the timetable, not us. I don't believe that it is
necessarily right to simply prolong a patient's suffering.
That can be pretty horrid, of course. But we can do things

about that. . . . This business of living vegetables bothers me. The term has been thrown around too loosely by people looking for easy solutions. We've blown this whole notion of suffering way out of proportion. . . . There are plenty of drugs and techniques for the relief of pain, and the person who is maintained on drugs and machines is not necessarily a rooted piece of . . . of radish. Yes, it's wrong to simply prolong a patient's suffering, but I also believe that to simply let the patient go by stopping all IVs and all medicines which might give him relief is wrong also. For example, it is very bad to stop IVs and let the patient become severely dehydrated even though one. . . . I feel every effort should be made to make the patient absolutely as comfortable as possible. I do not believe in killing the patient, and there's no difference in my mind between letting him go and killing him. Palliative operations are at times extremely helpful. For example, in the patient with an obstructive lesion of the colon, I believe it's a good thing even if the lesion has metastasized to the liver to perform a colostomy or an anastomosis bypassing the lesion. If the patient is in an oxygen tent and oxygen makes him more comfortable, then I believe oxygen should be given.

KANSAS CITY (UPI), DEC. 20 — HARRY S. TRUMAN'S IMPAIRED KIDNEYS INCREASED THEIR OUTPUT WEDNESDAY BUT STILL WERE NOT PURIFYING HIS BLOOD ADEQUATELY. DOCTORS SAID THE FORMER PRESIDENT WOULD DIE IF THE SITUATION WERE NOT REVERSED.

"THE BLOOD UREA NITROGEN LEVEL IS MOUNTING IN SPITE OF INCREASED OUTPUT," RESEARCH HOSPITAL SPOKESMAN JOHN DREVES SAID. HE SAID SHOULD THE BLOOD UREA NITROGEN LEVEL INCREASE TO A CERTAIN POINT, THE 88-

YEAR-OLD FORMER PRESIDENT WOULD GO INTO UREMIC
COMA AND "DEATH COULD RESULT WITHIN ONE WEEK OF
THIS COMA IF HE COULD NOT BE BROUGHT OUT OF IT BY
DOCTORS."

First MD: I believe it is our calling to cure, to improve, to
comfort. I do not feel that we should cut any patient loose
and place him in the hands of a radiotherapist or a chemo-
therapist who doesn't know him, and who would be able
to stop medications or the treatment he requires to keep him
alive, because he doesn't know him as a person. The surgeon
should stick with his patients to the bitter end, and not
transfer the care of the dying patient to any other individual. The surgeon should call the shots, and I try to live up
to that. I have been practicing surgery for a very long time,
first in Munich at the Haas Clinic, and since 1943 in the
United States. And in all those years, I must honestly say I
have never seen a patient who took too long to die. . . . It's
not really the horror show that we hear so much about from
the euthanasia people anyway. I'm afraid I don't buy the
arguments of those who know absolutely nothing about
medicine beyond what they read in the newspapers or
Woman's Day, or even those of some academic medicine
type in some school who couldn't treat a bunion anymore. . . . I'm just tired of it all, the arguments, the image
of hospitals full of patient-robots hooked to some tubes and
plugged into a wall.

KANSAS CITY (AP), DEC. 22 — FORMER PRESIDENT HARRY S.
TRUMAN IMPROVED YESTERDAY AND HIS DOCTORS SAID HE
IS SHOWING "REMARKABLE STRENGTH" IN COMBATTING THE

FAILING KIDNEYS WHICH HAVE BEEN A MAJOR CONCERN
FOR THE PAST WEEK.

TRUMAN, 88, REMAINED IN VERY SERIOUS CONDITION,
BUT WAS REACTING FAVORABLY TO AN INNOVATIVE FEED-
ING PROCESS INTENDED TO COMPENSATE FOR HIS MAL-
FUNCTIONING KIDNEYS.

"TRUMAN IS SHOWING REMARKABLE STRENGTH AND
TENACIOUS PSYCHOLOGICAL REACTION WHICH ARE A RE-
FLECTION OF HIS ATTITUDE TOWARD LIFE," DR. WALLACE
GRAHAM SAID IN A MID-AFTERNOON BRIEFING. "WE BE-
LIEVE THAT WE HAVE BEGUN A FAVORABLE TREND."

A SPOKESMAN FOR THE HOSPITAL SAID GRAHAM WAS
SPEAKING OF A FAVORABLE TREND IN CONNECTION WITH
THE KIDNEY AILMENT ONLY. THE FORMER CHIEF EXECU-
TIVE HAS ALSO SUFFERED COMPLICATIONS OF THE LUNGS
AND HEART.

First MD: Look, you just cannot keep a patient alive indefinitely on any machine, and that's just not possible medically. Again, we have all these instant medical experts con-
juring up frightening pictures of Frankenstein's monster
kept breathing and alive with electricity in his veins. It's
terrible. You just cannot keep a person going on a respirator
forever. When his brain finally dies, there's a helluva lot of
pressure built up in his skull, and he gets to lose large
quantities of urine, and his blood vessels collapse, his heart
stops. The longer he's on a respirator, the more prone he is
to lung infection. You lose his heart and you start it up again
but it is going to quit finally, and that's it. Nature takes over.
What is it, six days that a person can be kept going on a
respirator? I think that's the record so far. No. What you are
doing when you keep a patient alive is limited. It's part of

the plan, and you're not interfering, you're just doing what you're supposed to do, with the tools that have been given you. As I said, my job as a doctor is to keep people alive as long as I can. Every man has an allotted span, and all I'm supposed to do is get him through that, and if that means prolonging his life beyond what some people feel is appropriate then I do it, because I believe that everything, all of the effort, is part of the plan for his allotted time. And when I cannot prolong anymore, it's not me that killed him, it was just the end of his line, that's all. It's the Lord's will, who lives and dies. I haven't intervened with any purpose of beating death. All I'm doing is what I am expected to do . . . keep him alive until it's out of my hands, because that's just the way it is. His illness, his suffering, his dying, my efforts, they're all laid out well in advance. It's like you . . . when you have an automobile accident, the first thing you think is, God, if I had only left the house five minutes earlier this morning, or if maybe I had gone to bed an hour later last night, I wouldn't have been at that spot at that time, and this wouldn't have happened. But, leaving the house when you did, the time you went to bed last night, that was all part of the plan, and there's not a damned thing you can do about it. Death is a natural thing, a part of life. It is going to come to all of us, and it was charted that way a long time back, and the doctor who lets people die before the . . . before he is ready to, is doing the same thing as killing him by injecting air into his veins. There is no difference. They can call it what they want, but it's the same. I know a lot of Catholic gynecologists who prescribe oral contraceptives for their patients. The church has told them it's all right as long as the pills are given to regulate the menstrual cycle. So, if they prevent conception, well, that's supposed to be just a nice little bonus. And the patients take them with a clean conscience. It's the same thing for the physician who gives a heavy dose of medication to a dying patient, ostensibly to kill his pain. The stuff hastens his death, but no matter, the doctor's conscience is clean because he played the little semantic game. . . . He did it for the pain, he did it for the pain. . . . The intent is the same in all these things . . .

Frankly, I wouldn't want to take a chance letting someone go who may not want to. How the hell do we know what he's thinking? I mean really thinking. And the family. They tell you the patient can't stand it anymore, and wouldn't it be better if he were out of his misery. What misery? And whose? In most instances I'll bet it is the family who wants it over, not the patient, or at least some members of the family, and that poor bastard is lying there, maybe not able to really communicate his true feelings. I recall a doctor at a genetics meeting telling of a woman with Parkinson's disease who developed a severe urinary tract infection with acute pyuria. She went into a coma, was rigid, and did not respond to any stimuli. Her own physician ordered that she be left alone, with no food and no medication, not even water. Just let her go, he said to the staff. The nurses were upset over that. They talked with the patient's two daughters, and they found that the family was divided over what to do. The younger daughter wanted her mother kept alive as long as possible. The eldest wanted the doctor to allow her to die. With the assistance of the younger daughter, the nurses got after the attending physician. He started a program of antibiotic therapy, water and electrolyte replacement, bladder irrigations and nasogastric tube feedings, all that. The patient survived. In a couple of weeks she was oriented to time and place. And was carrying on meaningful conversations. I prefer to keep asking myself, what's in the patient's head? Is he composing a poem?

BOSTON (AP), DEC. 22 — THE SOLUTION OF AMINO ACIDS BEING ADMINISTERED TO FORMER PRESIDENT HARRY S. TRUMAN TO COMBAT FAILING KIDNEYS HAS BEEN DEMONSTRATED IN USE AT A BOSTON HOSPITAL TO NEARLY DOUBLE A PATIENT'S CHANCE OF SURVIVAL, ACCORDING TO A PHYSICIAN WHO HAS USED THE TREATMENT.

THE SOLUTION, CURRENTLY NOT AVAILABLE COMMERCIALLY BECAUSE IT HAS NOT BEEN APPROVED BY THE FOOD AND DRUG ADMINISTRATION, FEEDS AMINO ACIDS DIRECTLY INTO THE BLOODSTREAM IN AN EFFORT TO ELIMINATE NITROGEN WASTES WHICH MALFUNCTIONING KIDNEYS CANNOT ELIMINATE.

First MD: For God's sake. Am I to stop treatment just to satisfy a family that too often has its own motives for wanting it over? They want their anxiety alleviated, or the treatment is too costly, or . . . and it's cynical but true . . . maybe it's an inheritance, and it could be wiped out by the hospital bills. Are those considerations right? What do they have to do with the quality of life, another overworked term. The quality of whose life? This financial consideration, the cost of protracted hospital treatment, is a very . . . a very serious thing. Yes, it does cost a fortune sometimes to keep a patient alive, but if that's the way it is, then that's the way it is. To let a patient go because it costs too much to keep him alive is saying that he's got a dollar value, he's worth so much, and if you go over that price to keep him alive, then you're doing something terrible. That, to me, is immoral. X dollars is all we'll pay, they say. Because that's all you're worth. Any more than that, forget it. We can't afford you. And they'll also set some arbitrary time limit. . . . If you can give him a year, or seven months, Doctor, well go ahead and we'll go along with that. But less than that and you'd better stop, lay off him. For some people, I believe, even a week would be a precious gift . . . even an hour. And it's always up to us. Doctor, *you* let him go. *You* do it. *You* keep him alive. Doctor, *you* save him. And when they ask us to let him die, it keeps them clean. Would they withhold insulin from a bedridden, immobilized diabetic. The hell they would. But I'm legal. Like the executioner, arm of the law and all that. Blameless. But you know, I have never really believed that the man who pulls the switch on the electric chair is blameless. He's got a mind and a will and emotions. And he's a scapegoat, just like the doctor who listens to relatives who don't have the guts.

KANSAS CITY (AP), DEC. 24 — THOUGH IN A COMA AND STILL ON THE CRITICAL LIST, HARRY S. TRUMAN KEPT UP THE BATTLE FOR LIFE LAST NIGHT, AND A HOSPITAL SPOKESMAN SAID THE FORMER PRESIDENT WAS SHOWING SLIGHT IMPROVEMENT AND RESTING COMFORTABLY.

TRUMAN HAS BEEN RECEIVING A SPECIAL CHEMICAL DIET IN AN EFFORT TO RESTORE HIS KIDNEY FUNCTION AND STAVE OFF BLOOD TOXICITY. HOSPITAL SPOKESMEN SAID IT HAD SUCCEEDED IN DECREASING THE POISONOUS UREA NITROGEN LEVEL, BUT THAT AS KIDNEYS IMPROVE THERE ARE TIMES WHEN RAPID AND POTENTIALLY DANGEROUS CHANGES IN BODY CHEMISTRY MAY OCCUR.

MORE THAN 40 NEWSMEN, CAMERAMEN AND OTHER
TECHNICIANS HAVE MAINTAINED A VIGIL FOR THE FORMER
CHIEF EXECUTIVE IN THE GYMNASIUM ADJOINING THE
HOSPITAL.

"Any of you shitheads of the press want in the pool?"
"What is it, a buck?"
"Right. Get it up."
"Okay, let's have a slip."
"What'd you get?"
"Christmas Day, 10 A.M."
"Hey, looks good, babe."

First MD: You know, if a patient asks you to yank out a
plug, then he's thinking, and there's got to be something
there, even if he's flat out. And what about the people who
have recovered after their EEGs went straight, some of
whom would have been shipped to the morgue. I recall a
case in Israel where this teenager was wounded in the head
in the war and was in a coma for three weeks, with no brain
waves. He pulled through. And there was a Japanese physician who claimed he had fifteen patients who lived for
quite a long time after their brain waves disappeared. . . .
They breathed for several days after, and some of them
lived normal lives later on. No. You have this responsibility.
It's like a baby. You have to keep it alive, that's all there is
to it. You feed it, you just do. The person isn't merely a body,
he's a brain. Too often, you know, we tend to treat the
elderly like nonhumans, or former humans, and we decide
that there's nothing wrong with slowing up the treatment
when they're past a certain age. And when an old person

146

asks to be let go, too many of us breathe a sigh of relief. Why else do you think all the bright young doctors from Harvard aren't breaking down the doors of the geriatrics hospitals to get in? You don't win any Nobels in there.

BULLETIN BOARD, Neasden Hospital, London

The following patients are not to be resuscitated: very elderly, over 65; malignant disease. Chronic chest disease. Chronic renal disease.

Top of yellow treatment card to be marked NTBR (Not to Be Resuscitated).

The following people should be resuscitated: collapse as a result of diagnostic or therapeutic procedures — e.g., needle in pleura (even if over 65 years). Sudden unexpected collapse under 65 years — i.e., loss of consciousness, cessation of breathing, no carotid pulsation.

Dr. W. F. T. McMath
Medical Superintendent

First MD: We just don't have the right. There's entirely too much disregard of a patient's rights by letting him go, by not doing all you can for him. If he asks for it, I don't believe he really wants it, and if he doesn't ask, then we can't presume that he wants out. No doctor or nurse, no relative, no patient has the right to make that decision. It is innate in man to survive . . . even a suicide note is a cry for help.

There's entirely too much of that surrender mentality around nowadays, it's everywhere. Have a baby, get an abortion because you don't want the child, and it is that, despite what the women's groups would lead you to believe, that is what it's all about, surrender. You're a heroin addict, you take methadone. Forget the self-help. Look for the easy way out . . .

To the Editor:
One question, the greatest of all, is how to end the suffering of hopeless, helpless sufferers, and this has never been delved into. Here, a young woman lies stretched on a bed, immobile, bereft of the great motor engine of her constitution for the past three years, which places her in an absolutely paralyzed condition. She is unable to exert a single muscle in her body, besides suffering much pain, yet in full possession of the strength of her mentality, craves and yearns for that which would end her misery. And that misery is such as tongue cannot relate nor pen describe.

Masterminds of medical science, skilled diagnosticians, have exhausted their efforts in bringing about some relief or cure. Now, why should not the State take the matter in its hands and end the wretchedness of such poor sufferers? Let us just stop long enough to think that when a brute, the lowliest of the animal kingdom, becomes inactive and doomed to suffer, its suffering is put to an end, and here, a human being, the highest and noblest of created things, must linger and suffer on until the vital organs give way, which may be an indefinite number of years. What a cruel order of the universe.

Naturally, one's loved ones cannot bring this about. Your physician cannot do it, for he would be condemned. So the only means is the State. And who shall take up my case, as it requires a pioneer as in everything, would win an everlasting debt of gratitude.

If I were neglected for a day or two, death would come. You cannot imagine how I would welcome it. The care and medical attention I get, while it is kindly and meant, keeps life in me only to force me to endure the most terrible physical and mental suffering. There is not one thing on earth which could give me the faintest sensation of pleasure. Before I was ill, one of the greatest enjoyments was reading. Now I could not turn the page of a book. My suffering is too intense to let me listen while another reads aloud. The sight of my loved ones makes me think of what I have lost. And the sorrow that I read in their faces hurts me. No power can make life easier for me. The one thing I can look forward to is death.

Sarah Harris
New York, N.Y.
1912

First MD: A few years ago, I did everything possible for a 14-year-old boy who had been shot in the stomach, and he was dead, or so everyone thought. He was a star baseball player this spring. . . . That was a challenge, I admit, a challenge to my wholeness, to my skill, and, yes, I was fighting for myself, as much as I was fighting for him. But everyone has reasons for doing what they do, and maybe in the case of that boy it was more for me than for him, but I like to think not. He wanted me to save him. I know that . . .

To the Editor:

. . . an operation was performed, after an eminent physician informed me, "As sure as I'm a walking man you'll be a walking woman." Behold, it relieved me of my intense pain and later I was able to move a bit and sit in a wheelchair, and a change was brought about in my attitude.

As I look back on it, I believe it was the calmly rendered verdict of my doctors who led me to believe that I had no chance that caused me to cry out for euthanasia. My mind is now free, and I plan to write short stories.

When I asked for euthanasia, I would have hailed it as a welcome deliverance. Now I shudder to think what might have happened had such a law been enacted.

Sara Harris
New York, N.Y.
1913

If the disease be not only incurable but also full of continual pain and anguish, then the priests and magistrates exhort the man, seeing he is not able to do any duty of life and by overliving his own life is noisome and irksome to others and grievous to himself: that he will determine with himself no longer to cherish that pestilent and painful disease. And seeing that life is to him but a torment, that he will not be unwilling to die, but either despatch himself out of that painful life as out of a prison, or rack of torment, or else suffer himself to be rid of by other. And in so doing they tell him that he shall do wisely, seeing by his death . . . he shall end his pain. And because in that act he shall

follow the counsel of priests, that is to say of the inter-
preters of God's will and pleasure, they show him that he
shall do like a Godly and virtuous man. . . . But they
cause none such to die against his will, believing this to be
an honorable death.

— Sir Thomas More, *Utopia*

First MD: And when they say things like skillful neglect,
watchful neglect, careful neglect, passive euthanasia, and
negative euthanasia, and that they're leaving it up to the
individual to decide whether he should live or die . . .
well, they're really making the decisions, not the patient.
Whether it's positive or negative, active or passive, the
intent is, as I said, still firm. Death. I don't give a damn
what you call it. You know, a lot of coercing goes on in
situations like this, and my colleagues know goddamn well
it does, too. I'm sure most of it is rather unconscious, well,
maybe it isn't, either. . . . But it goes something like this.
The doctor might say to the family, we have tried everything in our power to cure this person, and we can't do anymore for him, and there are times when death is preferable
to a miserable existence, so what do you think? What I am
saying is that there is a suggestion here, just as there is a
suggestion when the parents of comparatively uneducated
groups are told by physicians that *maybe* your child needs
this, or *maybe* he needs that, and if he doesn't get it, *maybe*
he'll die. So the suggestion becomes more than that. It
becomes an implied threat, and the parents get guilty, and
they say, well, do what you have to do, doctor, or, you're
right, it *is* the only way, or, I don't know, what do you
think, we'll go along with you. No. There's just too much
influence from a certain clique that means well, I'm sure,

but who are playing the God game, calling the shots, running the show, influencing people to, in effect, give up their lives any time they want to, lives that they had no choice about acquiring in the first place. It isn't the same as buying a camera that you can sell later when you're tired of it. It's more like getting a gift from someone who thought enough about you to give it. . . . You just don't sell it or give it up, and if you do you're wrong. Hemingway said that the closer to death you are the more precious life becomes. . . . I think there's a lot of awfully good public relations going on behind this whole movement, and it says that death is better. It's a bit frightening.

To my family, my physician, my lawyer. My Living Will:

If the time comes when I can no longer take part in decisions for my own future, let this statement stand as the testament of my wishes:

If there is no reasonable expectation of my recovery from physical or mental or spiritual disability, I, the undersigned, request that I be allowed to die and not be kept alive by artificial means or heroic measures. Death is as much a reality as birth, growth, maturity, and old age. It is the one certainty. I do not fear death as much as I fear the indignity of deterioration, dependence and hopeless pain. I ask that drugs be mercifully administered to me for terminal suffering even if they hasten the moment of death.

This request is made while I am in good health and spirits. Although this document is not legally binding, you who care for me will, I hope, feel morally bound to follow its mandates. I recognize that it places a heavy burden of responsibility upon you, and it is with the intention of sharing that responsibility and of mitigating any feelings of guilt that this statement, this living will, is made.

First MD: Words are being put into people's mouths, without a thought of the consequences. They're opening a Pandora's Box, and we'll end up putting people away because we . . . because someone doesn't think they ought to live. Isn't that what happened in Hitler's euthanasia camps, with his orders calling for the extermination of all persons who were mentally defective or suffering from an incurable disease, and that was only in 1939, and they shot thousands in euthanasia camps, and there were rumors he would do in wounded German soldiers and unproductive workers to free hospital beds and conserve food . . . and then later, the Jews, millions, undergoing Hitler's gas therapy. It reminds me of that *Alice in Wonderland* rhyme, about I'll be judge, I'll be jury, said cunning old Fury, I'll try the whole case and condemn you to death. . . . I feel very strongly that too many of these people who are trying to set guidelines for handling the dying patient are people who have never had to make a decision like the one they're advocating . . . lawyers, clergymen, philosophers, teachers. Of course there are numerous physicians who are on that side of the fence, too, but there are many who are not, and for some reason their views don't get in the newspapers. Maybe it's the time we live in, values shot to hell, easy answers, no pain, take a tranquilizer. It's all very dangerous, the precedent that might be set, and I truly worry about it. There are simply too many questions that can't . . . deciding which patients should live and which should die . . . by what right does anyone assume to decide that? If the surgeon is faced with a prince or a pauper, does that influence his judgment? What if the doctor hates Jews? And the man in the bed is a Jew? Human nature. You can't deny it, and it works in doctors as well as in cabdrivers who won't pick up blacks. Is the kidney transplanter apt to go the extra mile for the professor, and not for the wino? Aren't they then selecting a strain, a breed, a molded human who fits their conception of meaningful existence? And what does that mean anyway? It's relative. Meaningful, as I said, to whom? Is a patient less a human because he's choking on phlegm and supported on a machine? Than when he was supported on food? You know, you can depersonalize a patient more by neglecting him. More than you can by treating him, by overtreating him. What some people consider ordinary treatment today is what often was considered extraordinary years ago, like penicillin. So, you go all out. No. We can't do anything else but that. We simply cannot. We have no right to decide whether a healthy, normal person should live or die. Why is it any different when a person is sick, retarded, elderly? There are too many shadings . . . how sick, how seriously retarded, how old? By whose standards?

RN: Euthanasia, I suppose, is really putting people to sleep. I don't know that I, as a nurse, could justify stating bluntly on paper that all patients over the age of ninety, or seventy-five or eighty, should be put to sleep. I don't think that anyone can do that because there are too many exceptions to that. But I do know that, personally speaking, I have been involved in this type of procedure for a number of patients for the last few years in intensive care, all of whom have been helped to die gracefully by medication, and it was ordered by a doctor and it was administered by myself and/or by a doctor, and I have not felt one twinge of guilt about any of that. I felt that it helped the patient, it just quickened their death by a few hours, it helped them to suffer less. . . . I really don't know if an unconscious patient suffers, I don't know what degree of unconsciousness patients stop suffering at, I really don't, because as they say when you put a patient to sleep, the last thing to go is their hearing. . . . Well, who knows if the patient lying in the bed isn't feeling something when you suction them or turn them when they are so . . . so very ill. And I did feel that in every case that I can think of that we did a merciful thing, and it was the right thing for the patient and the family. It was a decision reached at with much difficulty by the physician involved . . .

To give you an example of what we would do. . . . One might have a critically ill, elderly patient, perhaps an eighty-five-year-old man who had undergone major surgery and who had then suffered complications, who had ended up supported by machinery. In other words, a ventilator and on cardiac monitors, perhaps undergoing peritoneal dialysis because he is in renal failure and then it was decided that we attempt to remove these machines to see if the patient is viable. All right. Without them, the patient is nonviable, and at this point the family says, we just don't want to continue anymore. . . . We want this patient to die instead of being kept alive. What happens is that you remove the patient from the breathing machine. This is the first thing. Then you have in front of you a patient struggling to breathe, who cannot breathe because he is too ill. And gradually, because the patient becomes hypoxic, it sets up a chain of events, one of which is hypotension, or lowering of the blood pressure. Now, morphine is a calming agent, also a pain reliever, but it also drops blood pressure so that when you give a certain amount of morphine. . . . It's best given IV because given intramuscularly to an elderly patient it's not absorbed, it just sits in the muscle, you know. So you give it IV and within a few minutes the pressure is down even further and therefore the patient is more hypoxic and sinks gradually into unconsciousness. And then a further dose of morphine shortly after the first one continues this trend, and then, of course, as the patient becomes more and more hypoxic, you understand, the cardiac output is lower and the patient goes into shock, and dies. And this is absolutely justified, totally justified. Also, there was one instance I can remember in which the patient was conscious. This was a particularly horrendous incident when we had a patient with chronic obstructive lung disease, and it was the end stage, and he had been in and out of the hospital many times. He continued to smoke, though he had been told not to. He had so little lung function that he was . . . he was not even in a bed-chair, he was in bed for the whole of his life. He had no interest in life at all. He was brought in to us and he had an infection on top of it all, and it was decided by his private internist together with his family that we would not support this man, that we would not intubate him and give him respiratory care as we had done before, because this was just prolonging life that could not be prolonged. And so then what happened was that the man was very distressed and uncomfortable because he couldn't breathe. He couldn't get enough oxygen. So then, what happens, you see, normally, to a chronic obstructive lung patient. . . . You do not give them anything at all to suppress respiration because they need all the drive they can get. So what was decided was that since we couldn't . . . since we were not going to support him anymore, and that since he was in distress, we would give him a calming agent, the morphine. And in calming him down and relaxing and relieving him of his anxiety, because he couldn't breathe, we also depressed his respirations, and this finally proved . . . ended in death for this man. And he was conscious when this was first administered, and it was administered with the intent . . . with the idea to make him more comfortable.

I really have no qualms about . . . actively administering enough of a dose that I knew would bring a patient down. I don't have the hangups . . . well, they're really not hangups . . . that the doctors have. But the doctors are . . . their code is to prolong life, to preserve life, generally, and that's the way it has to be. And it's a very big person who can admit there is no more we can do for this patient, this patient is going to die and he's suffering horribly. It's a very big person, in my experience, a very rare person, who can do that . . .

KANSAS CITY (AP), DEC. 25 — HARRY S. TRUMAN'S HEART-BEAT BECAME MORE IRREGULAR LATE YESTERDAY AS THE FORMER PRESIDENT LAY IN A COMA, HIS CONDITION STILL CRITICAL.

RESEARCH HOSPITAL AND MEDICAL CENTER SAID IN A STATEMENT THAT MR. TRUMAN'S HEART CONDITION WAS "SLIGHTLY WORSE IN THAT HE IS EXPERIENCING MORE FREQUENT PERIODS OF ABNORMAL CARDIAC RHYTHM." BUT THE STATEMEN ADDED THAT HIS LUNGS SEEMED SLIGHTLY LESS CONGESTED.

"Oh shit, I missed out."
"Don't sweat it, maybe you can try for Mao."

RN: You know, I think it's worse to leave it up to the individual patient. A lot of them are in no condition to decide anyway. In terminally ill patients, things start to build up in them. They get very paranoid for one thing. And in . . . they get to a point, they say, leave me alone, don't touch me, go away, I hate you. And some of them will kick and bite and scream if they are able to. And some will lie there in a cross, tight, angry little mood, and if you put a thing of medicine on a bedside table, leaving it up to them, they'd likely just go *wham* and knock it flying. Besides, I think that imposes more guilt on the patient. They feel, well, gee, am I copping out by doing this? Shouldn't I really be staying and fighting? And the doctor who leaves it . . . that just reflects his own personal insecurity, his indecision and his unwillingness to make the judgment, so he's copping out, too, and he's aiding and abetting a suicide, and maybe committing murder, too. It's difficult . . .

You know, it's very hard to decide. Who has the right to decide who lives and who dies. Of course, some people say God has, but then there are people — patients and doctors and nurses — who are atheists and don't believe in God, so it really is hard, and I think that all one has to go on, really, is the clinical picture of the patient. If you know the patient has no lung tissue left and. . . . How can you transplant a pair of lungs into a seventy-year-old man who has got damage to systems and organs from the disease, from the progression of the disease? I mean, how can you do that, what can you offer?

Many, many times, the patient will ask for death . . . but in every instance that I can remember that they've said it, they didn't really mean it. And so what I've always done is I've sat down with them and we've talked it through. You see, many patients say this. A lot of younger patients who are just having a sort of crisis of an illness will say that. They'll say, oh dear God, I can't take it anymore, just put me out of this misery. But they don't really mean it. They're saying that to, you know, sort of frighten you, as a sensational kind of remark.

> Thou shalt not kill; but need'st not strive
> Officiously to keep alive.
> — Arthur Hugh Clough

> A door is open for us — death, eternal refuge where one is sensible of nothing.
> — Cicero

> The bounty of Providence has filled the world with herbs for painless death.
> — Pliny the Elder

> Incurables are a worry to relatives and an expense to the state. We ought to have the moral courage to put them out of the way. A little chloroform and it would be all over.
> — The Reverend Charles Francis Potter, organizer of the Euthanasia Society of America, 1938

Second MD: Right. As surgeons we do have that impulse to fight for life, to go that extra measure, even in cas which are almost desperate, and I'll agree with my colleague on that. And we do remember our oath and that sort of thing, but at the same time I recognize there are cases in which you doubt whether you're doing the right thing, keeping a patient alive. Maybe saving the life of a very old atherosclerotic, mental patient. The best example I can remember during my years of practice was saving the life of a mentally ill, a retarded child born with an annular pancreas. Yes, I do. I feel there are times when we must let the patient go, particularly from a surgical standpoint when we find there is totally incurable disease, such as cancer, and my God we should know when a disease is incurable, all these miracles notwithstanding. I think as a surgeon I am justified — let me put it another way — I am *not* justified in prolonging life by surgery or supportive treatment beyond what in the past would have been natural death if the condition is not remedial. If prolongation of life has to be the rule, then it must be comfortable, and I emphasize that word comfortable, for to me it means more than adequate, not just . . . okay. We have to prolong life, I suppose, but not dying, not prolong beyond all hope. So what do I do? Well, in the presence of widespread, inoperable brain damage, renal failure, and the very old patient with, say, far advanced cardiovascular and pulmonary insufficiency, I am inclined to relax and accept death.

Teenager: I think if you watch somebody die . . . I was convinced I would want to die if I had to be like my cousin, and she was just around my age, seventeen, and I believe if someone didn't take my life, I would kill myself. I don't think that would be wrong under certain circumstances, like we kill people in war and so on, and we take babies in abortions to improve health and mental attitudes of mothers, and we kill people in electric chairs because that's justified, or they shoot horses, and this is all right. So why do we have to have laws that say that suicide is always wrong and giving a patient something to help him die is wrong? This girl, my cousin, she drowned to death in her own mucus, and every day she'd beg me, she'd say, Karen, don't let them give me another radiation treatment, and she'd be crying because it was so painful. . . . Please don't do it again, please don't. . . . As a matter of fact, I think that with all that radiation treatment they disintegrated some of her cells, and they were causing other parts of her body to . . . I mean, you could almost break a finger off her, and her hair was falling out, she just used to cry all the time. And they brought mustard treatments, gas or something like that . . .

Second MD: What I say is that we must consider the age group, diagnose the condition and come up with a valid judgment, a valid *clinical* judgment, as to what the salvaged product will be, and if we need to we let the patient go, let him go, for there are times when this is the humane course, and in so doing we are not usurping the prerogatives of any God, this is not really the case at all. When the patient is suffering from a far advanced disease, when he is a human vegetable and a great burden to his family, to society, and especially when there is no hope of amelioration, well, yes, it is our moral duty to let him pass on. Look, doing a cordotomy on a cancer patient with metastasis is an unnecessary and fatal procedure, so let him die, and don't call it euthanasia, please don't do that, because we're not killing him, we're just letting him die, as nature wills it . . .

And, yes, keeping a dying patient alive indefinitely is a

costly procedure, a fierce drain on finances and on the emotions of the family. But, I don't like to think that that's the main reason I would agree that a patient should be let go at times. I hope that's not my main reason. I like to think, rather, that the decision should be based only on the patient's own welfare, no one else's, and that's where I disagree with some of my colleagues who seem to concern themselves more with the quality of life of the survivors than with that of the patient. The patient's welfare, the benefits that *he* will gain by living, this is the prime factor.

I don't feel that the doctor has the right to do something actively to help a patient die, even though I feel a patient should be allowed to die without the taking of extraordinary measures. . . . And I suppose it should be up to the patient, in the final analysis, but even at that I think the doctor is the only one who knows whether the patient can or cannot make it, and this is a helluva load to carry, but is there any other way? If you leave it entirely up to the patient and his family, you open the door to a lot more trouble than if you left it to the attending physician. And I think a doctor should be pretty sure in his own mind that the patient hasn't got a prayer before he quits. I've been in this business a long time, and I've never ever been wrong about when a patient of mine has been at the end of the line, and I suppose I'm one of those rare animals in this profession in that I've also never seen a miraculous cure. They've worked out just as I thought they would . . . they've died or they've lived. Someone has got to do it, and I guess that's part of the job, tough as it is, this making of the decision. It can't be any other way if you want to keep the proper moral controls operating. Dignity in death, that's what it's all about today, and dignity means the right to die as comfortably as possible, not obscenely, stuck full of tubes and pumped full of oxygen and hidden behind a wall of computers so that your loved ones can't see you. But it doesn't mean that the patient has the right to tell me when. I make that judgment, I just have to, when it comes to extraordinary steps, for hopeless patients who are deteriorating like snow melting on a warm day. . . . And by all this I don't mean that we should never use artificial means, that would be preposterous. Lord, all of us in this business have pulled plenty of patients through, and that's not miraculous, patients who would have died without assistance. You know, now it's possible to feed a person only by vein for long periods of time, so you keep that up until that patient is strong enough and until you can cure him surgically, and if you can cure him that's the crux of it. That's certainly not the same as filling a dead man's lungs full of air and calling him alive, or keeping his blood moving with an electric pump. If the rest of him isn't going to cooperate, then you have to let him go . . .

I think it has to be based on whether the man can live on his own or on ordinary treatment, and that means anything that can be obtained conveniently, inexpensively, and which offers reasonable hope of benefit. . . . And another thing, about a person's usefulness, or uselessness. . . . As I said, I hope I make decisions on the basis of the patient's welfare, on the benefits that he'll obtain from life, and as I said also there are times when you wonder if you've done the right thing in saving someone who, maybe like that Mongoloid, won't have much of a life. . . . But what I mean to say is that I try not to be influenced by how useful or how useless, in a productive sense, the patient will be. I try not to do that. I could not say, for instance, that paralysis would be tantamount to a life of uselessness. I suppose what it all boils down to is, if I can save him, I do it, if I can't, I don't. When I say save, I mean just that. Save. I mean able to live without artificial support, without continual artificial support. Diabetics need insulin, people need food to live, thyroid medication is essential, and all of this is standard treatment, if you will. Saved means the disease is cured or at least arrested for a while, or it has lessened in intensity. Too often there's a tendency to be unrealistic about those goals when deciding whether to make a fight for it. You know that word rehabilitation is a tough one, and that's where those of us who have to make the judgment have trouble . . .

What I fear is that the euthanasia movement will get carried away, and that there will be certain criteria for rehab, just as there now are for what constitutes death. You might be able to do that for death, but for what constitutes rehabilitation, that's a bit more tricky. . . . I think we all have a tendency to fight like crazy for the life of an elder statesman, because he's so highly visible, because his loss will be a loss to the world, maybe because saving him looks good for the surgeon, and what happens is that the patient isn't fighting for his life so much as the doctors are. But now what about that poor guy who hasn't contributed a damn? Do we fight as hard? And I don't mean to sound like my gung ho colleagues who go all out with everything they've got to the bitter end when there's no hope for some poor derelict. What I'm trying to say, all that I'm trying to say, is that I get worried about the possibility of too many guidelines about who should be saved and who shouldn't. I think this is pretty cut and dried . . . the judgment is a clinical one for no matter who, though that's hard sometimes, and if we lose sight of that we're only making this whole thing more difficult. As I said, there are times when you quit, when you just have to quit, when you don't do any more . . . and anyone who doesn't accept that is being unreasonable. . . . I don't like to sound like a mechanic, but you can't help it, and isn't that what it's all about anyway? If a car's running properly, or at least it's functioning reasonably well, you try to keep it that way, whether it's a Caddie or a VW, and if not . . .

KANSAS CITY (UPI), DEC. 26 — HARRY S. TRUMAN, 88, LAY "NEAR DEATH" IN A DEEP COMA LAST NIGHT, HIS HEALTH WORSENING STEADILY, DOCTORS SAID.

MR. TRUMAN'S HEART AND KIDNEYS WERE FAILING, HIS TEMPERATURE WAS INCREASING TO 104 DEGREES AND HIS VITAL SIGNS WAVERING WILDLY.

BESS TRUMAN, 87, HIS WIFE OF MORE THAN 50 YEARS, WAS AT HIS BEDSIDE IN A SIXTH-FLOOR ROOM AT RESEARCH HOSPITAL AND MEDICAL CENTER.

WALLACE H. GRAHAM, MR. TRUMAN'S PHYSICIAN, SAID AS ONE AILMENT WAS TREATED, ANOTHER ORGAN WOULD FAIL.

"TREATMENT WHICH HAS A FAVORABLE EFFECT ON ONE SYSTEM HAS AN ADVERSE EFFECT ON OTHERS," HE SAID. "IT'S VIRTUALLY IMPOSSIBLE TO GET A BALANCE."

A. Yes. Let them go, especially if they've got uremia. There is a very high cost factor in dying from that.

A. Twenty years ago, I would have done all in my power. Not today.

A. I use common sense.

A. I ease them out when they hit bottom.

A. And when life is no longer a pleasure.

A. I do it, and then I pray.

A. I let them hold on until they can see distant relatives.

A. We've been doing it for years. Why the recent interest?

A. A drink of water is all I give them.

A. I consult another doctor.

A. I write it on the orders: Dr. Black. Or Dr. Standstill.

AN FBI WIRETAP: "Now, like you got a guy to hit, and you tell him you're goin' to give him a shot of truth serum to find out if he's levelin', right?"

"How many guys you gonna con with that?"

"And what you really give him is a big belt of poison."

"Who the fuck is gonna go for that?"

"Well, if he don't, then you give it to him straight. You tell him, look, like you got four, five guys in this room. You know they're goin' to kill you. Tony Boy here wants to shoot you in the head and leave you in the street. Wouldn't you rather take this stuff in the mainline? We put you behind your wheel. We don't embarrass your family or nothin' that way."

"You ever have a guy agree to gettin' hit?"

"Yeah. This one guy went for it. There was me, Zim and Petie B., and we took this guy out in the woods. I said, look, you gotta go, so let me hit you right in the heart and you won't feel a thing. He says, Ralphie, I'm innocent, but if you gotta do it. . . . So I hit him in the heart and it went right through him."

"Maybe you're right, about the poison I mean."

"Sure. Look at Baretti. They hit him in the Surfside East. That man never should have been disgraced like that."

Greek: eu, good; thanatos, death; thus, a good death.

"How would you like to go out, kids?"

"Fast."

"Smiling."

"Jump in the ocean."

"Off a cliff."

"Quick."

"Fall out of a plane, through the sky."

"Oh, wow."

Laughter.

"Some ride."

"Whee."

"Anybody for dying in bed?"

Groans.

"No way."

"That's Hollywood."

"With my family around? That's awful. I worry about that more than death. I mean, I just imagine how my parents would be, sitting around my bed if I were dying, and that hurts to think about, how they'd be looking at me and crying. I just couldn't stand that."

"Oh, I don't know. I wouldn't want to die too fast and have, like, loose ends. I'd want to tie it all up, you know? Like I'd like to know six months ahead that I was going to die rather than not know at all, 'cause like there's so many things I could do in those six months that I had not done already, that I was planning to do, and I could do it all, right there and then."

© New York Times News Service

KANSAS CITY, DEC. 27 — HARRY S. TRUMAN, 33RD PRESIDENT OF THE UNITED STATES, DIED TUESDAY. HE WAS 88 YEARS OLD.

TRUMAN, AN OUTSPOKEN AND DECISIVE MISSOURI DEMOCRAT WHO SERVED IN THE WHITE HOUSE FROM 1945 TO 1953, SUCCUMBED AT KANSAS CITY'S RESEARCH HOSPITAL AND MEDICAL CENTER AT 8:50 A.M. EST.

HE HAD BEEN A PATIENT THERE FOR 22 DAYS, STUBBORNLY STRUGGLING AGAINST LUNG CONGESTION, HEART IRREGULARITY, KIDNEY BLOCKAGE, FAILURE OF HIS DIGESTIVE SYSTEM AND THE ENCROACHMENT OF OLD AGE.

A HOSPITAL SPOKESMAN SAID DEATH RESULTED FROM THE "COMPLEXITY OF ORGANIC FAILURES CAUSING COLLAPSE OF THE CARDIOVASCULAR SYSTEM." THE FORMER PRESIDENT HAD BEEN IN A COMA FOR THREE DAYS.

NEW YORK (AP), DEC. 27 — DAY AFTER DAY AFTER DAY, HARRY S. TRUMAN, AGED 88, AND SICK BEYOND REPAIR, CLUNG TO LIFE.

HIS PHYSICIAN, WALLACE GRAHAM, WAS IMPRESSED, SAYING THAT MR. TRUMAN'S "REMARKABLE STRENGTH AND TENACIOUS REACTION" REFLECTED THE FORMER PRESIDENT'S ATTITUDE TOWARD LIFE.

OTHER DOCTORS AGREE THAT A STRONG WILL TO LIVE AND A POSITIVE PERSONALITY COULD AFFECT A PERSON'S PHYSICAL SYSTEM ENOUGH TO POSTPONE DEATH . . .

"MANY TIMES, PEOPLE SEEM JUST READY TO DIE, AND

THEY DO," SAID DR. WAYNE MEISNER, A PSYCHIATRIST AT
THE NORTH SHORE HOSPITAL ON LONG ISLAND.

AS FOR MR. TRUMAN, MEISNER SAID, PART OF HIS
STRENGTH WAS THAT HE LOVED PEOPLE AND WAS LOVED,
THAT HE WAS "ORIENTED TOWARD THE WORLD AND HAD
LOTS OF OUTSIDE INTERESTS BEYOND HIMSELF AND NO
FEELING THAT HE WANTED TO LEAVE THIS 'MISERABLE
WORLD.'

"BORED PEOPLE DON'T WANT TO LIVE. HE WAS NOT
BORED. TRUMAN WAS ALWAYS LOOKING FORWARD AND HAD
A STRONG COMPETITIVE SPIRIT."

Charlotte Rigney, 45

First of all, she was eighty-four years old, and she was
basically an extremely healthy woman. I can't ever recall
her being sick in bed, in my whole life. She was, I presume,
in bed when I was born [laughs], and she must have gone
to bed when my sister was born, who's two years younger
than I am. She had me at home, my sister in the hospital.
She was extremely energetic, hyperthyroid type, I guess,
probably. . . . So she simply wasn't anyone you would
imagine giving in to sickness. She just wouldn't have it,
that's all there was to it.

Now, when she was probably around eighty-two, her
dentist noticed there was an ulcer in her mouth, apparently
caused by her dental plate. And it turned out to be malignant, and she . . . I didn't see her at this time, she was
away from here and she was under the care of a doctor in
Buffalo, and she had cobalt treatments for about I think
six months. They were believed to have cleared up the

cancer and . . . because she was the kind of person she was, and she had so little to do with doctors all her life, she did not go back for checkups after cobalt treatments after they thought she was in the clear. I think she was completely impatient with the whole idea of being sick. I think she always had the attitude that it just wouldn't happen to her. . . . You know, it wouldn't dare. Anyway, she should have gone back six months later. And I still blame the original doctor. I feel that he should have followed up her case. First of all, if he had been treating her he should have known her personality, after all, if she was in her eighties, and it was a heavy winter in Buffalo, that it was not easy for her to get onto a bus, say, and she probably wouldn't have bothered to take a taxi, things like that. I feel that he should have followed that case up. And he did not. He did not. He never pursued her coming back to the office for her checkups. I can see maybe a doctor if he had some conversation with a younger person about something or other like that, but he knew she was older, that she might let things go, that she might just, you know, say forget it . . .

Do you think that maybe she was playing a game, that she had an idea something was wrong and she didn't . . .

No. I don't think so. I think she thought it was over with. And she just did not go back. Now, there was a point about a year later when she knew that there was something wrong . . . again. I know the reason she didn't do anything about it then, and this was purely a family situation. My sister had gotten married in the meantime, and her husband wanted to move to Phoenix. My mother suspected that there was something back again . . . this was probably in the middle of her eighty-third year. They were planning to go to Arizona, she knew . . . and she knew that if my sister found that the cancer was back that she would not go. And she thought it might interfere with the marriage. She was living with my sister. So she didn't say anything. Well, they delayed another month, anyway, and it was October before they finally left . . . and I went to Buffalo. I brought her back to live with me, and within two days of the time we got here we saw Dr. Evans . . .

Now, I had never seen in her mouth. She just wouldn't show anything, and as a matter of fact I . . . it didn't even occur to me to ask. I imagined something tiny, an ulcer about the size of a cold sore maybe. So when Dr. Evans examined her, he asked me if I had ever seen it, and I said no. In the first place you just wouldn't ask my mother to look. She was extremely independent, and she handled her own affairs, and if she wanted to show it to you she would show it to you. At any rate, Dr. Evans called me in to see it and it was unbelievable. It looked . . . I've never seen a cancer so I don't know what a cancer normally looks like, but the cancer . . . in her mouth . . . the whole side of her tongue looked like it was covered . . . it was ruffled, like the fungus that grows on trees? I didn't believe that it could be this large, that anyone could eat, or pretend to eat. . . . I didn't know how she had been eating all this time and I didn't know how my sister could have not seen it. She did tell my sister that she was having trouble with her plate but that she was going to wait till she got with me, where she could have a dentist that could follow her up and so forth. She was just fantastically inventive in the way she got everybody to not be aware of her condition. She must have been in great pain at that point. But she was an unusual woman, and I can remember as a child her cutting off the end of her finger and not even. . . . I mean she just held it under the running water and I can remember the bowl full of blood because the blood was just gushing out. . . . I mean she really cut it. She had put her hand into the vacuum cleaner and the fan had cut it off, and I can remember her telling me to get the doctor on the phone. And she never cried. She was . . . you know she had her tonsils removed with no anesthetic, when she was in her twenties, and when my father found out that there had been none used he almost killed the doctor, I mean he almost physically attacked the doctor. He was so angry with him. Anyway, she was eating very soft foods like mashed potatoes and soups and so forth.

Well, Evans scheduled an operation as soon as possible, and he did operate and he removed a portion of the tongue and a portion of the gum. And he said, after she had been in the hospital for a few days, that it appeared he had gotten it all, and that it was quite remarkable. I think the only reason they felt there was some hope was because at that age the cells should not be multiplying, and that if they took enough . . . and they took beyond the point that was cancerous, according to his description . . . that they could prevent further occurrence.

Well, at the time she was in the hospital, she did have a heart problem, it may have stopped briefly or accelerated or something. I don't know enough about physiology to understand exactly what happened, but he did call in a specialist, and they gave her some heart pills to take, which she continued to take after she left the hospital.

She was a very cooperative patient in the hospital, and I think she was frightened. Everyone is. But I think she had resigned herself at one point that she wouldn't come out of the operation. We did talk a little bit, I don't say we talked a great deal. . . . After all, when you're eighty-four you don't. . . . Anyway because she was alone so much when I got her home I felt that maybe she might be dwelling on things, like, well she was eighty-four and you've got to think in terms of you may die. And I asked her one day what she thought about in the daytime . . . and she said, well if you're asking me whether I think about dying all the time, I'm not. At any rate, at home the situation was like this. Her mouth was still sore, and she was on liquid foods, and we were supposed to go back to Evans for a checkup. Well, there was a very bad storm the day she was supposed to go back, and I've often wondered whether this could have . . . and I had trouble with the car and we couldn't get in that day, so we had to reschedule, like three weeks from now. I would hate to think . . . but the worst situation was that I couldn't have . . . I couldn't afford to have the car fixed. Finally, I bought another car. I really couldn't afford it but I bought it, and I borrowed from a couple of places to buy it, because I felt that I absolutely needed a car if she was going to be sick. . . .

At any rate, I brought her in to Dr. Evans and he looked at her. . . . Well, she had been back for one office visit and she checked out all right then and he was very pleased. And it was then he gave her something . . . some medication that he hoped would retard. . . . Anyway, this next time he found something again. And he said she would have to go into the hospital and have a biopsy. By the time we got back to the hospital, a few days later, for a biopsy, he looked at her and said he could do nothing . . . it had gone too far.

Did he tell her that?

No. He didn't tell her. He told me.

And you never told her?

No. Not really. When we got back home, she was in and out of bed. She would get out of bed and try to fix something. She was terribly active, and she loved to do the dishes. And I was going back and forth to work at the time, and I let her do what she wanted to do. Evans told her he was going to try a medication that was going to try to retard it. That's what we told her. He could not operate anymore, because it would have meant taking the whole jaw and she simply could not survive that . . . there was no point putting her through it, and he wouldn't recommend doing it, and I wouldn't ask him to do it if there was no chance. Also, if she did survive it, at eighty-four to have the whole jaw and part of her neck . . . well, she would have to spend the whole rest of her life in the hospital. Anyway, she was taking the heart pills and pain pills and whatever Evans had given her to retard the growth. I think his feeling was that if they could keep it from getting much worse she could live on liquids for a while, and she was not very enthusiastic about food anyway at this point. Incidentally her top weight in her life was about one hundred eighteen, hundred and twenty. She was a very slim, wiry woman, and by now she had gone down to the eighties. Maybe seventy-five or seventy-six, I don't know. At any rate, I could pick her up very easily.

So I was away every day, and she was sick enough to require nursing care. She was in and out of bed. And I didn't want to have her in a nursing home if I could avoid it.

Anyway she began to get progressively worse. When I say that I mean she began to spend a little more time in bed than out of it. [Her voice breaks.] She used to heat soup for herself, or make an eggnog after she came back from the hospital. But she was getting to the point where she preferred not to eat. She didn't have the energy. And she was starving to some extent, I suppose. I think she . . . in a way . . . phased herself out. I think that she knew. . . . We kept talking in terms of hopefulness, that the medication might retard the cancer. But she was a very intelligent person. And she knew he could not operate. . . . However, she went along with the fantasy . . . for us, rather than herself. So that we could talk in terms of next summer and what we'd do, that sort of thing. Well, by this time we had gone to another doctor, not a surgeon because there was nothing more to be done on that end, and this doctor was very nice, youngish, in his thirties, and she liked him, and Dr. Evans said this was good. The extent of this doctor's care, Dr. Segal, was to prescribe medicine for her that would build her up, vitamins because she was getting practically no food, not even liquids. She would drink maybe a quarter of a cup at a meal. There came a day when I called the doctor's office and said that I didn't believe she was capable of even getting into the car, and she had said, do I have to go? Do I have to get up and get dressed? We had an appointment with Dr. Segal, and it was a terrible effort and I didn't want to force her to go out even though it might have been good for her to get out. So, Segal came to the house instead, and he examined her and said to her, are you taking the medicines and so on? [She wipes at her eyes, which are filling.] I found out afterward that she wasn't taking her medicine. This is the way we had worked that out. . . . I would leave them in separate cups with a note saying what time of day to take them. My Carrie would come home from school — I would never put more than enough out for her to take — and Carrie would come home and put the rest out. So that there was no chance of her forgetting that she had taken something and then take too much like the heart pills. At any rate, we did find afterward . . . I found pills that she had tucked in drawers, inside the pillows and like that. Now these were pain pills and whether she figured that the pills were prolonging things. . . . However, I've read since then, reading about people who are older and sick. . . . I don't know whether I would have made a different decision if I. . . . I should have known more than I did. . . . I have found that they do hide medication. Now I don't know why this is. Believe me she was not fuzzy. She was not at all fuzzy, not vague or anything. She didn't not recognize anyone or anything like that. Well, when Segal came to the house he said, in the other room, that it was a matter of time. He said . . . I can't remember the whole thing . . . he said I don't know what to recommend at this point. He said she will eventually get to the point where you'll have to have a nurse here or take her to a nursing home, because she'll have to be fed intravenously. And he said the cancer will get larger and will fill her throat and she won't be able to. . . . But he said that at this point it wasn't necessary. Then he said, and these were his words, he said the most merciful thing that could happen would be for her to get pneumonia. I didn't understand this because I didn't know about the pneumonia you could get from lying in bed. I thought this would mean like from a cold and I said to myself how in God's name can she possibly get a cold and get pneumonia when she's in the house. . . . You know, medical people assume that if you're reasonably bright and you've been out in the world you know a lot more than you do about medicine. But if you've never been involved in sickness you just don't know. And since I had never heard about pneumonia except the kind you get after you get a cold . . . it never occurred to me. Well, by now she was having difficulty getting up, for the bathroom. So we got a bedpan, and we used that for a couple of days, and she hated it. First of all, she was very thin and very bony and it hurt her to use it, and I got padding. . . . We got some sponge rubber, but it still was very uncomfortable for her. It hurt her to move at this point, she was so frail. So I said when I'm here wouldn't it be easy for me to carry you into the bathroom and she said yes. And I carried her into the bathroom. I think this was the day that I made the decision that . . . I didn't consciously make the decision, but I think this was the day I decided in my own mind [she begins to sob]. It's traumatic at this point, I'm sorry. . . . I think this was when I decided I would rather have her dead than alive. Not so much for her as for me, because I just couldn't stand to see her suffering like that. I couldn't stand to see her in a position where she had to be carried around by someone . . .

Incidentally, before she went into the operation and she considered the possibility that she might not recover or she might be . . . terminally ill, you know . . . she had said to me that she would rather have an opportunity to . . . commit suicide, I guess is what she meant. She would rather take too many pills. . . . She said if there were a chance to have more pills I would rather take them than lie in bed and be sick. And I said to her that I would feel the same way . . . I would feel the same way. And I said . . . are you trying to . . . tell me that you would . . . would want me to help you? And she said . . . and she said, I'll tell you something, I've always thought that, but, she said, now that it was a . . . a possibility, I wouldn't want . . . she wouldn't want me to get into trouble doing it. She said there was always the chance that I . . . she said I would like to do it, but I would not like to have you in a position to . . . in a position of. . . . What she said was that if she were going to have to lie in bed sick . . . that she would want the opportunity to take an overdose of something. But she did not quite . . . want me to become implicated by making it actually available to her. I mean, she did spell it out, but she didn't, you know. So, I felt that I knew how she felt about it. . . . She was asking me to, but then she wasn't . . .

So, say two days before she died, she was quite clear and talkative, and the only time I was impatient with her . . . and I've been so sick about it afterward . . . I got angry with her because she wouldn't take her medicine. At that point she said, maybe I ought to go into a nursing home where they know how to take care of me, and I said I didn't mean to be impatient, it was just that it upsets me so because you won't take the medicine. . . . I think she knew that the medicine wasn't doing her any good. And I think maybe she knew that I knew it but wouldn't admit it. . . . I couldn't let myself admit it, and I had to insist that she take it. . . . I was trying to keep up this fantasy . . .

At any rate, I felt this was such an undignified thing for my mother, who had been so active and who had taken care of everybody else all her life. Anyway, I had taken a week off and was working at home. . . . She was too sick to stay at home alone, and I didn't have a nurse yet, I couldn't find a nurse. . . . We had a visiting nurse come in, two times a day, one came early in the morning, one later. . . . And it was the visiting nurse who told me about turning her over so that she wouldn't get pneumonia. . . . So I didn't . . . didn't turn her over. . . . Then I knew . . . that was the kind of pneumonia the doctor was talking about . . .

And when Segal came to see her again, he said . . . you

know, you can stop medication if you feel like it. . . . And I did stop the medication . . . and she just lapsed into a coma. On Friday, the visiting nurse came and spoke of moving her, and I said, I'll do it . . . but I didn't do it. She was in the coma, and we went into the room and I said something, and when I did that she lifted both eyebrows . . . and the nurse said. . . . She must be able to hear us . . .

FOUR

The Caretakers

The loneliness of each individual human being in serious illness, and most of all when near to death . . . is one of the limits of the human condition. *"On mourra seul,"* said Pascal. I attempted to say the same thing in a lecture once: each of us dies alone. An academic critic thought that simple remark extremely funny. I wouldn't wish him or anyone else — and nor would any of you who have been compelled to witness it — to have to undergo the full extremity of that condition.

> — Lord C. P. Snow, "The Hospital as a Humane Institution," an address at St. Barnabas Hospital for Chronic Diseases

If, together with adequate physical care, the dying person had sufficient human companionship, most of his anguish would be prevented.

> — John Hinton, *Dying*

TO: NEWS MEDIA
RE: BETATRON

The 42 MEV Betatron is the first unit of its size in the western hemisphere. The complete unit weighs 22 tons; the head alone, 6½ tons.

The stand and head rotate 190 degrees.

In a room behind the head are units for cooling the electromagnet, which heats up as the current passes through it. 7000 volts is the current used to activate the magnet.

The equipment was made in West Germany, assembled and tested there, then shipped to the Medical Center and reassembled.

In a room over the Betatron is a large frequency transformer to stabilize the energy to 50 cycles per second.

In the Betatron room are two television cameras operating on a closed circuit; one shows the entire room, while the other is focused on the patient and the Betatron head. The television screens are located in an adjacent control room from which the radiotherapy technicians monitor the treatment. During the course of the two-minute treatment, the patient is alone in the Betatron room, with a heavy door made of metal sealing off the facility. While the dosage is almost entirely concentrated in the beam directed at the tumor, the air does become slightly irradiated. While this is of no harm to the patient, who is scheduled for only a few treatments, the constant exposure would prove dangerous for the technician. The room is also provided with telecommunication so that patient and technician can talk during the treatment.

Unlike the smaller Betatrons in use (the 18 MEVs), nearly all adjustments on the 42 MEV Betatron are made electrically, since the equipment is too heavy to adjust manually.

Patient Status Report

NAME: OMER F. MARCOUX
M DOB: 4/6/21
DIAGNOSES/PROBLEMS
   ACTIVE & ESTABLISHED
     RETICULUM CELL SARCOMA
       SEVERITY: SEVERE
       PROGRESSION: PROGRESSING
     LYMPHOMA
       SEVERITY: SEVERE
       PROGRESSION: PROGRESSING
       COMMENT: THORACENTESIS CONTINUE CYTOXAN REFER
         TO RADIOLOGY FOR FURTHER MGT

DR. MARINO (4/16/72)

Eileen Fryer, 24

The physicist gives us the numbers, and we monitor the kicks. Push this button here and it starts the machine. Like, some people only come in once and you might give them a thousand rads, and that way they don't have to come back. The doctor draws things up for us, and he writes down how much dosage and so forth, field signs on the back of the chart, and it all goes to the physicist and he does all the calculations, and that's where we get the kicks from.

We talk to the patients before they get the treatments. They know they can talk to us while we're setting them up. It takes eight to ten minutes to set someone up, so we talk to them, try to calm them down, you know. We have to calm them down because they're really scared of the machine. They're afraid mostly that it's going to come down on them, or something like that, and we have to settle them down. They don't feel anything in there, but the only thing is that noise, and when you close that door on them they get really uptight, and they want us with them and so on, but, of course, we can't stay in there or we'd be wiped out.

We can talk to them over the intercom if we want but we don't usually do that. I've only done it once. It scares them more, hearing that voice coming out of nowhere. We can see them but they can't see us, and to hear that voice is a little eerie. Might make them think there's someone in the room, sometimes, and they'll move and that's not too good. Often we'll just turn off the machine if they get really upset in there, and we'll go in and talk to them, try to calm them down . . .

And you can talk about lots of things to help these people who are so frightened, and you just play that by ear. God, I wouldn't particularly want to be under that thing either. The thing you've got to make them realize is that the machine isn't going to come down on them, like I tell them we've got plenty of nuts and bolts in it, and there's no way it's going to fall. And you've got to explain as much as you can, depending on their own intelligence, why we can't stay in the room with them, about how the beam is directed at them for only a few minutes and that we're in there every day and the accumulation isn't good and so on, but I try not to tell them that it could wipe us out, like that, because that gets them more upset. And they all want to know how come the beam kills the tumor and nothing else, and we try to tell them about that, if we can. . . . But mostly what you try to do is get them away from talking too much about that monster over their head, that's pretty scary.

They hear that noise, though, and even though they don't feel a thing they hear that. Even the ones who've had the treatment for a couple of days worry about the noise. Patients are very perceptive, you know, all their sensitivities are exaggerated. Once they get in the hospital, and especially when they get under a machine like this one, they start to imagine all sorts of things. Well, even the ones who've been in treatment before will notice that this particular machine makes different noises every day. One lady, I'd go in and stop the machine and she'd say, it's a different sound today, I'm really scared, there's something wrong with it today, like that. And if the treatment is a few seconds longer one day than it was yesterday, they'll notice that too. The patients know. Don't ever figure they don't because they do, they know what they've got and they generally know what you're doing to them in there. They're just scared of it, that's all, and most of them just want to get it over with, graduation day we call it here, that's all.

And that's why we have to be so . . . so able to talk to them. We talk to them more than the doctors do, you know, because we're with the patient all the time, and so are some of the nurses. But some of the doctors, well, most of the doctors in radiology, they don't know one patient from the next one. I like to try to look at them as either a relative, or as a. . . . One patient of mine, he drove a cement mixing truck, and I'd ask him about his job, and I told him that when I was a kid I always wanted to ride on a cement truck because I never could figure how the things worked, and I meant that, I always was baffled by that thing rolling around on the back.

And he made a bet with me. . . . What we did was I knew, I noticed, that he had this thing going for one of the older nurses. . . . She's a widow, Mrs. Myles, and she's still pretty well stacked, and this Mr. Marcoux, he was a great old guy, about fifty or so, and he was feeling real down one day just before he came in for therapy, and he was saying he hoped to God it was going to do some good and all that. He wasn't always that way, and most of the time, when he wasn't in pain, they kept that pretty much under control, he would tell me these real filthy jokes, you know, and he was some stud in his day, I guess, and maybe he still was, I really don't know. But anyway, he used to talk a lot about it, and we all got a kick out of him and we went along with it, because I think that's a good thing, if it keeps his mind off his trouble, then I don't have any objection to that at all. Well, this one day he was complaining about the pain, it was running around his back, he said, and the swelling in his groin was getting worse, and he said, I just hope it works. I told him it must be rough to be that way, and I just told him to hang in there and that we'd try to do the very best we could for him, and I made him look at that stupid sign we've got up there that says your hospital cares, and I told him I just wanted him to know that there were a lot of hospitals in this city that could give him this treatment and we were glad he came to us because there's a lot of competition and we try harder. And I told him we needed thirty, forty patients a day on this unit just to pay for the machine, and he got a laugh out of that. Well, I told him that the radiation works a lot on people and that I bet it would work on him, and that he'd be back in shape again. I told him there was no guarantee but that I'd bet on it with him. He said he doubted it, that he was not going to make it, but he asked me what I'd bet. I told him I'd bet that two days after the treatment he'd feel so good he'd grab Mrs. Myles right by the ass. Well, he did get a laugh out of that. . . . If I lost, and he didn't start chasing Mrs. Myles around, then I was supposed to guarantee him that I'd spend one whole week showing him porno pictures to get him back in shape. . . . Either way, I told him, it was a good deal for him.

Well, the day we wheeled him into the Betatron room he was so-so, and I was trying to get him to tell me about his cement truck and getting him to promise to give me a ride on it and all that, and I tried to kid him about his days as a stud, and he did come out of it a little, said with a little chuckle that he was going to be a priest once, and I asked him which church, the one near the convent, and he said no, too much trouble fighting them clothes they wore, and I told him that street clothes were in now so he shouldn't have to worry if he got the urge to put on a collar, foolish talk like that . . . we had a nice back and forth way with each other. He was a little concerned about the treatment

188

and the room and being alone and so on, so I just told him to lie there really quiet and just think of Mrs. Myles. And I said that when the noise started up that I'd be outside there working the dials and having my coffee, too, because I didn't want him to think that I was giving that up just because he was lying in here. And I said that when he heard that noise to just imagine he was with Mrs. Myles on a jet going someplace together alone. And he said something about me watching out where I pointed the beam, that those were the family jewels and they were hard to replace, and I told him I knew all about a girl's best friends and that I always took care of my friends. He laughed again, and then I told him I had to go out and get the door closed, and I told him again to just think of Mrs. Myles and her ass, and he just looked up at me and he said, I got a hard-on just thinking of it. And I said, good, that'll give you something to hang onto while I'm zapping you . . .

Well, he died the next morning, and I just went home and cried like a baby, and all I could think about was the last thing he said about his hard-on, and about a joke he once told me about a guy who died with one and they couldn't get him into the coffin . . .

Nurses clearly need more training in the emotional needs of their patients and help in achieving sympathetic personal contacts with them.
— *The Lancet*

Empathy toward the dying patient is easy to talk about and has been an in thing over the past few years, possibly starting with *The Cancer Ward*. Perhaps all the talk has actually helped to increase empathy toward these patients, I can't say.

> But, through personal observations I see that 99 percent of what the nurse learns in school about caring for the psyche of the patient is not practiced outside teaching hospitals by anyone except the idealistic novice nurse during her first few weeks on her first job.
>
> — Donna Ledney, RN

Dorrit Briggs, RN

She is a primary nurse in the Oncology Unit at Boston University Medical Center. A responsive, soft-spoken young woman whose quiet eyes do not reflect, even when she speaks of it, the often hard death from slow malignancy they have witnessed.

I guess I got into this because my mother died of cancer. And I can remember her being at home and we needed nurses around the clock. And also she was in the hospital, in and out, and I was a child who could go into the hospital and see her. So I got into nursing and probably in cancer, although I didn't recognize why at the time.

My mother died at home, and I think that was a really nice thing because when she was sort of sick at the end we still felt a part of her life. And a part of her care. But when she died neither my brother nor I were allowed to go to the funeral, and it was just like we were alienated from what was going on, and we were immediately taken to a part of New York City and cared for very well by very good people. . . . But I think I felt that alienation a little bit, and then we came home and my mother wasn't there, and there was a whole house full of people, all of which I can remember vividly. I was about five or so. And I think one other thing I can remember quite well was going to school and coming home and thinking, well, it's almost spring, it's kind of warm out, and. . . . I had my leggings on, my woolen pants all winter . . . and I was thinking, I'd like to change into overalls, so I'll go home and ask Mommy. And all of a sudden it hit me . . . Mommy's not there.

When I had just graduated from nursing school, I had an experience with a patient who died and I had a long-term involvement with him, and I think that was a very satisfying experience, and helped me a lot in facing death. . . . It was a painful process, and he was a young person. He had Hodgkin's disease, and he came into the hospital one day, fortunately when we were not busy. And I pulled a chair up next to him. Usually, I was, you know, on the run, admitting patients, and there usually wasn't time to talk to them. But this day there was and I sat down with him, and the look of fear on his face was just something I'll never forget, and as his mother left him that day. . . . He was probably twenty-two, huge guy, about six-seven, basketball player. . . . And as his mother left I said to him, what helps you, Ralph? And he said, someone to talk to, and so I said, well, I'd really like to talk to you. What are you afraid of? And with that he just started talking about his, you know, fear of death, and his fear of the unknown after death and just not knowing what to expect in terms of dying. And yet, knowing his diagnosis and even feeling that this hospital was going to be his last one and that he would die in the hospital.

What did you tell him?

I really tried to listen to him. He was very open and really wanted to talk to someone. In fact, later he said that

I was the first one he'd talked to openly, you know, about death. And then later I asked him what his religious background had been and if he had seen a minister or a priest. He came from a Protestant denomination and he hadn't been to church for a while. And I have these very strong convictions in terms of afterlife and so on. And I just wanted to know how he felt about this, so I asked him if he felt there was such a thing, just to try to find out where his place was, and then I asked him what he felt about God, was God a personal being to him, or just some far-off force. I asked him what he thought about the Bible. He said he just hadn't attended church for a long time, that he had sort of given it up, but that recently he had been thinking about, you know, things . . . again. And so he talked about that and he said he really wanted to know that God cared about him and that he could relate to him in a personal way. And so I told him that he could do that if he wanted to, and I brought him in a Bible and I read him some Scriptures, psalms, and so forth, and he was comforted quite a bit by that. Several weeks later I went back to him. You know, I took care of him in between times but I can remember one specific night, and I just went in there and he was kind of having trouble breathing. And I sat down again with him and it was the middle of the night, and he said, you know, I've been thinking a lot and it just seems like I can't reason out why everything has happened to me the way it has, and I can't know what's ahead, but I can believe there is a God, somehow I can rest in that. And two days after that he died, and I was taking care of him. And it was really a beautiful experience. I was holding his hand, and he just stopped breathing. It was a very peaceful death. He didn't struggle or anything.

How did you feel about it?

I felt because we had talked about it a lot and we had talked through some of his past feelings in terms of religion . . . the chaplain had also come in and talked with him and I think that helped a lot . . . and I just knew him as a person and I felt like I had gotten involved in his life, and not just on a professional basis.

Were there any other experiences like that?

Well, just recently I had an experience with an elderly patient. And I was on the floor for about a month and got to know this person quite well. She's probably eighty-two and her husband had died three years previous to this admission. And I met her on the floor when she came in and she started crying almost immediately. And I just asked her what was the matter and sat down on her bed next to her. And she said that her husband had died and that since then she'd been very lonely and really missed him and she wouldn't care if she lived much longer herself. She had cancer of the lung. She was up and around getting radiation treatments then, but as the months progressed I was on another responsibility and so I wasn't on the ward, but I kept following her every few days to see how she was and she began to get progressively worse.

One day particularly . . . she was very, very apprehensive, and she couldn't settle down, she couldn't be comfortable in bed, and yet she kept saying that she wasn't afraid. She talked about it a lot that day, and the chaplain stayed for hours that night with her. The next day, she was much better — in terms of peace, not her disease — and during the next few days before she died I talked with her a lot about her funeral arrangements. She had written a poem and she recited it and said she wanted to have that recited at her funeral. And then another thing she did was that she had an angel that her niece had painted, it was on the other side of the room and she said she wanted that angel put on her coffin when she died. So I wrote a note right then and there and showed it to her and put it on the card that it was going to be put on her coffin, and then she . . . she had a bouquet of flowers and she wanted those to be sent to her niece who was just moving into a new house. So I wrote a note again and put that there. She asked for her nephew several times and I went and had him called. We also talked about God quite a bit, and I prayed with her. It was a very . . . when she died. . . . Oh, the morning that she died, I went in about eight o'clock and I just took her hand and about two minutes later, she died. She just stopped breathing. I don't know if she recognized me or anything because she was in a coma.

Were those experiences the first you had ever had with a dying patient?

The first one was . . . quite a few years ago. The first experience was when I was in nursing school. My attitude was different then. It was a lot different. I don't think we had a whole lot of help in school in terms of death and dying and how to handle it. A lot of it was sort of superficial, things like call the rabbi for this, the priest for that or, you know, the minister, or maybe you need the psychologist and so on. But you don't get a chance to work out your feelings too much. Except we did have a class on psychosocial aspects of patient care, but it didn't really deal with death that much, and so the first patient that I was assigned to as a student. . . . It was a very difficult experience because I was sort of left at a dinner time. There was someone else outside taking care of the twelve-bed ward and I was left in a single-bed room with this patient who was dying. And I didn't know what to expect, and my feeling inside was I just wanted to run away. And I knew his breathing was getting worse and I could just see his whole body sort of change and I knew he needed the touch . . . I remembered that. . . . The touch was the best thing. And I did touch him, but I was scared to death. And afterwards, you know, I went home and I cried and I cried and I just . . . I didn't talk to anyone about it. It was a really horrible experience.

What about the effect on you of all of these?

I think the first one I mentioned . . . the young man . . . brought about a big change in my attitude because I could see the value of spending the time really treating the person as a person instead of as some *thing* in a hospital. . . . Some disease or something like that. And, really, I not only learned from him but, I think, him from me, and we shared it together. I really felt like we met in, you know, our inner selves . . . our inner selves met in real communication, and that was what was important.

Are you comfortable working in this environment?

It's still . . . I think every person who fears death. . . . I was talking to a woman today. She's forty-two. She's still not really able to talk too much about death, and I sense that she's thinking a lot about it, and is making preparations and is able to cry some when thinking of her family. She has four children, and two of them are quite young. And you know, it's really difficult to go in and talk with her because I just wish I . . . that she didn't have to die, and could be a mother to those children.

Do you think that involvement is good for you as a professional? Could you do your job better if you were totally objective?

I think it's far more satisfying to us as nurses to get involved. It doesn't mean that every person gets involved to the same extent, but with what you feel comfortable with, and I think it's much more satisfying to the patient, too. There are still plenty of nurses who don't want to get involved, of course. But on the unit this is the thing we want to have. And we've set up, like, a dining room thing so that the patients can get involved with each other and can eat together . . . or the families can come in and bring food, or cook a little for the patients, or something, so that there's a common aspect. We're trying to work in an interdisciplinary way. We had the doctor, the social worker, the chaplain, the patient and the dietician and the nursing staff in yesterday, which ended our two-week workshop on the cancer unit. We just talked together for several hours about our philosophies and tried to explain to each other the roles that we have . . .

Your own feelings about death . . .

When my dad died I really had strong feelings about that. I can remember when I was told, I was about fifteen, that he had died. I just couldn't believe it. It was unreal. He had had a stroke. And I was very angry at God. I was

196

angry at people and I really expressed my anger at a particular person who was close to me. And I can remember saying, God, if you're real I'm going to find you, I don't care if it takes the rest of my life. And at the other end, I'd say, I don't care if I never find you . . . very ambivalent feelings, very angry at times.

I'm a Protestant and believe very much in an afterlife. I believe I can know God personally through Jesus Christ, and that his death is very significant insofar as my own relationship to him is concerned. And that he is a personal being I can relate to. I *know* that I will have everlasting life. It really is a great sustainer. It helps. . . . I was brought up with a strong faith. Both my mother and father really believed very strongly. And we went to church very regularly. But I think it was at the time that my father died that my faith became stronger. After, you know, having worked through some of the grief I realized that the faith I had was very dependent on my father, and there was neither my father nor my mother around anymore to sort of depend on. So, if God was real he had to be real to me and to meet my needs in whatever thing I needed.

Religion has a different meaning for people. I certainly think it's helpful to have some direction in terms of this for your own life. Patients are always asking, why me? And families keep asking it. The same thing. . . . Why did this happen to me? It's a question we can't answer . . . we have to know only that there's meaning in whatever has happened.

What about the person who doesn't have that faith?

I imagine there probably are a lot of defenses, and I think that people have worked out ways of facing death. I remember one patient I talked to who was an atheist, and she said she had worked out the hereafter. She said, well, it was all right before I was born, so it'll probably be all right after I die. It's the first time I really heard it that way . . .

This has done something for you, dealing with these patients?

That word "enriching," I think that's very appropriate. If you can listen to the patient. . . . I've learned so much just listening to what the patient is saying. And many times the patient can't talk to the family at this particular time, although I believe this can happen . . . to say the good-byes, and I love you. It just helps so much as far as the separation is concerned. And the guilt aspect. The family can say to the patient what they really want to, and vice versa. But sometimes that's not possible. And sometimes the nurse or the doctor sort of becomes the friend of that patient, the friend that the patient confides in. And to be able to have someone share that much with me . . . well, I really appreciate that. And I'm grateful for their trust. That means a lot to me personally because I really . . . I just believe that communication on a personal level is the most important thing.

Jacqui Kellner, RN

She has just come out of an operating room at Beth Israel Hospital in Boston. She is dressed in a loose-fitting green gown, and a surgical mask dangles from her neck. A strikingly lovely girl, she reminds one of a television nurse.

You know, I *have* noticed a number of things since I came to America, which will get me back to the topic of the dying patient. One of these is the attitude of nurses toward patients, it is different here. It's completely different. In England, there is much more patient contact by the nurse. In many ways she is responsible for the instigation of procedures and treatments that are carried out, and she may suggest them to the doctor, whereas here I had to break down a number of barriers before I was accepted in that role, in an American patient-doctor-nurse relationship. So, that is different, and therefore the way she interacts with the patient is different . . . in that many times if the patient will say to her, nurse, have I got cancer?, her immediate response is, I don't know, I'll have to ask the doctor, or she'll say, has the doctor spoken to you, or, of course you haven't, don't be silly. Whereas in England, the nurse would say, if she knew, well, yes, you have, does it bother you? Would you like to talk about it? So, the whole approach is different.

I've been working in intensive care, and I've been very interested in the reactions of the nurses working with these patients. Because most of them, I would say 50 percent of them, the patients, in surgical IC units never make it out the door, except feet first. What it amounts to is, first of all, a feeling of anger that you've spent all this time, all this hard work, and in spite of all of this hard work, this patient is going to die, and how dare they die, you know. And so that has to be worked out. And then the nurse has feelings to work out toward the family, who are very demanding, who want her to spend time with them when she ought to be spending it with the patient. And she's got things that have to be done every hour, every half an hour, which are repetitive things and if she gets behind on them she's a whole hour or hour and a half behind with her treatments, and she gets very compulsive about these things, so she gets very angry at them, and she gets very angry at the doctors, too, for first of all making demands on her that she cannot meet, not only emotional but physical demands, for not spending time with the families and the patients as they might. Many of the surgical staff don't have the time to do that, I mean, when they're on all day and all night in a big hospital and they've got sixty patients to look after, to spend one minute with one of them is going to keep them from doing something else. . . . And she gets very angry at them also because she thinks many times that they are doing what she might consider unnecessary lifesaving procedures on a patient who is too old for this.

And that leads into saying, well, who can decide, you know. Am I the one to say this doctor shouldn't do this? Or, is he the one who should decide? After all, this is a living person in this bed. What right do any of us have to decide? So, she becomes very confused, and I think all of these things add together to the way she reacts toward the dying patient.

Do you think the majority of girls, at least those in your experience, would be averse to working with the dying?

Some of them. I think so. Some of them. Now, what has happened in our experience is, in IC, that once a patient has been pronounced DNR — or do not resuscitate — that the general feeling then is push them out of the doors because, you know, what good am I going to do for them because they're dying anyway. And this may in part be true. . . . If you have a comatose patient who is not going to respond, who you cannot sit down and counsel with about dying, who in fact is just lying there, really, just waiting to die . . . then that's true, they're best out of the unit because that's bad utilization of acute beds anyway. But, on the other hand, there may be another type of patient, one comes to mind from last year which . . . who was in the unit for some time. . . . He was married to a nurse himself, was very acutely ill for a long time, had complications after complications after complications, all the way through the book. I mean, you could predict them all. Finally, he was left in a condition whereby he was alert to a certain amount, could feel pain, was kept on a machine. . . . And nothing more could be done, and no one knew quite which way to turn. So there he was, and everyone would come in and kind of half wish he wasn't there, and we all built up this barrier against looking after him. We had to sit down with a psychiatrist and have a number of counseling sessions ourselves about it because we felt we just weren't doing anything for him . . . that the more we did for him the more upset we became inside because it seemed as though we were prolonging his suffering. And yet we had to do it because we were nurses, and it's our job. And there he was . . . and so we had a very interesting situation come up with people coming to me all the time, and saying, Jacqui, please don't assign me to him anymore because I'm no support to him or his wife. And what ended up out of that whole thing was that finally the decision was made that that was it, and I, in fact, was very much involved in that decision and was very instrumental in . . . in releasing him from the machinery . . . and he had a very quiet, peaceful passing on in the presence of his wife.

This was something I had talked with Dr. Ross about when she gave a talk to us. She had commented that she found it unthinkable that so many intensive care units restricted visitors from coming in, particularly when the patients were terminal, and this has bothered me a great deal, and I have always taught the girls that I have been responsible for teaching upstairs that the families have to be allowed in regardless, almost, of what else is going on. . . . I mean obviously there are some circumstances which would mitigate that . . . if there were a dreadful cardiac arrest going on in one of the beds . . . but they need to be involved, they have a dreadful need inside, because in a way they feel guilty because they have nothing to do with the care of that patient, and it really helps them to be in the room, to be with that patient, apart from being a comfort to that patient. We found that in the patient I just mentioned that just having his wife there was certainly a great help to her, where she was a nurse, and believe it or not she was a tremendous help to all of us.

Nurses sometimes say, I hope he or she doesn't die on my shift.

That's absolutely right. I think everyone is a little bit afraid of the unknown. I don't know, I've watched many, many, many people die. I think one of the good aspects of English training, English nursing training, is that you get a good deal of clinical experience. One night, my first year of junior nursing, I laid out three people, just in one night. [Laughs.] So to me it's like the turning off of a light . . . and I'm not sure of my personal feelings, about where that light goes when you turn it off. I mean, everybody has a place for it to go, and I suppose I have my own, but I do think some of the younger girls are afraid of death, and I think they're afraid of how they might respond when they see a beloved patient die. You know in intensive care you become very attached to these people. . . . You begin to get to know them intimately, in a way that on the floors you might not. You get to worry about what would happen if his mother leaves her two-year-old child home without a baby-sitter because she has to come in here and see him, things like that that you wouldn't get involved in otherwise. . . . Just to further clarify that, we had a patient upstairs in intensive care who was a young man, thirty-five, nobody became emotionally involved with him. . . . One might think they would since he was in our peer group, but nobody did. He was a bartender over at the Exeter Hotel here, and he had cirrhosis, which sort of goes with the job, but he was a very nice person. . . . He subsequently died upstairs. When he died, 50 percent of the unit went to the funeral, and sent flowers. So that just shows you how much one gets attached to patients without being in love with them. And the other patient I mentioned, a number of us went to his funeral, too, and I've known the kids upstairs to get involved to the point of doing washing, baby-sitting, children-watching so that families could come in. . . . It's different upstairs. But you know, there's the fact that one always lays out a dead patient, and it's unpleasant, and some people don't like doing that, and then there's the ones who say that you'd better leave him, you never know what you're going to get in that bed space . . . and that also has to come into consideration.

Can you remember the first patient who died while you were nursing?

Yes, I can, as a matter of fact. I was about . . . well I was sixteen, and she was a little girl of three. And her name was Anne, and she had leukemia, and it was in a children's hospital outside of Nairobi. The family didn't have the money to send her to England, and there weren't, really, the resources to treat her, and I remember when she died and how very much upset we all were. Yes, I don't think I'll ever forget that . . .

Were you afraid?

No, I was curious, I wasn't afraid. I was curious because I had never seen a dead person. I had seen dead animals. But I couldn't quite . . . I wanted to see what the difference would be between this little tot sitting up and looking at me and the dead child. I was there right when she died, very peacefully, and she knew she was dying, there was no question about that, although she never talked about it. But she knew . . . and she was happy.

Do you think you're different from most nurses? You seem to have plunged sort of matter-of-factly into it all.

I think maybe I am a little different, actually. I've thought about this from time to time. It *does* bother me when people die. I mean, if anybody is crying over a dead patient it's me. But it's not . . . I'm not really crying because they're gone. It's almost a sort of relief that they're gone, a release more than a sadness . . .

How do you feel about what all of this has done for or to you? Has it been more positive than negative?

Yes. I think so. More positive, I think. The only thing that I wish. . . . You know, there's a lot of talk about euthanasia, and as I said, I don't know who has the right to say this patient will live and this one die, but this keeps coming up. . . . And people keep saying to me when I say they shouldn't be doing this surgery on an eighty-five-year-old, they say, well look at Paul Dudley White. So, there are two sides to it. I do think that somewhere along the line the rolling stone has got to be stopped because I understand how the doctors feel, it puts them into a very tight situation. They, perhaps, take the stomach out of a very old lady who has been bleeding, who up to that time has been doing her ironing and her shopping and having a great time, and then all of a sudden, because they took her stomach out, she went into respiratory failure, and then she has a heart attack, and then a number of other events happen. . . . None of which you can say, well, gee, we'll just stop right now, because you can't, you have to go on and on. And then at the end of it you have so much suffering, and that's the negative part of it all. If anything is negative, it's my feelings about that.

Are there some patients that you feel should just be left alone when they're dying? That you shouldn't get involved with?

Yes. Yes. I have worked with some doctors who have been very outspoken about this. Mostly internists who say, we'll leave this patient alone and let him die. Maybe a patient with chronic obstructive disease who has no future. I've nursed many patients who are in terminal condition now because they're . . . I mean, you can breathe for them with a machine but you cannot give them extra lungs, and this type of patient should be allowed to die. . . . And I guess there are always exceptions to the rule that you face death with the patient because there are many people who will say, am I going to die? And what they really want you to say is, no, you're not. Even though they know they are. I know that Dr. Ross says that everyone will eventually accept and know . . .

I think of one patient, a girl, upstairs, a young mother, after having had her first baby. . . . She had an unspeakable complication which happens in one of every five million people perhaps, and she went from one thing to another thing to another thing, and we were all distraught and beside ourselves because she was only twenty-five, with her first baby, with a young husband, and they had only been married eighteen months, and it wasn't right, you know. Everything we did . . . it just seemed to be getting worse and worse and worse, and she . . . I used to feel. . . . Well, I was on the night she died, because I didn't feel I could let the responsibility for her care the last night fall with one of my younger girls. So I stayed up, and we set ourselves sort of standards for each hour because she was deteriorating so much. And I thought, early in the evening, well at least . . . at least let her see the baby before . . . because the baby was going home . . . and I said, well, at least we'll get the baby in . . . which was unthinkable. Imagine, getting a newborn into an IC unit. Well, we got the baby in, and she saw the baby, and I thought, well, thank God, she's seen the baby, so that's that . . . and the baby went home. She was gradually deteriorating, so I thought, well, at least let's keep her blood pressure such and such, and let's keep the machine at such and such a setting. . . . And I'd do that for an hour and she'd go down and I'd think, oh my God, let's do this and this, and it would change every hour until everything was so low that I just stood there with the tears rolling down my face and I thought, you know, there's just nothing we can do, there's just nothing. . . . It doesn't matter which way we turn . . . this woman, she is going to die. And she . . . by this time she was barely conscious, and she . . . I was talking with her about the baby, and smiling, and we were planning how . . . her going home with the baby. And I thought to myself as I said it, my God, I really shouldn't be saying this, you know, I should be saying that she's dying . . . and is there anything that she wanted me to communicate. She really couldn't talk . . . she was tracheotomized by this time . . . and yet it wasn't appropriate to do that, because this was the last thought that this woman had . . . that the next morning she was going to wake up and everything would be different, that she was going to wake up and she was going to go home with the baby . . .

The times you've talked it out with patients, did you feel that was being too clinical?

No. I get very much involved . . . inside. And I know that that's. . . . Sometimes I did feel that I was being a very bad nurse because I used to think a nurse has to be objective and clinical. But I learned differently. A nurse can't be objective and clinical, because if she is she isn't a nurse, she's just a person who flicks pages and signs charts and that's not a nurse.

Do you think there's a lot of that?

Yes, I do. Particularly in this country. A tremendous amount. Particularly with the new breed of degree nurses, some of whom are very, very good, but some of them are designed to sit behind a desk and become administrators.

Many of the nurse's aides are now counseling the patients because they're the ones who are in the rooms. But things are changing, but slowly. A few months before I left the intensive care unit to do operating room work we started a program of nursing workshops, and we would go out and visit all the patients we knew would come into the unit after their surgery, which included the major abdominal surgery and the chest and heart surgery, and I would go in . . . the doctors were aware we were doing this . . . and I would go into a room and try to bring this patient out, find out what he had been told about his operation, and so many times he hadn't been told anything. They didn't even know where the incision was going to be . . . this was before the operation, of course, the evening before. . . . And so I wonder if these basic things are being dealt with . . .

Do you miss working in the ICU?

Yes, I miss the involvement with the patient, the feeling of helping them in a concrete way. I suppose I probably have a need to do that. I guess we all have our needs, and I know what mine are. And I know that you could argue with me that running the OR and presumably raising the standard of care is offering the patients better service, but it's not the same as . . . as talking to someone who's in pain, or making them comfortable, or suctioning them when they're choking, or starting their heart going when they're arresting. It's not the same at all, and that's what I miss. I think I'll eventually go back to it. Intensive care is a thing of the present. It's going to be worked upon and enlarged upon and it's here to stay. One gets satisfaction out of small things . . . patients advancing by millimeters is what you get out of it.

And what about when they don't advance?

Yes. That's when we all get down. We've established these counseling sessions on a regular basis so we can talk out our anger and our fears. It is true that when you have a number of patients in the unit who, as we say, don't move, because they're absolutely and chronically and desperately ill . . . then the tone of the unit goes down with them. The morale goes down with them and you think, oh, I just don't seem to be making any progress. But it changes. You get this feeling which comes on after an eight-hour shift, when you've really worked physically very hard. . . . Because, you know, chest patients . . . and positioning and treatments all take a lot of physical activity and you feel very tired at the end, after eight to ten hours doing this. . . . And the figures are coming back the same and you've done nothing, so you think, oh my God, this is terrible. Well, if the next day you come back and you've kind of forgotten all that a little bit, if the patients have changed, then it's all right. But if they're still at the same level, then you begin to get depressed, and this anger starts building up, and the outcome of that is that the patients generally die and everyone feels relieved, and then the whole cycle starts over . . .

I think of a Harvard student who had just shot up a bad bag, and he was paralyzed, totally, and subsequently died . . . a nineteen-year-old boy, only child, and you can imagine the feelings the kids up in the unit had, because most of their friends smoke grass now and then, so it hit close to home. And they do get very emotional about young people. . . . Another boy had an ascending neuromuscular disease where one muscle goes, then another, a viral disease thought to be brought back from Vietnam . . . and his wife was a nurse, and she rushed him into the hospital when he complained that his feet were going numb and that he couldn't move them, and then it was his knees, and then his hips and by the time we got him he was just about breathing on his own, and we just caught him in time. We kept him upstairs, twenty-one years old, newly married, a big, hulking, handsome soldier, until he got better and we sent him home. But through all that time, he, of course, went through an emotional psychosis. . . . There he was, totally dependent on women, where he had just come out of the company of men. So he had a great deal of difficulty adjusting to that, and he was totally dependent, I mean he couldn't even wipe his nose. He just could blink his eyes and that was all. His wife became pregnant, and so he was resentful of her. It was his baby, but it was just bad timing, and the feelings of the unit toward him started out with a feeling of wanting to get him better because he was so handsome and so gorgeous and everyone fell in love with him, you know . . . and it all went through to complete and utter rejection because he started to behave so badly that no one could bear to even go into the room with him . . .

Religion seems to sustain a lot of patients and a lot of nurses.

That depends on the patient. I'm not an atheist, I go to church, quite a bit for people of my generation, about once a month. My son goes to Sunday school and we say prayers, and I do believe there is a God, but I'm not so sure he created the heaven and earth in a week or whatever. I sort of base how I react to the patients on the way they react to me. If they are very religious, then I will adjust to that, and I will talk that way with them. But I don't bring it up unless they do.

Do you think working in this sort of environment has helped you arrive at any conclusions about your own death?

I've thought about it, and I just hope I'm allowed to die with dignity because that's what I fight for for many of my patients, and that's something that bothers me, these patients who . . . I'd like to die with dignity, that's all . . .

Do you fear it?

Yes, I think so, because, you see, no one ever comes back to tell you what it's like. One talks to people who arrested and who were resuscitated, and they'll say, I was having a dream, something like that. But they can never really say, well, gee, I was in this dark place and there was this gate and someone was opening it and saying, well come in, you know. I suppose I do fear it. Wondering . . . wondering . . . I suspect that once the time comes I'll say, now wait a minute, wait a minute, I've got to learn my lines. But that's my other career, I guess. I do a lot of amateur theatricals . . .

There obviously have been a lot of incidents, but is there one that sticks in your mind that has influenced you? More than any other?

There is one, yes. One that I looked after in England. It was really . . . in fact, it was the teaching of the ward sister on that ward that influenced me more than anyone else that I will ever meet in my whole life. There was this lady . . . the patient was a lady and she was hit by a truck, right in front of the hospital. She and her husband were coming to visit her youngest who was having his tonsils out, and she had four boys, age eight and down. She had a head injury and went into a coma from which she never woke up, and I remember going onto the floor that day, and I was just eighteen, it was sort of my first big assignment, and the ward sister sat me down and said . . . now, Miss Field, she said — you see, you don't get called Jacqui or anything like that in England . . . it's Miss Field, or nurse — she said, I want you to know that this patient is in a coma, and if she develops an infection in her chest it will be as a result of bad nursing care. This ward sister was well in advance of her time because it's just been in the last couple of years that the theory has sort of come to fruition that if you don't move a patient he'll get pneumonia. Well, she really didn't know that then . . . it was just sort of instinct. And we loved that patient, we turned her and we bathed her, and we had no IC unit then, and that patient never did get a chest infection . . . but she died. She died because she had a catastrophic event in her head . . . and that really influenced me more than anything else. I think it . . . well, for one thing I was very upset when she died, and the sister sat me down and she said, well, you know, it doesn't matter how fine a person you are, whether you are a doctor or a nurse, there are just some times when you cannot do anything, the patient is going to die, and all you can do is make them comfortable . . . and, she said, I know you have done that. So, you see, it's not all futility and frustration.

You know, I think there are a lot of nurses who are . . . who just look upon nursing as a glamorous way to catch a husband, which is unfortunate but true, actually. I've always prided myself in being a fairly good judge of character and I've managed to keep those people out of the ICU because they are no good at all, they're just no good to you. . . . They do their job but they really don't give the patients the support they need, physically or emotionally. I think, too, there are the types of nurses who do go into it for an administrative job, and you can spot them, it becomes a career thing. They're interested in being a head nurse, sitting at a desk, they don't make rounds, they don't have patient contact, they're not interested in the families. These people don't go into it other than the fact that to be a nurse in America is, you know, it's about like being a doctor is to a man, I suppose. It has a sort of status ring to it, and besides the money is good, nurses get paid well, and so perhaps that's the reason. I find it hard to even think about people like that. . . . In England, the majority of people are like me. We do it because we want to be with people, to be with patients . . .

William Hauger, 22

He is a first-year medical student at Boston University, and on the first day of class he buried his brother. Jeff Hauger was twenty when he died of acute leukemia, a "double miracle," according to his doctor, Lewis Weintraub, a hematologist at University Hospital, who treated Jeff during the last six years of his life.

Jeff was given one to two years to live when his condition was diagnosed, but he survived for ten, making him one of the longest-enduring leukemia patients in medical history.

"My father told my older brother and me about Jeff as he drove us to school," says William Hauger. "I didn't believe it. It was all unreal to me. But I remember using my lunch money that day and I bought Jeff some Oreo cookies and a comic book."

The family decided that their life should not change, and Jeff was not told of the seriousness of his illness at first. When he was sixteen, the pose was dropped, and Jeff's disease was discussed openly. "From the beginning, his attitude was he was going to beat it," recalls his brother. "He never asked, 'Why me?' or felt sorry for himself. We talked about his life and not death. He was more interested in making it easier for us. He had a feel for life. I remember one Christmas my junior high had a contest, and the kid who sold the most wrapping paper won a $25 bond. We lived in a Jewish neighborhood, so I sold just a few rolls to my family. Jeff went door-to-door and sold more than anyone, and he won. He was warm, just a funny guy."

I'm probably unlike a lot of students I know in that I had no physicians in my immediate family, really, and yeah, I'd say that in my personal case my brother had more to do with my going to medical school than anything else. Although it would be wrong to say it was like a get-out-there-and-save-the-Gipper type of thing. I wasn't that unrealistic. But he was my avenue of access into health care, you know, and other than that I probably wouldn't have gotten the idea of being a physician. I hadn't thought much about it til I got into college.

Jeff was diagnosed when he was ten so it was a long time. He lived longer than anybody else with this particular diagnosis, and it was a sort of unique situation in that from the time we were kids we lived out in the country, in Jacksonville, on the St. John River, and our nearest neighbor was five miles away. My older brother was pretty much gone from home by this time; he was six years older than me and he was at college. So Jeff and I were really playmates more than brothers. It was a really close relationship. Our family was really close then because that was, you know, all there was around.

Was he aware that he had leukemia from the very beginning?

Well, that's a very hard thing to determine. He knew . . . he could put the name leukemia on it himself when he was about fourteen or fifteen. He probably really knew when he was sixteen, I mean in all of its consequences. He probably knew long before that, though, because I can remember him asking me when he was about thirteen or fourteen and he asked me about leukemia, said he looked it up. For one thing he was a smart kid, and for another thing you can't go to a doctor's office once a week and hear what you hear and see what you see and not start to get an idea of what you've got. Although really it was just a, quote, blood disease to him and then it was laid straight on the line between him and his doctor. And he was living it from then on, even before that, but after it was presented to him with no holds barred he was about sixteen.

And he probably lived better and did better than people who had no problems. He was an all-state basketball player and things like this. He lived with it and came to grips with it, there's no question about that. The thing about it is. . . . It's hard to say but there was a sort of unwritten agreement among the family not to really talk about leukemia as a. . . . It was just sort of something that existed and wasn't

215

really a killer, if you know what I mean. Because you know it hadn't killed him. And we all really kind of felt that if anybody was going to beat it he would, and he certainly felt that way. But then the last year, well, these things start to catch up to you, and I think he really knew what he was up against that last year. And we talked openly about it. He had, really, few restrictions on himself, and he did what he wanted to do, when he wanted, and he wasn't much of a baby. He just wouldn't do it. . . . Like if Mom said stay in tonight, you're too tired, he'd say no I'm not going to stay in tonight. [Laughs.]

And this whole experience has, you feel, had an effect on you and your career?

I think the thing is that so many of us are so innocent. We know death; like your grandfather dies, maybe when you're a child and by child I mean up to sixteen or seventeen, and you might have to go to the funeral, you might have to see the open coffin. Now I personally hadn't. But I think if you really come right down to it, a lot of young medical students have not really seen death as it exists. I mean you see someone alive now and dead a second later, and it's especially going to have a big influence on you when it happens a week before you start medical school. Actually, the day he died other students were in classes, and I missed the first week. I think I'll never forget that.

I don't think a physician can really deal with death unless he's really thought about it. I don't think about it, you know, death is something that happens to somebody else. I'm young, and I think you think about it when . . . well, when you're about fifty, maybe, that's when you really think about it. And if a physician can't think about death, how can he possibly relate to it? You know, death is. . . . Like, I think physicians really avoid it because it's . . . like it sort of emasculates them. If you can't save the guy, well, maybe you're not really the good doctor you're supposed to be, that sort of thing.

And I think that if you can sort of impart to a dying patient that, okay, we both know we've crossed a certain point, without really saying it . . . that, you know, I will be with you to the end, and to the end I'll still be doing everything that my profession has taught me might help, and aside from that there's nothing else I can do. . . . But I will be there, I will be there to talk to you when you want me, I will be there to stop the pain if it becomes a matter of pain until death. . . . Sort of the feeling that even though we both know you're not going to make it you're not going to be deserted. And you can see this. I've worked at City Hospital drawing blood, and thank God I did for the month before my brother died because it really was a sudden thing at the end . . . and I'm not so sure I could have dealt with it as well as I did, as well as I think I did, if I hadn't had the experience in the hospital, at seeing it happen to someone else at City Hospital before. And you see it, you see doctors avoiding it when they see a patient is at the point where he's biding time until death, they avoid the room like the plague. Just the experience seeing some of those patients at City, a tube down their throat, the noises they make . . . stuff like that. If I had to see that for the first time with Jeff I'm not sure I could have stuck it out. So as it was I was able to stay with him the last twenty-four hours instead of having to leave the room because I was upset.

And you know the other thing is you don't see it if you see the person a lot. I'll give you an example. Jeff died in

September, and my older brother had been away for a long time, married, in the army, so he's really been away from the situation for about six years prior to the death. He came in and saw Jeff a few months before he died, and he was still relatively healthy . . . I say healthy, but as healthy as you can be with leukemia. A photograph was taken of Jeff and his niece, my brother's daughter, and then my brother took that photograph and after the death had someone make a painting of it. And my father, when he saw the painting, said, you know, there's something I never realized before . . . and he looked at the painting again and he said that there was death in Jeff's eyes, which we really couldn't see because we'd seen it accumulate so. . . . But the picture makes it look . . . you can just see that he's very tired, you can just see the death. . . . And my brother could see it easily . . .

I don't know what I'm going to do yet, it's too early in medical school. Maybe hematology is a possibility simply because I find it interesting and not so much because. . . . You know, it would be so nice to say, well, his brother died of leukemia and he's going to go out there and be a great . . . and ten years from now he'll win the Nobel prize. . . . I can't really look at it that way and it would be a mistake for others. Probably the main reason I chose medicine was more in terms of career and personal satisfaction. If you go into it with the right attitude it's interesting work all your life, not like any nine-to-five thing, and there's always something new if you're willing to look for it. And there are those who say a large part of being a doctor is an urge to feel needed, and I certainly wouldn't contradict that. I feel that urge too. As I said, there's no medical background in my family, and my father's been a furniture salesman all his life. . . . You know a lot of kids in medical school, they got

218

their doctor kits when they were four years old, and there was no question what they were going to do. I was a geology major in college, and that's a long ways away . . .

I really think that if you have a model to base things on it's different. I have a model. Like this guy, my brother, really went through it, in a way that was . . . noble is the wrong word but how else can you say it? Like he had three strikes against him before he started and yet. . . . And they can't really say why he lived ten years, when others live a year and a half, and I can't really come to anything else but a sort of personal drive. He was totally aware of what he had.

His disease was open-ended . . . there really was never a point when there was no hope until the last two days, but then, when you come to the last two days, he had a brain hemorrhage, slowly went out, was conscious, less conscious, and suddenly unconscious, and then in a coma . . . and at that point I felt very frustrated and I felt like maybe. . . . Well, at that point there was a possibility, though we didn't know, that this thing could stabilize and he could become a vegetable for three months. And at that point I became very frustrated, and felt, sort of, wouldn't it be best to let him go out now. . . . Fortunately it never came to that, and he went on to die about eight hours after.

Jeff was hospitalized his last two weeks mainly because he wasn't coming around too well to a new three-drug treatment. Basically, what it was was that the disease had caught up and it looked like it was going out of control. And the particular three-drug sock they gave him, it's particularly bad on the circulation system and leads to a big possibility of hemorrhage. Now, he had had some GI bleeding, and the doctors knew he was in bad shape, if for no other reason but that the disease was out of control. He had showed some GI bleeding which Dr. Weintraub indicated to us might be a bad sign, in that if you bleed GI you can also bleed intracranially and when that happens you're in trouble. So on a Sunday morning . . . and he had also been in a lot of pain, just sort of a typical end-stage leukemia thing, but we really hadn't been warned that he was near death, just that it was a critical situation. Now on a Sunday morning . . . my parents live about sixty miles from here, in Westminster, near Gardner, and my mother, who was a big factor in why Jeff did so well. . . . He called Sunday morning, my brother, and all he could say over the phone was, I'm very frightened. It's hard to say, and yet in retrospect there can be no question that somehow he knew he had been hemorrhaging . . . because he said he was very upset, very frightened and near tears on the phone, and they said, why, have the doctors said something? And he said, no, I'm just scared. Well, they came in like ninety miles an hour and when they got there, Dr. Weintraub had done a lumbar tap, and there was blood in that, typical signs of hemorrhage. But when Jeff first called there had been no medical indication that he had had a hemorrhage. And they walked into the room, and the first thing he said to both of them was, he said, I've been going for a long time and I just want you to know that I love you a lot, and that I know you've done all you can for me. He was sort of saying good-bye. And he wasn't just sort of, he *was* saying good-bye. I was at my fiancée's house in New Hampshire, and they called me, and so I came down with her, and when I walked into the room he said, hi grub, and he said it's been ten years and I've been fighting a long time and I think it's almost over. And I said, well, you haven't given up yet, have you? At this point I didn't know that anything particularly new had developed. . . . There's no question he was saying his good-byes.

And what kept him going so long was that he had a lot of drive. You know, he was a goddamn good basketball player, and did everything he wanted. This was his way of convincing himself that he could function normally. . . . I remember he'd go to games and play and then be sick afterward, throw up and stuff, but he didn't care as long as he could play. It's not all medicine and cells, a lot of it must be brain . . .

And see my mother was sort of the central power figure in the house. . . . She was our boss so to speak, and was very close to Jeff and me. And she more or less stayed close to Jeff from the time it was diagnosed. She wasn't a domineering mother, but she was always where he could turn. She spent a lot of time at the hospital, and you know he spent a lot of time there, over ten years. But he would lie to her about how he felt. He never really felt well, but he never really complained about not feeling well. But I could always tell, when he'd be cranky, that he wasn't feeling well. Yeah, he was quite a guy.

Charles A. Fager, MD

A neurosurgeon, he is on the staff of the Lahey Clinic in Boston and is a member of the Harvard Medical School faculty. In 1965, he operated on Johnny Nerud, a successful thoroughbred trainer who had suffered a subdural hematoma after a spill from a stable pony. Out of gratitude to the surgeon for restoring his health, Nerud named a year-

ling after him — "Dr. Fager" — a money horse, all speed, who won seven of his eight starts in 1968 before ending his racing career.

Dr. Fager is one of 2,000 board-certified neurosurgeons in the United States, practitioners of a medical specialty in which death is a not uncommon occurrence.

You mean that most neurosurgeons are either very sadistic or they're that interested in death? [Laughs.] Actually, we really don't face death as much as we used to years ago because the quality of our work has improved so, and we do so much better a job than we used to do. My colleagues are always saying, oh, if you need a donor for a heart transplant call the neurosurgeons, which is a lot of baloney because those are bygone days. Oh, it's true that a bad head injury, or a bad brain hemorrhage. . . . Yes, those still occur, but from a standpoint of what we do to them surgically, we don't get too many deaths . . .

I had a terrible case just this morning, a twenty-eight-year-old girl with a huge vascular malformation in the right temporal lobe, thirteen weeks pregnant, her first pregnancy, and it was one of the most difficult cases I had had in a long time. . . . I had to take it all out, and I wasn't entirely sure I could get it all out, and what troubled me about this girl was that it's in an area where I could produce a rather serious deficit, mentally and from the standpoint of her extremities. I could make her hemiplegic. And I don't know yet how it's going to turn out. She was just waking up when I left the hospital. But as I talked to her, and her husband and mother, yesterday and the day before, I said the thing that my feeling about this was . . . she had to have surgery, she had two hemorrhages and there was no way out. . . . But my feeling was that if she does not do well and if she's going to be a vegetable, I would much rather see her die, because I've learned that there are far worse things than death. And we see this time and again with brain problems. We still see this sort of thing when someone has a serious brain injury or serious encephalitis or a very serious tumor . . .

Have you found your work depressing? An abdominal surgeon told me once that all the neurosurgeons he knew were seeing psychiatrists.

I've been practicing neurosurgery for twenty years, and I had four or five years of residency before that. And I've never found it particularly depressing because even in the early days the problems were so challenging that you couldn't get depressed, because if you got a case that you knew was going to die and you pulled him through, and he was in great shape, that really outweighed all the other problems that would have been terribly depressing. I haven't found it that way, no. I see these people with abdominal cancer and they're far more depressing to me than some of the brain tumors I see.

Can you remember the first time a patient you dealt with died?

Yes. I can remember in my formative years, as an intern who — and you know how impressionable interns are — I remember the first case on the ward that I was in charge of who was dying, and it was an elderly man, and I remember his wife. I don't recall the details of why he died, but it was obvious he was going to die, and I remember this man, and the thing that strikes me so much about the recollection of it is that she was grief-stricken, but she was also very much at peace. Apparently they were very close and they had talked about this quite a bit, because I remember being at the bedside and he had died, and the tears were coming down her face and yet she was obviously very tranquil, and not so emotionally disturbed as people I have seen since then . . . and I'll never forget that old lady. I'll never forget that tranquility.

I can't say to you that I haven't had great tragedy, personal tragedy, in some of the later cases that I have lost, that have died as a result of surgery that I have done. This is something a surgeon lives with. And you keep going over and over some of these things you'll carry all of your life. You know, a case where you feel you could have done it differently, and the patient might have lived. And that you just live with, always. You never forget those. I know I don't. And you learn from those deaths. Yes, you learn. Everybody learns something. I think there are very few times you repeat a serious mistake. I'm sure I repeat mistakes as we all do. But there are very few times you repeat a serious one. People don't like to think that their surgeon makes mistakes, and it's not something you talk about, but goddammit there are days when Johnny Bench doesn't do so well or when Bill Russell isn't as good on the court, and there are days when your manual skill is not always as good as on other days. Sometimes it's distraction, sometimes it's failure to concentrate somewhere along the line. I've always told myself I have to concentrate every single minute on every single damn thing I'm doing. . . . But the human brain isn't always that good.

And after you've lost a patient, how do you go on?

I feel . . . I feel that it's a personal defect, that I've done something wrong, something I shouldn't have done. But you go on. And I don't know what makes you rise above that but you do.

As a student in medical school, what were you taught about dealing with terminal illness?

Nothing. Absolutely nothing. You found your own philosophy, and your own thoughts about it, and I think mine have matured over the years. When I was younger, I didn't feel as strongly. . . . Let me put it the other way. When I was younger, I felt very strongly about doing everything possible about keeping a patient alive. And I have changed considerably. I have watched myself change. . . . You come out of medical school with this raw idealism, and you've had this drilled into you till you're blue in the face, and you're taught that under no circumstances are you to give up. [Laughs.] You see, the problem is — and this is the one that torments us sometimes — you think you've got a patient who's terminal, and by all rights he should be terminal and everything scientific tells you that this guy is not going to live, and please God take out the tubes and spare him the suffering and spare the family. . . . And lo and behold, once in a while he gets better. I still have a family who'll never let me forget it. A man who had a tumor in the hypothalamus, and I operated on him and he had every complication in the book. He bled from the stomach and we gave him twenty pints of blood for a bleeding ulcer, he got pneumonia, he got empyema, he was as terminal as any patient I have ever seen, and I said to the mother, who was very determined that this man should not die, and to the daughter, who was so emotional she couldn't think straight . . . I said, I really think we should let him go quietly in his sleep. And they were horrified, and they said, you can't do this, you can't do this. And he got well! And they have never let me forget it. And I won't, and I've always wondered what I should say to people in situations like this. And by all rights that man should have been dead, I have never seen anyone so terminal get better. But I try to be honest. I see terminal people and I try to be honest with them within the limitations imposed by their families because families still will say we don't want him to know, and I still have to respect some of their feelings about it. Many times they feel they know a patient better than I do, and many times they do. But I might say, well, I'd rather tell him that he may have a malignancy that I can't do anything about, and that we're going to be sure he gets enough medication so he doesn't suffer, so he'll be comfortable. I've seen it happen too many times, when you keep lying to them and they keep getting sick all the time, and they've lost confidence in everything and everybody. . . . So I like to tell them when I can, when the family permits me, and it surprises me how many of them take it so well. I don't think you have to tell a man he's going to die next week. But I think you have to be reasonably honest with him.

Some of the patients I have in the hospital today. . . . I have two or three young men with malignant brain tumors. I've removed the tumors but I know they're going to grow back. And I've told the families this. One is a young man, twenty years old, and the mother is being insistent that I couch it in different terms to her son. So I said to him, what I think I want to do is give you X-ray treatment for this, because this tumor could grow back and we want to do what we can to suppress it. Another man I've told that it was malignant, that I'd removed it, that these generally grow back, that I don't think there's anything to worry about right now, that we'll see how things go as time goes on, and then you and I can face this together if you have more trouble. . . .

But even with all this, it's not depressing. And even in the early days of neurosurgery . . . well, was Harvey Cushing* depressed? The challenge, as I said, was so great that you couldn't be. You were taking something that hadn't. . . . Well, you couldn't help but win, because you were entering a field where everybody had died. And again, as I said, I see these people with cancers of the pancreas, that the surgeon knocks himself out on and he works like a dog, they're so sick, so much sicker than our patients, and our patients are apt to be confused, even euphoric at times, so that there's a pleasurable aspect to it. . . . They're often quite gay in an unrealistic way. No, the only thing that depresses me is when I've fouled up.

Has any of this been of value with regard to your own personal feelings about death?

I'm sure . . . I say I'm sure, no one really knows until he's facing it, but I think I can face it very reasonably. I hope that somebody, if I'm having a painful affliction, will be kind enough to give me enough medication so I don't suffer. But other than that I feel I'll get through it. I feel I've had a very full life, I've done everything I've wanted,

* American neurosurgeon (1869–1939) who served as surgeon-in-chief at Boston's Peter Bent Brigham Hospital and who originated new techniques of brain surgery.

I've had the experience of being able to do surgery, and my personal life has been so rewarding, my children have been so successful, and we've had such a marvelous family that I feel fulfilled. I think maybe a lot of people die frustrated.

Why did you choose neurosurgery?

Well, I found it very difficult to give up medicine. I just loved it, I loved cardiology when I was in medical school, and one of the hardest things was to give up medicine. . . . I liked to do things with my hands, and I always had surgery in the back of my mind. I liked to operate and I've always enjoyed doing things manually. So I got started in general surgery and I got some exposure to neurosurgery cases and I saw that general surgery in those days involved hernias and gallbladders and I couldn't see . . . and stomachs . . . and I couldn't see spending the rest of my life doing that. And I loved neurology, I just loved it from the word "go," and it was a natural for me, something a little different and with a challenge. But there's also an element of medicine in neurosurgery which I found that general surgery didn't have, which is neurology. Oh, there are a lot of things about it. . . . You may get bugged by crazy phone calls, by people, and sometimes you just want to tear your hair out when you know there's someone over in that hospital who's in critical condition that you have to face and you just have to face it. And you just live with it. I've been very fortunate in that I've had a marvelous home life. If it weren't for that I don't know what the hell I'd do, because I know some men who don't, and I don't know how they get to the OR and keep cool. I've thought of that many times and, you know, one of the things. . . . The clinic has talked for a long time about being under one roof so that we don't have to go around so much to different hospitals and so on, but one of the things I like about being in my car is that I can think about that case I'm going to operate on, and I can leave this office and nobody touches me in that car, and I can take my time and think about what I'm going to do tomorrow . . .

There are things . . . I'm thinking of a perfectly beautiful young woman in her early twenties, and she had a very bad arterial venous malformation, similar to the case I did this morning, and she came with her husband, no children, and we talked the thing over and she was having intense headaches, intense, driving her crazy. She had to take codeine and Demerol. Such a strikingly pretty and charming girl that I could never forget her. And I did arteriograms and I looked over the thing and I thought that I could remove it . . . I thought I could remove it. It was in the right occipital area and very large and you could hear it with a stethoscope. It was . . . the blood was just pouring through it, it was an arterial venous fistula, and it would go psh, psh, psh, like that. . . . And I heard it as soon as I listened to her. She had been around to a lot of doctors, complaining of headaches, and nobody had made the diagnosis. Her husband said, well, I'd like to take her to visit some relatives in the Midwest for a while before you operate on her. I said, okay. But they changed their minds and said let's go ahead and operate. I talked it all over with them. I told them she was faced with a danger, and I operated on her and it was a . . . it was really . . . it turned out to be so much more than I ever dreamed, and I got into an impossible hemorrhage that I could not control, and she died. I managed to stop the blood and get her back into bed, and she just died the next day. And . . . I felt that I hadn't prepared them adequately for that. This was my feeling, that I had not prepared them for that. They had a lot of confidence in me, great confidence in me. They felt I was going to do this and pull it off, and I thought I could and I don't think that I had analyzed the situation as satisfactorily as I could have. And I don't think I prepared her for the possibility that she might die. And she never regained consciousness, and I never had a chance to talk to her again, and that hurts.

Elisabeth Kübler-Ross, MD

I phone Dr. Ross at the South Cook County Mental Health and Family Services Center in Chicago Heights, where she is medical director, and she tells me she is just in from the Coast but to take a late Illinois Central from the Randolph Street station near the Loop anyway and get off at Homewood, then take a cab to Flossmoor, where she lives. "Wait for me at my home if I'm not there," she says. "My children will be there."

At the Homewood station, far south of the Loop, the cabdriver says, "Yuh, the death lady," and knows where she lives.

She is waiting when I arrive, and I climb over piles of shoes and toys to get to a high-ceilinged living room that is being refurbished. Children are playing noisily elsewhere in the house.

Dr. Ross received her MD degree from the University of Zurich in 1957, and in 1965 she joined the University of Chicago as assistant professor of psychiatry and later as assistant director of the psychiatric consultation and liaison services. A member of the advisory and editorial board of the Thanatology Foundation, she is a peppery little woman caught up in her subject, which is terminal illness and the attitudes of the dying. She has dealt with hundreds of patients near death, and in 1969 she published a definitive work, On Death and Dying.

The Death and Dying Program that she started at the university several years ago has drawn medical students, doctors, theological students, pastors, chaplains, nurses, nursing students, hospital administration students, psychology interns, respiratory therapy students, dieticians, social workers, and social work students. These health professionals attend seminars where a different "teacher," a dying person, confronts them each time from behind a one-way glass partition. The patient has volunteered to share his personal feelings, hopes, and despairs with the students, and hundreds of terminally ill, ranging in age from sixteen to ninety, have taken part in the program, which is often a therapeutic experience for the patient as well as a teaching tool for the staff.

"Originally, I thought it would be simple to ask terminally ill patients to share with us their needs, fears, and fantasies," she remarked in a lecture in the Menninger Foundation's Department of Education a few years ago. "I had several students in a seminar on 'Crisis in Human Life' and my own idea was that we would stand around the bedside to listen to the patients and collect enough data for the students to write their seminar papers. But we soon encountered a crisis of our own in that we did not get the staff's permission to see a single dying patient in a 600-bed hospital. The staff, in effect, denied that anybody was dying. When I pointed out very sick-looking patients to them, they

asked, 'What do you want to talk to them about?' When I
answered, 'About dying,' they looked at me as if I were the
one who needed a psychiatrist.

"After denial came rationalization. 'These patients are too
sick, or too weak, or maybe they feel like jumping out the
window, but you cannot talk to them about dying.' When I
did not give up, there came a flood of hostility, and I was
soon given the nickname of 'The Vulture,' with the implica-
tion that I must get a kick out of talking with patients who
had only a short time to live. Because of this tremendous
resistance and hostility of the hospital staff, we became
more serious about what it is really like to be a dying
patient in a large hospital. What we learned basically is
that the patients, once we were allowed to contact them,
were quite ready to talk about dying. Indeed, they needed
to talk to somebody. Many of them said, 'Since I am beyond
medical help, I'm treated as if I had a contagious disease.'
Most patients felt terribly isolated and lonely. From the
start, we conveyed to the patient that it was all right to talk
about 'it.' It took only this cue for most patients to begin
talking about dying — sometimes within one or two minutes. The patients shared with us then what it is like to be
dying, what kinds of needs and fears, unfinished business,
and hopes they had."

Approximately 200 of the 500 patients Dr. Ross and her
students interviewed had never been told of their diagnosis,
so it was natural for her to ask them to help her teach
medical students how a patient should be told of impend-
ing death.

"The patients shared with us how helpful it is to be
honest and frank with them from the beginning of a serious
illness. They made two important points. The first was,

'Don't put it in terms of black and white. Don't tell me there is nothing else that can be done. Tell me there is some hope.' Second, 'Convey to me that you are not going to desert me.' If a physician can give hope and convey he is not going to desert these patients when they are beyond medical help, patients can then move quickly through what I have called the five stages of dying."

Dr. Ross identifies these stages as denial and isolation, anger, bargaining, depression, and acceptance.

In her living room, she pours us brandy and talks about what her work has done for her.

It has enriched my life beyond any description. I can't even put it in words. Dying patients, you know, develop a very interesting philosophy, perhaps, of life. They have one talent. And I don't have a scientific word for it. They are able to throw overboard all the baloney. We know that if I meet somebody we have to talk about trivialities to get to know them, and it takes a long time . . . we have to be sociable. Do the handbag and the shoes fit my dress? All these little nonsenses that we spend so much time and energy and money on. For the dying patients, this becomes totally trivial. And the more we work with them, the more we become that way.

I think of my Swiss old-fashioned upbringing . . . if you called me and wanted to meet with me, like today, for example. Years ago I never would have dared to invite you here. Because my house looks a mess, the dining room is full of kitchen stuff, you have to climb over shoes there, I can't offer you a dinner because I don't have a stove. It would have become a very big complicated issue and I wouldn't have even known how to tell you that, you know, discreetly, without being rude, that I can't see you because my house doesn't look like it ought to look.

Today, it's that you come to see me and you don't come to see my house. You don't come to see whether my kitchen is clean. You come to talk about what we are talking about. And therefore all those little details are meaningless. And it is this kind of philosophy that I think rubs off in many ways. I went to Los Angeles last night. I came to the hotel at one-thirty in the morning. I was dead tired. I carry a little bag, not a suitcase. I just had my papers, and nothing to change. And I told the driver to wait outside, I wanted to see if they did have my room reservation, and it was in a bad neighborhood and I didn't want to be stuck alone. And I said, I'll give you a signal if he has my reservation so you can get my bag out. Well, it was one-thirty in the morning and he was probably tired, and I gave him the signal, and he drives off. And there I stand, you know, in this hotel at one-thirty in the morning. I didn't have the most basic things with me . . . I didn't have a comb or a toothbrush, nothing. All my lecture material was gone. I had no idea if I'd ever get my bag back. Well, the next morning I was picked up, and there was a big group of important people there and I had nothing with me. Well, I'm sure that ten years ago I would have been a nervous wreck, and would have worried stiff about what was going to happen to all of my things. So, I said to myself, so I don't have a bag, so I'll improvise. I can do without it, and I'll just share my experiences with these people. I don't really need those notes. So I'll sleep in my dress, it wouldn't be the first time, or the last time. It's not the first time I've been without my toothbrush. And you know I slept like a log. And I didn't worry, and things worked out okay.

Then I went to the airport, and the woman said sorry

you don't have a ticket, and I said what do you mean I don't have a ticket, I just paid $246 for a round-trip ticket last night. Well, I'm sorry, she said, there's some problem. . . . So there I stand and the plane is ready to take off and I have to end up paying another $132 for a ticket that I had paid for the night before, and I'm not getting paid by anybody for all that. Well, sometime ago I would have been very upset and not known what to do. So I said so it's better than breaking a leg and that would cost me a lot more . . .

All of this . . . you become extremely, I don't know what you call that. . . . You accept things that you can't change without spending so much time getting aggravated and upset and having sleepless nights which is not going to do anything anyway . . .

I think that what is happening is that if you identify often enough with your dying patients that what you regard as meaningful and valuable. . . . Well, you really learn, and this is what I said in my book. The dying patient as a teacher . . . they teach you a lot more than what it's like to be dying. You can't work with them for any length of time without getting into a stage of acceptance, and that does not only mean that you are finite, that you're only a tiny little snowflake in the wind, not terribly important . . . but that all the things we think are important don't really count at all. Like if I'm dying. Does it really matter if I have six pairs of shoes? Or . . . just so long as I have one pair. Or a woman who doesn't speak to her husband for a week or some such nonsense. It puts it all in a very different perspective.

I was never really very materialistic. And growing up in Switzerland is a bit different from here. But you know, working with dying patients makes you begin to appreciate things terribly much, and it's this kind of thing I think I got out of it. You also become much more religious in a very peculiar way. And I think I'll have to define what I mean by religious. I'm one of triplets, very ecumenical, I presume, although I don't know what you call it. We were raised . . . not at all very religious. We were taught that the only thing that counts is what you are and how you do things, not what you do. You could be a cleaning woman or a shoemaker, it wouldn't matter as long as you were at least a good cleaning woman and a proud shoemaker. Pride in your work, that was the kind of philosophy I was brought up with. It doesn't matter how high up you go but how you do what was assigned to you. More philosophy than religion. It also didn't matter whether you were a Lutheran or a Presbyterian or an Episcopalian, only that you were decent and honest and in a sense that you did to your neighbor what you wanted your neighbor to do to you.

It didn't terribly matter whether you went to church as long as you applied what one ought to do outside of the church. So, you know, going to church was never an issue. Once in a while, we went. . . . We were triplets and searching for some identity, and one married a Jew, one a Catholic and one a Protestant. That shows you how really irrelevant it was what we were . . . more of an emphasis on what kind of human being and personality you are. Well, when I came here to Flossmoor, I was kind of looking for a church which I could belong to, not for my needs so much but because I would like to raise my children to at least know what it's like to belong to a church. And I'm not really looking for a church but I'm looking for the right minister . . . that means something to me as a person, and I wouldn't really care which church he belongs to. Well, I met one and I told him I'm a triplet, one of whom married a Jew, and one a Catholic and one a Protestant, to give him some background, and his answer was, well, it's too bad only one of you married the right guy. Do you understand that I would never put my foot in this man's church? This, to me, is not a religious man. This, to me, is so judgmental and so narrow-minded that he turned me off. I told him so. I told him, you are not my kind of minister, and I walked out.

Well, I'm still not belonging to a church. But, what I mean when I say I've become much more religious. . . . It is still not important to me whether I go to church or not. But I can spend, for example . . . I make a house call on a very, very desperate woman here in the neighborhood, who is dying, who has had a very tough life, and she is alone and lonely. And I feel very good when I can sneak off half an hour and hop in my car and visit this woman. And I just sit with her sometimes, and she just holds my hand, and I let her cry on my shoulder and be with her. To me, that is almost like a religious experience. I feel very close, very comfortable, very happy that I can do that. And this woman is like a new human being, and I said to her whenever you need that very badly and you're down in the dumps all you have to do is call me and I'll be over, and I know that she is going to do that. She has done this, once or twice. And they don't exploit you. But they know that they'll never be deserted, that there will always be someone who's going to sit with them, when they're down. So in this sense I have become much more religious.

So this has all had a positive effect on you. Some people might think such work could make you depressed.

Oh, no. In fact, I think I am much happier, much more fulfilled. I have always been stubborn in the sense that I have always done what I believed in doing. Nobody ever was able to put me in a mold. I'm also much happier now than when I was in academic medicine, although it sounds much less good to be. . . . You know, what am I? I have no fancy title, I'm not in academic medicine anymore. Now I can do what I really love to do. I work in a clinic, where I serve indigent people. Most of my patients pay nothing. Some pay fifty cents or a dollar. I can help the poorest of the poor, and the most desperate of the desperate. I see almost exclusively psychotic people that nobody wants in the first place, and a group of mentally disturbed, handicapped children, and I love it. I really love it and I remain a physician this way . . .

My big problem is that I have trouble saying no. That is my biggest problem. So when I'm flooded with requests for lectures and workshops and seminars and committee hearings and what not. . . . It would be very easy, for in three months I could have a lecture or a workshop every day, from Honolulu to Italy. . . . So in order to remain a physician and not become an author or a lecturer, which is not me, I made this commitment to this clinic, five minutes from my home. I can see needy people, I never have to make bills, and I never have to say this will cost $25 or $50, which I could not do. And I remain a physician and I give them two and a half to three days a week, and the rest of the time I travel and try to turn other people on, like you were, and I feel naturally extremely lucky and fortunate, because you know very well that there are many people in a lifetime who work very hard, as hard as I do, who never see the fruit of their labor. And I've done this through a chance happening — nothing planned, nothing expected, nothing in the way of a research project. I've done it purely to help some poor students who were in trouble. . . . That's how the whole thing got started, and it grew like an avalanche.

And everything you've learned from the dying patient you've been able to use in treating all kinds of other patients with other ailments?

Sure. You know, when I look back at my work with blind people, for fifteen years. The stages of dying . . . my blind patients went through them. First the denial — I can't possibly be blind — and then the anger and the rage — Why didn't the doctor do something before, why didn't I go to this and that clinic, why didn't I take better care of my diabetes? And then the bargaining — If I could at least have some light perception, if at least I don't need a white cane, at least I don't need to learn braille, if at least I could keep on the job. . . . And when this was no longer possible, the tremendous depression, and hopefully, if I was able to help, the acceptance. Only you don't even have to use drastic examples like blindness. A boy who loses a girlfriend. He is in a state of shock or denial. That guy couldn't possibly have stolen my girl. She couldn't do that to me. Then he's angry as heck at the other guy, then he bargains and sends her flowers or theater tickets, and if it doesn't work he gets very depressed, and then, hopefully, he finds a stage of acceptance when he finds another girlfriend.

I think of when a newspaper I worked for went out of business, and we all went through a lot of that. Maybe this is a universal experience.

It is. Human beings are alike all over the world.

Do you think it's all helped you to face it when your time comes?

Oh, I'm sure I'm much more comfortable. If I were to die today my big grievance would be my husband who just had a coronary, out of the blue sky, he's only forty-four, and my small children, they're too young to go out without a mother and father. I'd be very concerned about them, you know, and we don't have any relatives in this country to rely on . . .

What is it about death that we fear today?

Take the young generation today. They are so aware that we, the grown-ups, the older generation, have made such great strides in medicine and science, have made fantastic progress in that span of time. . . . We have also created, for the first time in the history of mankind, created what man has always been afraid of as long as he has existed. That is a catastrophic, destructive death. Do you understand the fear of death? What the fear of death is, psychologically speaking? You have to understand that not only to understand the language of dying patients but in order to understand what it is that is happening in our society. Then you try to analyze why we, at this time in this society, have such a hangup, and that we have to write a book on death and dying. Isn't that odd? We can't conceive of our own death. We can only conceive of it as being killed. When you try to ask people what they are afraid of . . . what is their gut reaction when they've been assigned to a dying patient. . . . I've asked at least twenty thousand nurses: You've been assigned to a terminal patient, so what does this patient do to you? I would say that over 90 percent of the nurses' response is, and this is all over the country, I hope she doesn't die on me. Now what does that mean? That means basically, concretely, that if she dies five minutes after lunch, it's okay. Not on my shift. And why do we feel this way? The reason we feel this way is what we are really afraid of is our own potential destructiveness. We are terribly afraid that if she dies on my shift maybe I goofed . . . maybe I gave her too much medication . . . maybe I didn't call the physician in time . . . maybe I should have noticed a change in this direction. It's a feeling of our own potential destructiveness, what the Nazis, in a sense, acted out. . . . That which is in every human being. And you have to understand that because if you don't understand that the real fear of death is a fear of catastrophic destructive forces bearing down on you and you can't do a thing about it. The atom bomb is one of those catastrophic forces that can reach you out of the blue sky. The tragedy is that this last generation has made this a reality. It's not God-sent, it's not epidemic, it's not the plague that used to be catastrophic, destructive death. It is now man-made. Pollution. The atom bomb. Bacteriological warfare. Years ago, man faced up to his enemy, he had a chance to kill him instead of being killed. And we're faced with this man-made destruction which we cannot hear and smell and see and we must defend ourselves psychologically. America is the most death-denying society, and we can only live if we use denial. If I were to really accept that we have created all of this and that it can happen here, I couldn't have children, I couldn't have plants for the dinner table. So I use denial. We don't talk about it. We isolate the dying patient, we send the children to grandparents when someone is dying. Ten Viet Cong killed and *only* one American. . . . You've read it every day in the newspapers. We develop antiballistic missiles in the belief that it will not happen to us. It shall happen to thee and to thee and to thee but not to me, and we have wars far away, the farther away the better. But denial doesn't last long. You can't maintain it for a long time . . .

The tragedy is that the older generation has to send its own sons out to kill and to be killed, and they cannot remain in a state of denial. They are in rage and in anger against the society, against parents, the President, everybody. They are in an almost pathetic depression. They are in a hopeless depression, without being aware of it. They wonder about whether they should get married and have children because the children may have to go to school with a gas mask on. So why have children? They have no air, they can't run around New York anymore, so let's have sex, live it up, enjoy this, and have an abortion if by chance you get pregnant, let's take dope, and get a kick and have fun before an atomic bomb falls. I'm exaggerating to make a point. To me what we call the generation gap is two generations out of phase in two stages. . . . The pathological denial, which is much unhealthier, and the more realistic but very sad anger and depression, but a heck of a lot more realistic in terms of this earth. And instead of judging them, with the lessons we have learned from the dying patient . . . if we used the same therapeutic approach there would not only be peace but there would be a much better understanding that we could do something about. . . . But, you see, we judge them . . . sex maniac, dope, the bad guys, every label in the world, you can't understand what they do. It's not socially acceptable, but it's a lot healthier . . .

How did you choose this work in the first place?

It's hard to tell. I think I got into it basically after the war. I grew up in Switzerland which was like an island of peace, and all around was this war of destruction and killing and people trying to swim across the river into Switzerland, and the Germans machine-gunned them down. . . . And I grew up this way. . . . My father and brother were both in the Swiss army, and they came home and told me how many they were able to rescue. And whole families were killed and they watched it and couldn't do a thing about it. . . . This impotent feeling that whole families are gunned down and you're a few yards away and can't do a thing. And I swore to myself . . . this was when I was about thirteen . . . that when I was old enough and able to leave the country physically, if I could walk or hitchhike to Russia and Poland, I would do relief work, to help.

I worked as a cook in eight countries, I worked as a mason . . . did everything you could do after the war. I was very happy and fulfilled, feeling like, you know, I'm really doing something to reconstruct this country, this crazy world, and it was during these trips that . . . and doing this work which I did for several years . . . that I. . . . You know, sometimes without food for three days and hitchhiking through Europe . . . that I came to the concentration camps. And I think that if you have seen these camps where millions of people have been killed, and you see carloads of baby shoes and carloads of women's hair that had been taken off, you have to become preoccupied, not so much perhaps with life but with death. I think that what started me to think when I saw these camps was the potential of the human beings. . . . Why do some people turn into beautiful people? Some are superhuman and some become monsters. And to me this is the question, really, of life and death. . . . If you have lived a meaningful life that you can be proud of, then it doesn't matter one whit whether you're four years old when you die or seven years old when you die. If you have lived in a way that can say maybe I've never achieved greatness, or, I'm not anything superspecial but I've done the real best I can . . . then you can die any day.

I've seen people, young people, who had done what they believed in, and who died in a beautiful stage of acceptance. A thirty-four-year-old man who had never been much in terms of society, never made much, had been a truck driver. . . . His philosophy was, why should I have a lot of money? People with a lot of money get ulcers, he said. I have a roof over my head, I have food for my children, I have clothes to keep me warm, I've never wanted more. Well, this was his life. He had been decent and honest and hard-working, but not killing himself, not killing himself to make more. And he died with the same kind of decency and pride . . . beautifully.

FROM THE PETER BENT BRIGHAM HOSPITAL
Theology students are given the opportunity for clinical experience in the Hospital through a field education program supervised by Dr. Samuel Bojar, Senior Associate in Medicine, Division of Psychiatry, and the Reverend William G. Leach, Hospital Chaplain. Currently, twelve graduate students from Harvard Divinity School and Episcopal Theology School, a Catholic chaplain and a Lutheran minister are participating.

Each student sees a minimum of five patients a week at

the Hospital. Dr. Bojar and Chaplain Leach hold a didactic session with the students every Tuesday to help them understand the emotional and religious needs of the patients. An open-ended discussion is held each Saturday for two hours during which students discuss the role and identity of the chaplain, the meaning of health and sickness, life and death, and the theological implications that arise in a clinical setting.

Although each student is under constant supervision, he is expected to become a part of the Hospital's caring team and to act in a professional manner. He is given a free hand in establishing his own style of ministry and is expected to recognize his own strengths and weaknesses, limitations and growth potentials.

The project places special emphasis on having the students understand the world of the physician. They attend teaching seminars about medicine and are offered a variety of clinical experiences. These include seeing films on childbirth, or witnessing critical operations, or an autopsy. They become acquainted with the doctors and acquire a better understanding of their problems and feelings.

The project also places particular emphasis on the world of feelings, interpersonal relationships and the spiritual dimensions of the human situation. The role of the minister as a clergyman rather than a psychologist is stressed.

The supervisors of the Brigham Project see field education as the grounds for what they call "functional theology." Each year some of the students who take part in the project describe it as one of the most meaningful experiences of their educational careers. In the past, students have been called upon to baptize patients, to counsel with them, to meet their practical and spiritual needs, and to occasionally officiate at funerals. The work of the students is greatly esteemed and appreciated by the Hospital Administration, the Medical Staff, patients and their relatives.

Peg Rizza, 24

She is a student at the Harvard Divinity School.

. . . at least two and a half years in field work, and the field work can be any sort of Christian-related ministry that you have in mind. You can work in church, or in pregnancy counseling, and my first choice would have been in a Catholic girls' school teaching literature because that's the thing I'm most familiar with, poetry and literature. And the reason I didn't do that . . . well it's a rather complicated personal reason . . . the reason I didn't do that is the same reason I'm in divinity school, that I wanted to do something completely different, that would help me to come to know a different dimension of myself that I know exists, but that I had never explored before. The dimension that made me go to divinity school was that I wanted to believe that there was something besides this literary jet-set life that I had been leading for the four years before. And the reason that I am working with chronically ill and terminally ill patients is that it's a dimension of . . . of real life. It's a part of real life that I had never even considered.

Now, I do not have the kind of personality that can go into a hospital. . . . I mean, I'm terrified of pain, if I see someone throw up, I'll throw up, if I see someone cry I'll cry. I'm very squeamish . . . and if you had said to me five months ago that I was going to work in a hospital I would have told you you were crazy. I'm not suited to that kind of work. But somehow I felt it was some sort of test of myself to be able to do it. And I also knew that if I ever did, by some odd chance, go into the ordained ministry that I would be expected to work with sick people because this is one of the duties of a minister, to be able to go to sick people, to dying people. I really . . . I have to say that when I went into it I didn't know what I was doing. I mean, I had a lot of idealistic reasons, but I didn't know just how painful and energy-consuming the whole thing could be.

So, the first patient I had was a woman dying of metastasized cancer. She was a young woman with two little children. When I first visited her, she did not look very sick. She had been in the hospital about six months at the time, dying very slowly. She was having hourly shots of Demerol, a lot of pain. She didn't look bad. I mean, she looked like any other person, she looked like she might have been there for the measles or something. And when I first saw her she like continually pretended to me that she was cheerful. Like she always put on this very cheerful act. And I sort of went along with her. She'd say, when I go home. . . . I have access to the patients' medical records so I know what condition they're in, and I knew she was dying, that she had maybe three months to live. . . . And she kept saying, well, at Christmastime we're going to go skating, and next spring we'll put the boat in the water, and my kids are going to do this and that. She kept asking me questions about myself, and every time I would go in her husband would be there, and they would be playing this little game, and be treating me like I was their little guest. By the way, everyone in the hospital thinks that I'm not twenty-four years old, they all think I'm like sixteen or something, and they all think I'm a candy-striper, because I don't wear a collar, no clerical collar. I don't believe in doing that until you're ordained. We're supposed to wear collars but I just refused to do it. So they always had some confusion about my identity. And she wasn't aware of what she could talk about with me, she was always very confused about why I was there. And I came and visited her four times a week and she never knew why.

So, finally, I decided I would go to visit her sometime outside of visiting hours, like early mornings, when her husband wouldn't be there, so I could talk to her alone. And I still . . . this was like in my third week of working and I still wasn't sure what my pastoral duties were, like I still wasn't aware. . . . Was I supposed to pray with these people, was I supposed to go in there and make them talk about their death? Was I supposed to be like a shrink? Or was I just supposed to go in and cheer them up by talking about the weather? Or what? And so about the fourth time I went in, she said, how old are you? And I told her twenty-four, and she said, oh, you look about sixteen, and she said, what is it you do anyway? And I told her I was a chaplain, and there were a few seconds of silence, and she burst into tears. She was just crying and crying. She said, what am I going to do, I'm dying. I have little children. What am I going to tell them? And she said, I'm really sorry to be crying. And I said, Oh, it's all right, it's all right. You can cry, and I'm sitting there, of course, really trying not to cry myself. And she said, when my husband's here I can't cry, I have to pretend that I'm not worried when he's here, because he doesn't think that I am dying. Well, I knew her husband knew, but he apparently had been denying it all the time, and she had been going along with him, and they had to play this elaborate little game, pretending it wasn't happening. At this point . . . she had been crying for five or ten minutes . . . and one of the nurses came in and said, oh what a baby, cut out that crying. What's the matter with you? Cheer up, buck up. What if your husband could see you like this? And there it went, you know, sort of like all the freedom and honesty that she had been allowed for those few minutes completely evaporated, and she had to put on her little game again.

Well, she was transferred to another hospital for a while, and then came back to the Brigham again after two weeks because she had some sort of relapse . . . her blood count was pretty bad. So she was brought back to the hospital and put in sterile isolation because she had a low white count and that made her susceptible to illness. And no one went in to see her, ever, because they had to go through this elaborate sterilization process, putting on mittens and gowns and shoes, and you had to wash with this ointment, and no one went in. Like she was alone all day in this private room. So I went in to see her. I didn't find out she was there until after about eight days, and I went in, and boy what a mess. Like she was reduced to about half of her former size. She was like decaying, her body was decaying. There was nothing left of her. She had tubes everywhere, needles. I mean, you could tell she was really sick at that point. She could barely speak. She had sores all over her mouth. Well, I went in, and she said, how did you find out I was here? And I told her that I had just found out that morning and I rushed in to see her. And she said, well, she said, my own chaplain was here yesterday so I doubt that I'll be needing your services, my own minister was here, he came to give me confession and communion. And she said, two weeks ago he offered me communion and I said, no I'll take communion at Christmastime when

I'm out of the hospital, but he came in again yesterday and offered me communion and I said I would take it. And then she like winked at me, and she said, you know why I took it, don't you? And I said yes I do know why. And she said, I think I have two more weeks to live. But she was very cheerful, there were no tears. And she said, very calm, I don't even mind. She seemed really at ease, not talking about her children anymore, and she started talking to me about herself, like she said she had a desire to sing all the time, because of the drugs she was on. She couldn't eat anything, and she said she had a constant desire to sing, and she just talked about herself. What finally happened was she was dismissed from the hospital, and as far as I know she's still alive . . .

What about your own feelings during all of this?

My own feelings. My own feelings were that I was slowly coming to realize why I was there. And when other people sort of thought I was there as a student nurse or a candy-striper or something like that, that it really made me uncomfortable. I realized that I was there in the name of God, as a Christian. When I first went in and started seeing people who were really gross, like they smelled bad because they were ill and because they wet their beds and threw up and had scars, I really thought that would gross me out and that it would forbid me to go because I would be squeamish about it all. But it wasn't true, and even when this woman was dying I didn't feel what I thought I would feel. I thought I would feel really horrible and depressed and like I would want to run out of the room and all that. But I didn't. And I found slowly . . . I began to understand what it meant to go there as a Christian and to be with a person. You know, if you go to someone who's in pain and in a state of unattractive . . . health . . . like someone who's in a mess, you can go in there and sort of pawn off your strength on them, try to cheer them up. You can say, I'm strong, dominant, a person who can walk around and I have my health and I'm going to give this to you, it's going to be like a gift from me to you. Well, that puts you in a dominant position and they are just a mere receiver. And that is just how I started out. Like, I'm going to help these people. I'm going to cheer them up, I'm going to add a ray of sunshine to their awful days. But it didn't turn out that way. When you go and you understand your position as a Christian as opposed to say a psychiatrist or as a non-Christian social worker or something, you go to be with that person . . . to be *with* and that means you're going to accept them even though they're in pain, you're going to accept them even though they're unattractive and smelly. That means if a person screams at you and says, get the hell out of here, I can't stand the sight of you, that means you're not going to get mad or hurt. It means that you're not going to stand around expecting them to be grateful to you. And it didn't take me very long to figure that out. It was surprising how quickly I figured that out . . .

I've now had, like, five patients a week, and if I may say so it has all made me more conscious of the potential of my own death than ever before. And I realize that every minute of your life you are denying your own death, just by continuing on and making plans. And now, without being morbid, I think I am more aware of the possibility of my own death than I was say five months ago. And I have not seen anyone, yet, who has had a good death. You know the French have an expression that you make a good death, that you die with dignity. I've only seen people die in the hospital, or have been dying in the hospital, and there's not much dignity involved with that. And if I may say so, the one woman I saw went through a rather classical . . . in Kübler-Ross's own terms of sort of denial and then depression and acceptance and depression . . . and like that was not particularly enlightening to me. But I have seen people in terrible pain who have been sort of a lesson to me. I feel much braver now than I ever did. And the one way that it's really helped me . . . and I can't say that I feel any more comfortable about the prospect of my own death, I mean I still feel the self-preservation instinct and all the rest . . . and I still have to admit that when I leave a dying patient's room I wish that this person were getting better, I wish I could do something for this person. . . . It has helped me to understand that to be with a person in their pain, and I don't just mean in their pain after surgery, but the pain of knowing that you're dying, the pain of knowing that you're leaving your loved ones. Being able to be with a person in pain without trying to dominate them in some way . . . by dominate I mean like trying to say that I'm going to put myself in the position of this beneficent giver, I'm going to give them my wisdom, my skill, my training, I'm going to give you some sort of fruit of my self that will make you feel great, that will make you get better. Being able to accept the fact that a person's pain and end are inevitable has been very valuable to me. I've even noticed it in dealing with my own friends. Someone will come to me and say, I'm really depressed, I have this terrible problem. . . . I have a choice, I can say to them, well you have that problem, why don't you see a shrink? Or why don't you go to the library and read this book and that'll help you out. And then if a person doesn't do that I get mad. Or if they do and it doesn't work for them I throw up my hands in despair and it makes me feel awful. I've learned not to do that. I've learned to accept the fact that pain is a state of being just as much as happiness, that it has its own beauties, it is acceptable, and it certainly has to be acceptable in the eyes of God or it wouldn't keep happening . . .

I do feel that if death were sort of more out in the open. . . . Why are there so many books out about sex and not that many about death? And I know that sometimes even if I just mention it in passing to some friends that, you know, I'm working with terminal patients this semester, they all go, ugh, how awful, you must be so depressed all the time, how can you stand it, I could never do that, and so forth. It's considered almost . . . pornographic or something. And it's not.

Ned H. Cassem, SJ, MD

Dr. Cassem, who received his MD from Harvard Medical School in 1966 and his BD from Weston College School of Theology in 1970, is an assistant in psychiatry at the Massachusetts General Hospital, clinical instructor in psychiatry at Harvard, and an associate member of the Youville Hospital medical staff in Cambridge, Massachusetts. A Jesuit priest, he serves as project supervisor with the Boston Theological Institute's program, Pastoral Encounters with the Disabled and Critically Ill.

Youville Hospital, formerly named Holy Ghost Hospital, is a 305-bed chronic disease and rehabilitation facility founded for the incurably ill by the Sisters of Charity

(*Grey Nuns*) *in 1895. Born and raised near the institution, I recall vividly Sunday walks with my mother past the brick walls and the landscaped courtyard, and how she taught me to bless myself as we went by. Since then, both the hospital's function and image have changed radically, and today Youville is a leader in the vital field of rehabilitation and care of the long-term patient.*

In the fall of 1970, the hospital began a cooperative venture with the faculty and students of the Boston Theological Institute to try to answer the needs of the patients. Divinity students from seven graduate schools of theology come weekly to the hospital to participate, talking with patients and listening to them. Weekly seminars are conducted by a psychiatrist and two BTI professors, and at half of these one or more critically ill patients and/or their families are interviewed by the psychiatrist.

"Though the conditions of all those interviewed are quite serious," a hospital spokesman explained, "some have not yet entered the last phase of their illnesses, and death may not be imminent. The personal problems brought out during these sessions often open the way to recognition of a family disagreement or a troubling breach of friendship, which, when discussed, can be the first step to reconciliation. Burdens such as these are a tremendous relief when lifted from the mind of a seriously ill person. More often, the staff is helped to view the patient as a person and appreciate him as such. This is the primary purpose of the interviews. In essence, it is a learning situation in which the patients are the teachers. Patient reaction to the seminars is quite favorable. They welcome the opportunity of talking with someone who cares, and the majority are relieved to have people to talk to who do not want to have superficial conversations or play games."

Seventy out of approximately 7,000 hospitals in the United States have similar programs.

You know, too often the past has shown that severely ill patients are treated like inanimate objects. They have become no more than manifestations of their charts, treated on an impersonal basis as they move through tests and X rays. We've got to train hospital personnel to help patients live, rather than allowing them to merely exist while awaiting death.

Some people who work in hospitals may say, realizing that it costs to take care of someone who's dying and that it's difficult to put down roots and get attached, they may say, why should I get involved with this patient at all? They say, after all he's just going to die. The best answer to that question was given by Cicely Saunders [Dr. Saunders is a pioneer in the development of approaches to the dying patient; she opened St. Christopher's Hospice in London in 1967], and she said, "If you don't know the answer to that question then you don't have enough maturity to be in this kind of work." And yet the answer does require some elaboration . . .

The reason all this is so difficult for some is that you put down roots, you do become attached to the patient, and you do lose them, and that hurts. It's a loss, there's no way of minimizing that, there's no way of getting around it, and not only is it a loss but there's a psychological law that operates when a person responds to losing someone or something in his or her life . . . and that is that all our losses are cumulative. If I have a human relationship, a friend, and he dies, he's killed in the war, or he dies of nephritis or a heart attack or something like that, that is not discreet, it brings back into my mind, certainly into my unconscious mind, every loss that I've ever had before, every wrenching of my attachments that I've developed before. And that's why it is extremely difficult for a nurse, say, to face some of these difficulties, to face getting involved with them and losing them . . .

And losses don't have to be losses through death. There are losses of relationships, of boyfriends, of disappointments, of jobs. . . . If someone is very sensitive to what his unconscious tells him, he would realize that when he thinks of the things he's lost and how he's been disappointed that some of those memories would return in the wistful hours or moments following the death of a patient. I remember a physician, a sensitive guy, a good internist, taking care of patients, and in the times following the death of a patient he would ask himself these questions: Why am I in this business at all? Shouldn't I just get out of it? Feeling very depressed. That wasn't his whole feeling, but it would fluctuate, and within a couple of hours. He remembered driving home and thinking of himself as being very inept, of not being able to help anybody, and what did he have to offer, thinking that he ought to drive his car into a tree or into a concrete abutment. And then if he allowed himself to think, he thought of other times in his career when he felt that. And one was early in his residency when he had the feeling of being inept . . . there wasn't enough knowledge, there wasn't enough in medical school to help these people, and why was he in it at all. And so the new loss, the failure that had nothing to do with his competence, of someone who had a terminal, relentless disease . . . that triggered and brought back all of the feelings, all of the gut feelings, of everything that had gone on back in his career. And with him I remember trying to get what his associations were to that, just allowing his mind to go anyplace . . . it's a good way to let yourself hear what the unconscious tells you. And one of the things he remembered was the interruption of his basketball career by an injury, and that came back. So that all those things are related in the unconscious . . .

If you don't do grief work, and you don't grow through losses, they mount up and they take their toll on you in later life. The inability to grow through loss, it's been said, is the royal road to dementia. You have to grow through it, but the inevitability of it is one of the reasons that nobody wants to deal with death. But after all, after thirty, life is just one loss after another, and if you think about that it's true. And people . . . they get upset because they lose their youth and they think their memory is failing and they're not as appealing or attractive, and how are they going to come to grips with this? And if you don't deal with it, if you don't work it through, then you really are on the road to senility and the inability to deal with later life . . .

For the dying person, we often are trying to help them say good-bye. How does one adequately end a relationship? It's a very serious question. And I think people need some help with that. For instance, if you have . . . spontaneously, people do this and they have for years but it's good to figure it scientifically . . . if you've had a good friend, and you've lived in the same part of the country, and you worked together, were in the service together, the war, went through school together, and the time comes that he will be transferred, or you will be, how do you say good-bye? You know that you'll stay in touch, you know that you'll see one another, but there are some separations that are quite abrupt and quite complete in terms of the amount of time you actually shared with each other. What's very important is for the two people to review the relationship, to review the times that have gone by, the good times and some of the bad times, so that certain things, subtle things, happen in the personality.

What we often do because losses hurt so much is we don't say good-bye to anybody. The day comes and we disappear. That was more common to us in our youth. Talking to kids I'll find they'll do that pretty often. They have to say good-bye, they just don't show up on the last day. They don't really say I'm not going to see you again, or I may never see you again, or our paths may never cross again. . . . What should be said is, I want you to know the relationship was meaningful, I'll miss this about you, or I'll find it hard to go down to the corner for a beer, it won't be the same, I'll miss the bluntness that you had in helping me sort out some things, or I'll just miss the old bull sessions, or something like that. Because those are the things you value. Now what does that do for the other person? The other person learns that although it's painful to separate it's far more meaningful to have known the person and to have separated than never to have known him at all. He also learns what it is in himself that is valued and treasured by his friend. And some of those underlying, corrosive feelings of low self-esteem that plague people are shored up . . . you put a solid input into people. I think I owe it to my friends that when they leave or when we're separated or when we part that I want them to know what I valued in them or what I'll miss about them because though I may say to myself, surely he'll have no problem of confidence, I know all too well, from my experiences, that everybody has problems with their confidence, everybody has a time in their life where they say this is a one-way relationship . . .

There's a lot to learn from the patients. The interesting

thing to me is that after eight years . . . I've only been working with cancer patients, I've dealt with death for a long time but I've only done work with, specific work with, cancer patients and the terminally ill for eight years . . . the patients keep me in it. I think the physicians are so dumb. And they're so antagonistic. At least they were in the beginning. That really has changed, and I guess the better I know them the less true that is. But the overall opposition to doing anything for patients has been so enormous that anybody in his right mind would have never pursued the field. But the patients . . . the patients have kept me going, and other direct caretakers have . . .

So what is it? What is it about these people? Subjectively, I noticed that when I ran the seminars at Youville, not always, but probably maybe 90 percent of the time, that when I left there I noticed something very interesting. I came to the hospital in the evening at around six o'clock, tired, often feeling drained, and wondering what it would be like not only to go through a seminar but then to have to go through four hours of supervision, and after to have to be there from six to midnight. It'd be just like putting in another day's work. And I found that when I left there at midnight I felt enormously refreshed, exhilarated, far less fatigued than when I set foot in the hospital. I'd come there to begin with after having seen very sick, mentally ill patients all day long, working with them almost exclusively on an individual basis.

What do you attribute that feeling to?

Well, as I review it, I think it's very valuable because in part it's the answer to the caretaker who asks what he's supposed to get out of it, dealing with dying patients. The question that I always entertain and sometimes put to those patients is, what kind of human resources do they have that allows them to face, to confront, wasting neurological diseases, quadriplegia or death, sometimes debilitation, humiliating circumstances of death, and I'll often come away from those intensive interviews having dealt with an individual who's absolutely phenomenal . . . someone who in the midst of feces and saliva and bad odors and weakness and all the humiliating aspects of being ill so preserves a dramatic human quality about him, sometimes a sense of humor, and other times dignity and real reflectiveness, some real bits of human wisdom, a flair for describing what life is like . . . that I really am edified. It's inspiring. Those people just inspire me. You really do learn that lesson from them. Resources of the human spirit are enormous.

You're a priest as well as a psychiatrist. Has that helped you, do you think, to deal with dying patients in a way that other caretakers might not?

I think that this has certainly been very helpful to me. I think, though, that I always try to walk a fine line because I guess I feel put upon all the time by the accusations of my psychiatric colleagues, not so much in Boston but much more what I hear in New York. And that's that anyone who has any kind of sincere and deep religious conviction is basically someone who hides his head in the sand, is running away from problems. I can certainly confess that I have no greater insight now as to what lies beyond death than I did when I started. But there's one practice that I'd always had that's common to the Jesuits and was common to St. Ignatius who founded them. He called it the examination of conscience, but for me it's one of the most valuable parts of the day, and usually when I'm driving home at night it starts. And I just review the day. Many times things are so hectic or so demanding that I haven't had any additional time to stand back and reflect. . . . I'll usually ask myself, where did the Lord touch me today? How did he touch me? What did I come in contact with that really moved me? Or upset me, or made me angry? What was it . . . what was it? And I reflect on that in a prayerful mood. And there are often things to be thankful for, lessons that I have learned, people that I admire, and in whom I felt that I got closer to some of the mysteries of . . . of. . . . I think what's profound in the human spirit, of people who are very courageous, or very dignified or have some profound sense of peace. And also something exciting . . . meeting these people, how they're able to extract, in the most abominable circumstances, really creative solutions, not denying solutions but really creative and constructive ones in their life settings. I admire them, and I think about that in the same way I might think about. . . . I also learn something about cardiology or maybe chemistry, things that are kind of wonderful or mysterious or sort of awesome, and I thank the Lord for the chance to get some further insight into the mysteries of the universe, and into the mysteries of people. . . . I think the way in which my religious convictions . . . part of it is learning to respect what the Lord made and to be curious about it, and to admire it and to thank him for it and to have a sense of worship about the wonders I find . . .

Have you ever been depressed working with this kind of patient?

Many times. Because it doesn't always work for people. I may be called . . . I have been called to consult on patients and I sit with them and I try to work with them and they don't seem to have any resources that they can call upon. It's very late in the course of their disease, they don't seem to have any capacity to face what is there, and they don't seem to have done very much about developing their potential, their human potential, to deal with debilitation or to deal with loss. I feel that I may sit there at the bedside, listen to what they say, try to draw them out, try to lend as much compassion and support, but come away and feel drained that . . . that . . . although the patient feels grateful perhaps, that I haven't had a feeling that much constructive has been accomplished. Now, see, I've changed a little bit in that. Over the years . . . I don't feel quite as drained, and what I've learned is that patients actually get more out of some compassion and understanding than I ever thought they did . . . but that's very, very hard to assess . . .

But I do get . . . at times I just feel discouraged . . . at the way some people died. It was not, I thought, very dignified. They could have been more of a man, or more of a woman; they could have exerted more autonomy, they could have been more angry, or it would have been more appropriate if they had acted this way or that. . . . But somehow, they didn't get a chance to do it. Now, maybe it wasn't their fault and most of the time I do feel it wasn't their fault. But that doesn't really help me. I feel discouraged by it.

These stages that dying patients go through . . . obviously patients die at various points along the way, without reaching acceptance.

The reason that Dr. Ross put those stages out is that it's work . . . you've got to work through this, you work that out. You just don't stop and say maybe that tumor isn't going to be malignant, I must have heard the doctor wrong. You don't stop there, and some people need help not to stop there. With enough time and help in working through the stages the patient will reach a plateau, where he is neither depressed or angry. He'll die with peace and dignity, but it shouldn't be mistaken for a happy stage, the acceptance. It is rather almost void of feeling. . . . It's really better to think of all the processes going on at once, each one being at different levels. . . . Denial would be low or high, depression would be here, anger would still be there and you might even have some bargaining going on at any point. But whether or not they're dying appropriately, that is, whether they're dying with all the capacities that they can exert, has to do with how much work they've been able to do prior to that . . . and perhaps how much help they're getting to do it in the setting. There are a lot of people who just don't get the help, haven't done the work, and who, I think, are dying in an undignified way. They die and it isn't at what they could, it isn't with the capacity, it isn't with the kind of self-affirmation and kind of self-resolve.

I think I'd like to be able to have someone say one of two things basically. Either, that it's coming, there's nothing I can do about it, I've exhausted all the possibilities, it's coming and it's there, and I've done some of the things that I felt I could do, done everything I could do . . . and I say yes, in a sense that there's a kind of affirmation of what's been meaningful. Or, they can say, I resent it, I fight it every point of the way, I know it's coming, to hell with it, and then go with their chins up . . .

So if a person dies in the anger stage that isn't so horrid?

They could die that way, yes. There are some people whose whole stance against life is anger. They are angry all the time. What you'd like is for someone to die *themselves*. Something that is characteristic for them, say, at the peak of how they are as a person, and if the person is most himself in a kind of angry way I would think he would have already done some of the work on the depressive aspects, but he'd do it in an angry way, and he'd come to grips with it that way. He'd say, what about this wound? To *hell* with it. I'll fix it myself. He gets so he cleans it, and he does it in an angry way, so he's worked something through. You know, Louis Lobel, a French spiritual writer, defined a saint as a man who lives to the limit of his capacities, and that's all the Lord asks of us. Sometimes we have a nervous system that's hyperexcitable, sometimes we have an upbringing or a background that makes us cantankerous, but we negotiate . . . and I would like to see someone just be able to stay at the limit of his capacity, or up as high as possible sometime during their terminal period because that's when they feel best about themselves . . .

And for the caretaker . . . well, he has to prepare himself and he throws himself in as a human resource. You take anything that comes and hope for the best, and try to offer the person every single human resource you have. And you may help them . . . you may help them. And the persons themselves. We always underestimate them . . . we always do.

But when you have people who know damn well that . . . they might say to you, look, this is painful, or this is so disfiguring that by God I hope I die. The best thing is for the caretaker to say something like, I can sympathize with that, I don't know whether it's going to be disfiguring, I don't know how long it's going to be painful, it makes me uptight when you say I hope I die because you know I want to see you live, and it makes me uncomfortable, and I guess I can't understand when you say that, and I guess I don't know what to say most of the time . . . but I want you to know I'm going to be here . . . I'll just be here. And they may say, it's hard for me to be here . . .

But, somebody told me a story . . . this is a lovely story. It came from a chaplain down near Taunton, John Smith, who is a great fellow and he runs a training program for some of his students, and he had one student who. . . . There was a man who had a very bad burn and the odor was terrible. It was infected and the student chaplain came in to take care of him — and this gets me into the other main point of what do you get out of all this — the chaplain came in to see him and he couldn't stand the odor, it just made him sick, he was nauseated, and he went to the bed and he couldn't talk to the man he was so repelled. It was just revolting to him, so he put his head down on his arm and he was silent for twenty minutes, and then he just got up and just patted the man on the shoulder and went out . . . he had to leave fast. So he thought, this is terrible, I've failed, I haven't been able to do a thing. He went in the next day and he talked to John, and John said, well, that's all right, we're just ourselves, we're weak, you know, we have these bad feelings and all this stuff, so go back in and try again. So, he went back in and sat down again and put his hand on the man's arm or something, and said hello.

Then the man said, Father, I just want to tell you how much that did for me yesterday when you came in and prayed for me like that, I really needed someone to do that for me. Well, you know the chaplain was astonished, taken aback . . .

So here it is again, what can we do? We're so helpless, we say. After all, is that really true? We don't have any idea of what we can do. I think that being in this after eight years, why I'm not so depressed all the time . . . although I'm still depressed, you know . . . is that I never know what I can do for a patient when I go to see them initially. I have a fair amount of confidence that I can do something, and I also know that I may not know what it is when I've left the bedside, and I don't know exactly whether I've done anything. But I'm more willing to say, well, maybe something will come of it . . . more willing than I was when I started. And I'll tell you why you get to know that. You get to know it for the same reason that you get to know you're okay as a person when your friends . . . like they'll tell you, I like this about you, I like that about you. . . . Some of the most moving and memorable moments in your career are when your patients tell you why it is that you . . .

I'm seeing a woman right now, cardiac surgery patient, and she's saying, I can't get through this without you, I can't get through the surgery, and then she says if it weren't for you I wouldn't have the surgery. And when she's through with it, she says, I wouldn't have been able to do it if you hadn't come and talked to me . . . you learn more about what you can do . . .

But, you know, I've found that I can't talk about the examples . . . when I'm talking before a group I usually use examples from some other doctors' patients, or from my students' patients, and I seldom refer to my own because they were so . . . moving. And I'm sometimes afraid that I won't be able to go on like that, although that isn't so bothersome to me. I guess it's sometimes bothersome to some people because they're afraid of their own feelings . . .

I remember, there was one person who said, realizing he was going to die, he said he'd miss seeing me, miss talking to me, that was one of the bad things. . . . And I remember this particular person said, you know, what I'll miss about you . . . I'll miss your calm. And many times I've thought of that and I realize that it's one thing you have to offer to people . . . and I've also been grateful to that patient many times.

I remember, especially at the beginning, saying, what do I have to offer to these people? Well, you have an awful lot to offer . . . if you're just willing to sit in there.

Is it possible to have no religious faith, and still die with dignity?

Oh, yes. It's always possible to go out with dignity and you never really have to have total equanimity with any of those things. I think that primarily what. . . . The spirit of people who do it well . . . the spirit that they convey is, it's all right, it's all right, it's difficult at times, and at times humiliating, and at times frustrating, and at times infuriating, but it's all right . . . and it's especially all right if someone knows about those things because that makes a lot of difference . . .

The Lord keeps pushing you, he demands of you . . . and studying theology you keep pushing back. . . . It's faith, faith, faith . . . faith is tried. The Lord expects you to pay for it. . . . He expects you to work on the ambivalence all the time. So I think we help people with the ambivalence by helping them bring to the fore what their fears are . . . and what are their fears? Well, we know the usual ones. That it's going to be painful, and they'll be isolated, it'll be undignified . . . they're guilty, it's unforgivable, their lives have been wasted, they'll go to hell . . . some are haunted by the thought that there is no reward. But what you must do for someone like that is to bring those things to the surface, and you sit with them. We don't have ready answers for that, and because we don't have ready answers people will accuse us . . . they'll say, there's nothing we can do about that, or that's a lot of phony emotionalism. I don't think that's true. There are resources that can be called upon, and growth that is possible . . . and you provide a chance to reflect . . .

Then you can die with a peace of mind that isn't religiously inspired?

Yes, I think so. I'm sure my psychoanalytic colleagues will dislike my saying this . . . because I think that people have anonymous faiths, and although I'd be happy to put that in the equation of, it's a faith in what's important, I would extend that to say that it's a faith in what is transcendental, what is bigger than we are . . .

And usually what the patient is preoccupied with is that there are things that are bigger than they. . . . What is important sometimes is what they're remembered for, and that's an extension of themselves, a form of immortality, if you want. . . . They may focus on what they've left, in the way of their children, in their work, their works. And some of those considerations are important to them, they may derive equanimity from saying, this is the way I've lived, these are the things I've felt were important, and even when

I'm put upon, when I'm hacked at, when I've got needles in me, when I'm weak, when I've got one last gasp in me . . . I'm still a man, still a woman, I'm genteel, I'm respectful, I'm gracious and I'm dignified . . .

So that brings me to something that the caretaker should remember, and everyone else who's dealing with someone who is dying. You take the opportunity, when you admire someone for the way he's doing something, and you tell him, for heaven's sake. And I've said to many a patient — and it's important that it not be false either — you tell them you felt they were under a lot of duress, but how inspiring it is to see them. . . . I've said to patients, I don't know how, I don't know whether I myself could do this . . . I don't know how I would take it. . . . I am stirred by the way in which you do this, the way you deal with this, I'm put to shame, it makes me feel small.

I had an interview with a quadriplegic, a young black athlete who was a regional tennis champion from the North Shore . . . he might have had some minimal movement of one arm, and certainly no fine movements of the hand. Bright, bright, a fantastic mind. And as I interviewed him I became more and more filled with a sense of awe, and I had the feeling I was dealing with an enormous and gigantic person. The brain was really phenomenal, and I took the opportunity to tell him that, that I had not heard descriptions of that sort before, and that some of the things he had told me were insights that I hadn't had the chance of hearing before. I was really stunned by him. If quads are given a chance . . . what comes out, the dimension, what the person is, what the spirit is like. You cut off a guy's body and you make him helpless . . . but you're willing to sit with him, you're willing to draw him out, to learn what he's like . . . wow. It's not only rewarding for you and reassuring . . . but it's also important to give him the feed-back . . . and that's one of the things you can do for the dying patient.

How do you think you'll approach your own dying? Has all this helped you?

Oh, yes, it has. I'm sure it has. I'm still a human being. I'm thirty-seven, and the way I want to die is with, as they say, with my boots on. There's no question about that. I plan to kill myself by working myself to death, and I don't want to go any other way. No bones about that. It's hard for me to think about having to face any other thing . . . debilitation, incapacitated, and so on. What if I had a stroke? What if I had a bad injury? You know, those things are gruesome . . . I think of that as gruesome. But dealing with these patients has forced me to first admit to myself that it is possible that one of those things might befall me. Now, I have to take that to two resources. One is the Lord. I have to be willing to say that if that's what I'm called upon to face then that's all right, I'll take it. Then, in the psychological resources, I guess what I've come to realize is that I have certain ways I have determined to go about that. . . . I will not be a whiner, and I will try and divest myself of those things that make it so difficult for care-takers. But I certainly will not divest myself of those oppor-tunities to be helpful, since I know that these people are so helpful if anyone'll listen to them. I have the feeling that somehow I still could be helpful, and not in any way that anyone would admit it because I know that caretakers don't like to admit that they're helped by anybody . . .

In fact, if I were a quad, I could be just as helpful as if I had a body, so long as I have my mind intact. People could still come with their problems and talk to me about them, and I could still help them with those. . . . But suppose I couldn't, suppose something had incapacitated me so that . . . what if I only came to consciousness or full awareness off and on? Well, then I still think there are ways of bringing the personhood of those dealing with me to the fore . . . helping them to be persons as well. I'd be mad at them if they tried to avoid me, maybe saying to them, hey, looks like you're avoiding this . . .

If I were told I was going to die . . . I don't know . . . I would be scared, I would be angry, depressed. I'd have to work it through, just like anyone else. I know that I would think about killing myself, I know that I would think about asking someone to kill me . . .

That sort of leads us to whether or not you tell a dying person he is going to die.

That question, whether to tell the dying patient he is going to die, that's often a pseudoquestion because it allows a person the luxurious illusion that if he formulates an answer to the question that that is going to take him off the hook when he's dealing with a person. As though it would make it any easier. How do you convey to somebody that the game is up, that somehow or other the natural resources have run out on them, and that they are going to run out faster than anyone expected? How do you convey that without trauma? You don't. You don't convey it without trauma to the patient, without trauma to yourself. If you want my . . . firm conviction, it is that if you want to know what side to err on it's unquestionably established by the investigative work that's been done with the patients that you err on the side of information. There is no question about that. And if you take any two men randomly and one hides the information from all his patients and the other gives the information to his patients outright, the patients of the latter man will do far better in the long run than the patient of the one who hides it. You can go one step better, if you're willing to endure more trauma. . . . You get the patient and the patient's family, and you give them all the information. There are doctors no matter where I go, and they'll stand up and they'll get angry, and they'll berate me and they'll say, you do this as an individual equation . . . all of which I agree with. But the evidence shows that the patient where the conspiracy of silence was not maintained did much better, is much happier. And, of course, they know anyway, that's the interesting feature. One of the patients I have, Mr. Casey. I saw him, and I asked him about his problem. He said, look, this amputation up here in my arm doesn't have anything to do with the disease in my legs and back. He said, I don't know what I have, I have no idea, and I thought to myself after he said that, my God then what are you doing here, and I asked him that. I don't know, he said, just a stay, I guess, and he went on with all that sort of stuff. On Tuesday — that was Monday when he said he had no idea of what was bothering him — on Tuesday he said, I'm riddled with this disease, I'm a goner. On Wednesday, he said, well, I'm a guy who doesn't like to know very much about my illness, and I don't ask a lot of questions. I asked him whether he'd like to know anymore from the doctor and he said, I don't know, I don't think so. On Thursday, he said, well, nobody likes to die.

Look at it this way. Caring for the disabled and the dying means caring for persons who are living on borrowed time, who feel pain, helplessness, disillusionment of lifelong dreams, and probably worse, the ache of loneliness. In fact, our prime task is probably to help prevent loneliness and isolation, and to do so we must be able to lower the sound barriers, understand the dying patient and speak with him comfortably. But this is difficult to do because we ourselves have never heard a death sentence, nor faced death, so we must be willing to learn how the dying do it. How about us? Do we have too many worries to listen? Or maybe we just convey that impression. Are we sometimes too nervous? Or don't we try at all?

You know, it's astonishing and regrettable that so many caretakers in the health professions, when they're faced with the care of the terminally ill, do not try. Try talking, try visiting, try listening, try sharing their lives with them. And it's essential for the health professionals to understand that grieving and dying are natural processes that have a natural predictive sequence, as Dr. Ross has outlined with clarity and eloquence. In addition to understanding them, we must be able to meet these patients on better terms, by listening, by chatting, by touching them, or by a single look or a smile. Young physicians, social workers, nurses, chaplains and other health personnel need guidance and practice to do this comfortably and well . . . and dying patients need caring persons to share their last days, to help them meet death with comfort, equanimity, dignity and peace . . .

FIVE

The
Dying

If that's the way it's got to be, then that's the
way it's got to be.
> — A reputed chieftain of an organ-
> ized crime family, after being told
> by an investigator that he had a
> godfather complex, that he
> shouldn't go to gangster movies,
> and that one day he would be
> killed

Daddy, I want to go to Jesus.
> — Last words of ten-year-old Clifford
> Jaeger, who drowned, with his
> two brothers and his grandfather,
> off Chappaquiddick Island

Lucinda Jackson, 68

The psychiatrist and I sit by her bed in the corner of a brightly lit hospital ward. We try to chat.

"Nausea."

"Nausea. And vomiting?"

"Yes."

"Could you tell us what it's been like for you?"

"I couldn't hold down a thing."

"Did it just come on suddenly?"

"Just come on suddenly, and kept up."

"Had it ever been like that before?"

"No."

"So you couldn't keep it down."

"No. And I wonder if some of the medicine had anything to do with it."

"Was there anything else? Any other symptoms? Aches, pains?"

"There was cramps, in my stomach."

"Lot of cramps?"

"Yes."

"Interfere with your sleep?"

"I didn't sleep."

"And you'd been active up to that point?"

"Yes."

"And what happened? What changes happened in your activity?"

"I just stopped."

"What did you stop?"

"Just things."

"Like what?"

"Physical therapy."

"Yes?"

"I had to stop. I couldn't get up."

"What else did you stop?"

"Just that."

"What were you doing, in physical therapy, I mean."

"Exercises."

"What kind?"

"All kinds."

"Tell me about some of them."

"Like using a walker."

"In a walker. You were using a walker?"

"Yes."

"And you had to stop that?"

"I was too weak."

"What effect did that have on your outlook?"

"It didn't bother me too much. I wanted to go home. I just felt a little bad, that's all. I wouldn't be worse off at home."

278

"How would going home help?"

"Just like being in my old surroundings, that's all."

"You were discouraged?"

"A little."

"How bad did it get?"

"I guess it hasn't gotten any further than . . . that. I'm still here, ain't I?"

"You're pretty chipper today. But I'll bet you weren't that way a week ago."

"No."

"How bad did you feel a week ago?"

"Awful bad."

"It would be helpful if you'd give me some idea just what that's like, to be in that state."

"Well, I can't very well. It's just that vomit. Whenever you eat and something goes down it comes right back up. When you do it all day and all night, it's more than you can take. It's very hard. Two weeks it went."

"Did you sometimes think it was going to go on like that?"

"I did."

"What did you think then?"

"It's all I could think of. That it never would stop. I wondered if it ever would."

"How can you stand something like that?"

"What else are you going to do? You have to stand it."

"Did it ever get so bad you thought you'd be better off dead?"

"Yes."

"It did get that bad?"

"It did."

"Did you ever tell anybody that?"

"No."

"I guess some of us don't realize how awful those things can be."

"That's right."

"When did you start getting better?"

"I don't know that I did . . ."

"But you do seem better than a few days ago."

"Maybe."

"You do feel a little better?"

"A little."

"And that makes a difference?"

"Yes."

"What do you notice mostly?"

"It's quieted down."

"What was it like for you when you were at your best, when you were feeling real good?"

"I was active, doing things around, staying home. Then I came here."

"Have you any memory of what the trouble was that brought you here?"

"Some. And I asked them not to."

"What happened?"

"They told me I was going to stay here."

"But I mean what happened to you that they brought you to the hospital?"

"They thought I'd get better, I guess. I don't know."

"Get better from what?"

"My fall . . . I guess."

"You had a fall?"

"Yes."

"When was that?"

"January."

"Did you break any bones?"

"Just some bruises."

"You make it sound so easy. Which ones did you bruise?"

"My ribs."

"Was that some morning you were going out?"

"With my dog."

"Your dog?"

"Yes. He fell, we both fell. He's dead now."

"Your dog is dead? What happened?"

"I guess he wanted to be with me, he just didn't want to be with nobody else." Her eyes fill with tears.

"He wanted to be with you, so that's how he came to be out with you. But what happened, how did he . . . ?"

"I don't know. That's all I been told."

"Who told you?"

"My brother."

"Your brother. Was he trying to tend the dog before . . . ?"

"I don't know."

"How long had you had him?"

"Two years."

"What kind of dog?"

"Small collie. And I trained him so he could walk on his hind legs, stand up and bark."

"Is that right?"

"Yes."

"Did you have him from a puppy?"

"Two months old."

"What was his name?"

"Mr. Grits and Hocks."

"Mr. Grits and Hocks?"

"Yes. I used to call him that." She laughs.

"Was he pretty clever?"

"Yes. He toddled along with me. I used to keep him on a leash." She laughs again.

"How did you teach him to stand up?"

"Well, he just got up all of a sudden after dinner and I said, well, if you want to walk come on, if you want to stand, come on, and he did."

"He wasn't a talking dog, too, was he?"

"No, but he knew things."

"What color was he?"

"Buff and white."

"How tall was he?"

"Oh, almost as tall as I am when he stretched."

"I thought you said he was a small collie?"

"Not too small." She laughs.

"When did you find out that he had died?"

"Just a couple of days ago."

"Must have been kind of tough hearing that."

"It was, kind of, because he and I both fell together, and I warned him . . . I did."

"How did he seem after the fall?"

"Well, he went down fast. It wasn't long after that. . . . He was on the leash, and I had it in my hand, and I was going out with him, and he was at my side."

"Did you fall on top of him?"

"No. I didn't."

"How do you think he got hurt?"

"Dogs can get hurt going downstairs just like . . . same as I, can't he?"

"But a dog. They're usually a lot tougher than we are."

"Maybe that's true."

"So you didn't get much information, then?"

"Well, I asked where he was. That's the answer I got. That he was dead."

"Thinking about that fall again. Does it really make much sense that the fall . . ."

"Well, I don't know whether he had any broken bones or anything."

"That's pretty unusual, though, with a dog. It usually takes more than being on a flight of stairs, doesn't it?"

"Well, dogs do get hurt, too."

"All except for your dog, then, you were pretty much alone? Kept to yourself, did you?"

"Yes. After my husband died. That was ten years ago."

"How'd that happen? What happened to your husband?"

"He just went. That's all I know."

"Very suddenly?"

"Yes."

"Was he at home when it happened?"

"No. He was at the shop."

"He worked in a shop?"

"Yes. A janitor."

"What happened?"

"He didn't come back to me, that's all I know."

"How long had you been married?"

"Since 1938."

"And just the two of you?"

"That's right."

"Do you miss him?"

"Well, you do at first. You have to get used to it."

"How long did that take?"

"Quite a while."

"Do you think you ever really got used to it?"

"I'm not so sure."

"Hard for us to get used to things like that."

"That's right."

"Must think about him, from time to time?"

"I did, these past two weeks. Think of my dog, and then of him."

"They've been a tough couple of weeks for you, haven't they?"

"Yes."

"So you actually thought you were going to die."

"I did."

"Were you scared?"

"No."

"Do you think about it often?"

"Not now."

"What about during those couple of weeks?"

"I did then."

"If you thought that maybe you were going to die, did you have any thought about how it would happen, what would make you die?"

"Just go, I guess. Maybe from the fall . . ."

"And it doesn't scare you, that thought?"

"Not for me. I'm old now, so . . ."

"You said there were times you would be better off dead than to keep vomiting all the time."

"That's right."

"What about during the times you're feeling better, did those thoughts ever come to you, that you were dying, or that you'd be better off dead?"

"I wouldn't know."

"Is that, the vomiting and all, about the worst symptoms that you have?"

"Right now it is. I hope so."

"Did they bring you breakfast this morning?"

"Yes. They brought something. I ate part of it."

"How's the food?"

"It didn't taste very good."

"What about when you were in physical therapy? Did it taste any better then?"

"I never cared too much for it."

"It is difficult to be in the hospital. Are there some things that make it easier?"

"I can't answer that question."

"Any recommendations?"

"No."

"What if you were giving advice to nursing students?"

"I wouldn't."

"You wouldn't?"

"No. I think they'd be giving me some."

"Any ways of giving advice that are better than others?"

"No. Not that I know."

"Do you mind being given advice?"

"No."

"That's a nice robe you have there. It's bright and cheery. Looks like you're ready to start moving."

"I don't know about that."

"Any plans for going back to therapy?"

"No."

"Does that mean no plans of yours or no plans of theirs?"

"I'll go back when they want me."

"You will?"

"I have to."

Carol Whitehead, 53

The rec room of a Harvard teaching hospital in Boston. She is idling at a number painting of birds in flight. Her clothes match the autumn outdoors, rust-colored sweater, tweed skirt, and Desert Boots.

Well, I'm a nurse, you know, that is, I was, and I used to work in a cardiology department, and I joined the club, so to speak. I've got a myopathic condition involving the heart, and a lot of problems. Do you want to get technical? The condition is idiopathic, which is a two-dollar word meaning they don't know what the hell causes it, and I have this mitral defect, the left ventricle doesn't work right and so on when my pulse goes up over 95, you know. And they did four caths on me, and after I had the second heart attack they sent me in here, thinking I was going to have open heart surgery. But they couldn't do it because my heart is so grossly enlarged that I'm a poor risk. . . . So they stuck me in bed for close to a year, hoping to shrink it down. First few months they managed a fifteen-millimeter shrinkage, but after that nothing . . .

I used to work at this hospital, as a matter of fact, and they picked it up here on a routine physical. . . . I had an idea something was going on, of course, but you know how you put stuff off. . . . Well, some smart little cookie didn't like what he saw my pulse was doing. . . . And he did an EKG. . . . Crazy but I had never had one done before, because in the old days, you know, they didn't do much in the way of testing like that. Well, I thought I was always a pretty healthy goat and boy did I get upset when he told me there was a problem. . . . The strange thing was that I felt fine . . . except when I didn't feel fine. [Laughs.]

It's bad, then.

Oh, it's bad all right. Yeah. It's so bad, in fact, they've fixed it so that I'm not supposed to be alone, supposed to have nurses around and so on, supposed to check in here regularly as an outpatient and so on. And they don't do that sort of thing unless they think you're going to conk out. To get this kind of treatment you've got to be in the last throes of something or other. It's all bullshit, which I don't really go along with. But I do come in regularly because they are afraid I'll go into cardiac arrest at any moment. . . . But the hell with it, I go my own way . . .

It's okay if I stick with the diet, no salt and all that bullshit, but I'm off now, I know, and I'm heading for big trouble. The weight is starting to go up, and I'm on a lot of medication a day, and it's beginning to not work. . . . Lots of little signs like that . . .

It doesn't really bother me until I start choking, and then I get scared, needless to say. But so far, I've always managed to get myself out of it. [Laughs.] And that's what the boys upstairs figure. . . . If I can get down here fast enough if anything serious really happens . . . because I am a nurse, you know . . . that they can work on me and bring me out of it, keep me here a couple of weeks and then send me home again . . .

Last time they sent me home was around the fourth of July, and they didn't think I was going to last the night, or that if I got home I'd be back in a couple of weeks. . . . But so far I've fooled them, and I've made it this far without being hospitalized, so I figure I'm up on them . . .

You talk quite casually about it.

Well, what's the sense of worrying about it? Oh, I have my moments, like when I start choking, and I wonder if I'm going to come out of it. I have spells of that, and they don't know what causes it. They've used a lot of emergency on me in here, and some think it's nerves, others that I'm going into atrial fibrillation, because they did catch me one time and they did an EKG and I was fibrillating. . . . And they found that while the fibrillation itself didn't cause the inability to breathe maybe my nerves got the best of me when I did feel the fibrillation, and that threw me into it. . . . And there's others that feel it's something they haven't caught up with yet that causes it. And when you're choking and can't breathe, that's serious . . .

And, you know, I'm a nurse, and I worked here in cardiology and I know an awful lot and the doctors have never tried to hide anything from me. Every cath they've ever given me I've never had any medication, and I've been wide awake while they were doing it to me. . . . And they've discussed it all. And they know I know, even though they don't come right out and say that I'm not going to make it, you know. But sometimes I'll say something to them, and that throws them a little because they do know me, and we all get along good, and no one likes to put it that way to people you like a lot. But there is one doctor who feels particularly bad, and we've known each other for years, and one day he came down to see me, and he was nearly crying, and he told me, you know, Carol, I don't think you're going to make it. He was terribly upset . . .

I've lived with this for quite a while. You either live with it or you don't live with it. You can't go through your whole . . . what's left of your life, worrying all the time. At least I can't do that . . .

And I figure I've got some time left. . . . No one knows how much. I've even decided to take a night course over at BU, in psychology, because I'm really interested in that. . . . I can't do nursing anymore, they won't let me, they figure I can't stand the pace, I guess. . . . But this one nurse buddy of mine said to me, she said, say, you're a smart cookie so why don't you go back to school, maybe take a course, so I decided I would. So nobody will hire me in a hospital, but what the hell. . . . I did work up until my first attack, but they wouldn't hire me today. . . . And I've tried, believe me. I'd certainly flunk the physical because they take stronger ones nowadays than they used to, and I'd be ringing those EKGs like gangbusters. . . . Yeah, it is pretty bad. If you want to see my chart, come on upstairs and I'll show it to you. . . . It's about this thick. You can go through it if you want, I wouldn't mind . . .

Do you talk much about your problem at home?

I do. But I don't think they like me to. It upsets my son and my husband. I knew I was having trouble before they diagnosed me, but I'd never admit it, and I hate to admit that I'm sick. Well, my husband would say to his friends when they'd ask about me, oh, she's okay, she's not too bad, things like that. . . . And after the first big attack, he'd say to people, oh, she's a lot better today, you know . . . and I knew I wasn't. And that kind of irked me in a way, because, you see, I wanted sympathy, plain and simple, just some of that old TLC I've lived with when I worked . . . I'll admit it. I do a little work, three nights a week in a greeting card shop nearby . . . and maybe that's why I go to the job. . . . The manager is a man, a nice guy, and he's very sympathetic and so on, and he's worried about me. I think that's why I like going to work when I know I shouldn't be going to work. Sympathy, pure and simple. I wasn't getting it at home, and they just don't want to face the fact that I . . . that I'm in trouble . . .

You just have to keep yourself up, that's all. I have to keep moving, and I've never asked the doctors what I can or can't do, what I should or shouldn't do . . . I just go.

The shop gets me out of the house, and that's good because I'm no homebody, and I just have to get out. I do try to restrict my diet. . . . Like I'm not supposed to drink, I'm not supposed to smoke. . . . But in fact they told me that it would be safer for me to smoke than to drink because alcohol makes your heart muscle even soggier. . . . I use normal precautions, I guess. If I have a problem, I have a problem. What the hell else can you do? What would you do if you had this thrown in your face? I was quite depressed for an awful long time when it first hit, but the doctors are wonderful, and I could weep on most of their shoulders. . . . A woman can do that, you know, but if I was a man I don't know what I would do. . . . Maybe a good-looking nurse . . .

I've got loads of things I want to do. . . . I've thought about that a lot. . . . And sometimes I don't really believe I'm going to conk out, even though the doctors think I am and even though I know the facts. . . . My brains tell me lots of things, but I don't feel my feelings go along all the time. Maybe I'm going to beat it, I don't know. . . . No doctor is going to pin himself down on the whole deal and say I'm going to have a heart attack on such and such a day, at such and such a time. . . . I could have one right now, this very minute while I'm talking to you, and that wouldn't be bad because I'm in the hospital already . . . wouldn't have too far to go . . .

You always hear those stories about cases where the doctor says you're not going to last a year and hell you live for six to ten. Well, I figure that maybe . . . sometimes I figure it that way. . . . I figure that I'm going to be one of those six to ten people. And maybe if I watch it I can keep myself living for that long.

But sometimes I do wonder for what. Like most people, I

do have other problems. . . . My husband, for instance, has been impotent for, I don't know, eight or nine years now, and I'm human, I've got feelings, and I've wanted to wander. . . . But I had three teenage boys when it all started . . . they're in their twenties now . . . and I didn't believe in that old saying, do as I tell you, not as I do, and so I behaved myself. . . . But lately, since I've learned I'm not going to live long, I've decided, well, maybe I'll do a little playing around. . . . And yet . . . well, I don't know. My husband is really a good Joe, and I guess we all have a tendency to want what you can't have . . . or maybe what you shouldn't have. . . . Maybe if I had it I wouldn't want it, I just don't know. . . . But maybe I'm being selfish and self-centered. But then, I figure, hell, I've had to give up smoking and I've had to give up drinking and certain foods and what the hell else is there left? People say moderation is the best philosophy in everything. . . . Well, I just want my moderation, that's all.

You know, even though I don't think my husband has any. . . . Well, he's still very possessive and. . . . This newer generation, you know, they've got a lot better attitude toward sex than we do, but perhaps they're . . . they're a little bit too heavy on it. Maybe they've gone too far the other way, because I am honestly not convinced that young people, what with all the license and so on, are really able to handle it . . . I really don't. . . . I don't know what I'm holding onto this bottle for. . . . It's Isordil, for the angina. . . . It's a nitrate. . . . I don't expect to have any trouble today. [She tosses the bottle of pills into her open handbag.]

Insofar as that impotency thing is concerned, I've asked him to see a specialist a couple of times, and he says he has and that there's nothing to be done about it. . . . And he's told other people, I hear, that it doesn't particularly bother him, so he's just letting it go on that way. . . . Well, I don't argue the point. . . . Sex is something that you can't force. . . . It either is there or it isn't, and he doesn't want to do anything about it, so I'm not going to push him. . . . And obviously, I'm not a very sexual person, or I wouldn't have let it go on for so long . . . without playing around. So it's partly me, too. But I've had lots of opportunities, believe me. . . . What woman can't these days, right? I've been working and if you want to take that road, well, there's plenty of married men who want to do a little playing around. . . . Right now, there is someone I'm sort of interested in, and I don't know whether I'll do anything about it or not . . .

But I have noticed I'm saying more and more that I am going to live my life the way I want to live it, and I think that philosophy is working with me a little. . . . Well, emotionally, I think I'm better off than I was when all this heart business started. As I say, I was pretty upset at the beginning. . . . That first day, they didn't think I was going to make it, and they were going to put me on Valium and morphine around the clock because they were worrying about me dying and so on and wanted to keep me on a hippie high. And I could hear them talking in the background. . . . You've got to be careful of that stuff, you know. . . . Patient might look comatose, but they can hear it all. . . . And they said I wasn't going to make it, wasn't going to climb out of it. . . . Another time, they had this emergency on me, and I was practically out, not able to breathe or anything, and the surgeon wanted to do a trach on me, and I heard someone else say, but she looks so good. . . . That's another thing, everyone says, you know, you look so fantastic, you'd never know you had any problems. . . . They'll say that all the time. Oh, you look so good, even the doctors will say it sometimes. And sometimes the nurses. But one doctor here, he's okay, and he said to me, he said, people have just got to look at you with X-ray eyes. Last time he checked me out, a couple of days ago, he told me my EKG was off, my weight was way up, everything was off, and he was afraid I was going to come in with a congestive heart failure in a day or so, and I had told him, yeah, and everyone tells me how great I look. Well, maybe I do, but makeup hides a lot. But that attitude annoys me, it really does. I always get sympathy from most of the doctors . . . they feel it, too. But never from the nurses and the aides. I get cracks like, what are you taking up a bed for? Things like that. You're not sick, they'll say. I've never complained much, like I never put on my light for what a lot of people put it on for, because when I flash that thing I want someone to move fast. . . . And when you don't bug them, they don't move . . . so they figure you're okay. Some of them are unbelievable. They've got time in, and they know no one is going to fire them, and God, if we ever get a national health program, a system like in England, it'll be like Civil Service in spades, I'll tell you . . .

But, as I say, I think I'm better, emotionally. I try not to think about it too often, what the hell is the use? I come in here every so often, just to work on some project, and I think being in a hospital gives me a sense of security. Although, everyone seems to be willing to spend time on the phone with me when I call. . . . And they act as though they're not rushed when I come in. . . . But basically I know they are, so I try not to call them, I'd rather come in . . .

Anyway, as I said, I hate being around the house, I do

as little housework as possible. . . . I'd go neurotic if I hung around there all day. And, of course, I'd do more thinking than is healthy. . . . My husband works nights, always has, and I've spent a lot of time alone over the years except when the kids were growing. . . . My husband would sleep a good part of the day, and we had to be quiet and so on so he could rest up, and he didn't have the problem of bringing up the kids. I did that, and that galled me a little sometimes because I felt they needed a father around more than they got. . . . And he had a friend he'd spend weekends with, and I felt he should have spent more time around the house. . . . I guess in lots of ways we sort of went our own ways, and even though he never was around much we were his life, in one way. . . . But I don't really feel he has ever been a husband or a lover, even. . . . He's more like a dependent child, like the children were. . . . I feel responsible for him, and he obviously likes that . . .

But I'm getting the feeling now and then, as I say, that life is so short and that perhaps I'd like something different. [Laughs.] But maybe if I went after it . . . maybe I wouldn't like it much . . . I don't know. I tell myself, well, you've got along and gone all these years without. . . . Maybe there's no point. . . . And I think that if you really want to know why I haven't played around, it's because of my neighbors. They're the ones who slow me down, really. But maybe I read too many magazine articles, and that's what gives me some of these foolish ideas . . .

I think that, generally speaking, I've had good medical care. . . . But, you know, when you know something about medicine as I do you just naturally feel that someone could have done it better for you than so and so did, or different. . . . Doctors and nurses, it's true, are the worst patients, they're really bitchy patients, and if you read my chart you'll see what I mean . . . I was a real bitchy patient for a long time upstairs. . . . But, hell, I was living in bed . . . no energy whatsoever, and every time I'd get up I'd start fibrillating and my pulse would just go flying and I would feel as though I were going to pass out, and I'd start having my choking parties, and when that happened at home there was no one around, and I wasn't sure those times whether I'd make the phone or not, or if I did make the phone I wasn't sure I'd be heard, because when I have those I can't talk for anything . . .

Yes, the medical care I've had is good, but, you know, I'm also on a lot of medication, a terrific amount, in fact. Want me to give you the list? When I get up in the morning I take digitalis. They told me to take a couple, but I only take one because it makes me so damn nauseous. As I say, I do as I please . . . most of the time. And I take Aldactone, four a day . . . four times a day. . . . And there's the Isordil, ten milligrams, four times a day. . . . I take Lasix, and those are strong little babies, you got to watch what they do to you. . . . I take them at noontime if I'm going to be around the house because they make you run for the john. . . . Three times a week I take them at night because they work better at night. . . . If I take them at night, I'm up every hour on the hour, so I don't get much sleep. I also take two Nembutal every night, and I'm trying to get them to switch that because I don't want to get the habit. . . . They don't seem to be concerned about the habit, but I am. . . . And those Isordils. . . . One day, I was having a pile of trouble and I took ten in a row and my doctor had a living fit . . .

But you need the stuff, I guess, to keep going. . . . Some days I have a lot of angina pain, and I say what's the sense of all of this. . . . But the next morning I'm usually okay. Maybe what keeps me from . . . maybe what keeps me going is the fact that one of my sons is still at home and my husband, and maybe I hate the idea of them coming home and finding a corpse or something . . .

I really don't know why I'm being so open about all of this. . . . I really haven't talked too much about it before. . . . Maybe it's like. . . . Well, there was a girl upstairs when I was in here last time. . . . And she was dying of CA, and this is something that surprised me. . . . She wanted me to be with her . . . because we got to be quite friendly, and even though she was half out of it, she would call to me. And the first week it was fine, I talked to her. But then they told me I wasn't going to make it. . . . And they were going to put me on a special drug, trying it out, you know, for six weeks, and whether that scared me or not, I don't know. . . . But she called for me again, and she had gone into this decline, and she started calling me again. . . . She wanted me to go to her, and I would get out of bed early when they'd let me, just to come downstairs in the lounge, to get away from her, and I had these awful guilt feelings for not staying with her . . .

Margaret Hennessey, 52

A small meeting room in a Cambridge, Massachusetts, hospital. The woman is dressed in a blue, soft bathrobe, hair neatly done up, with lipstick on, sitting in a wheelchair. Eyes that have worked overtime move nervously behind tinted, horn-rimmed glasses. Her face is powdered, and there is rouge on her cheeks. She is a slight woman, and she sits upright, slippered feet together, knees close, hands folded on her lap. A dozen folding chairs, six of us facing her. She has just been asked whether she would want to be told if she had a terminal illness.

Oh God, I don't know. I think so. I think you'd probably figure it out anyway. I think in this day and age that most people would be a little bit . . . I suppose I could use the word "dense" if they couldn't figure out when an illness is a serious condition and when it's getting worse.

Well, when you found the lump in your breast, did you know all about the seven danger signals and so on?

Gee, yes. And, well, I think every doctor tells you at that point whether it's malignant or benign, don't you?

Well, I think they should, but maybe I'm not like all doctors.

You know, I didn't realize that there would be a doctor that wouldn't. But over at St. E.'s [St. Elizabeth's Hospital, a Boston Catholic hospital] where I was before they seemed to be pretty definite about that point. I had the appointment with the doctor the day before my operation. I went into the hospital that next morning, and the day before the operation one of the doctors on the staff there, not one of my own, asked me did I understand the type of operation I was having. I didn't think any place operated without you being fully aware of the type of operation you were going to have . . .

Well anyway, he brought me in to the hospital and I had my breast removed, and uh . . . it was in February of '71, and I came along very good. Back to work and uh . . . in May of '71, well that was when we got the beautiful news that the office was closing. [Laughs sadly.] You know, I didn't have enough troubles. They decided they would close . . . gee, I don't know . . . I think they closed five of fifteen regional offices, and mine was one of them.

You lost your job?

Yes. So the office closed, the place folded up and everyone was dropped. There were no offers made. It was handled very brutally. We all fought, and in fact there's a lawsuit pending. I don't know how far it will go. It was very abrupt. In May, a man came down from Washington and announced the office was closing, and people could retire if they had twenty-five years of service, and they did have some inducements to get you out, for instance, if you retired they would give you a half year's pay, which is very attractive particularly if the salaries are very good, as they were in our office. So we all had the big decision as to what we'd do, whether we would retire if we had the twenty-five years, whether or not we would stay there and take our chances and see what they might offer us in the way of a position. Maybe we'd get an offer to go to New York, maybe we'd get an offer to go to Philadelphia, maybe to California. But everything was maybe, maybe, maybe, maybe. And they wouldn't tell us anything definite about what type of offer we would or would not get, everything was left up in the air. And the gamble was ours, you know? Whether we wanted to gamble on retiring or not retiring. But on top of everything else we had this time limit. We had to decide. . . . This was now May 15, when they had this big mass meeting, just as if they called everyone in this whole hospital and said, we're going to close the doors at the end of the month, you can retire or not, maybe we'll give you a job or maybe we won't, see? Well anyway. I retired . . . and at that point I was feeling pretty good.

That announcement must have been quite a blow.

Oh. Oh, I should say so. It really was fantastic. And the man who came in from Washington. I guess you'd say he had a lot of guts to get up in front of a lot of people and tell them that, but that's big business, and he was big business. He had been formerly president of some big company out West. I've forgotten his name. I wouldn't want to mention it anyway, but it was positively heartless the way they did it. And so . . . in fact, my boss at that big meeting, he got up and he said, what the hell is this anyway, some kind of Mexican standoff? And the big man, of course, didn't like it at all . . . he was just insulted that anybody would speak up and say anything.

Do you remember feeling depressed about that?

Well. I think you're upset at something like that. But I don't think I was depressed. It wasn't as if I was destitute. I had twenty-nine years of service, and I happened to be a person who had quite a good job there and could get a very decent pension out of the whole thing, so I wasn't going to be destitute. But neither was I at an age where I was ready for retirement. Well, May thirty-first came and we were separated. A few of us were hired back as consultants, three hundred or so. And I happened to be one of them. I was working in a department that was vital to the phase-out, and I worked every day full-time until about the middle of August, and that was really the end. Well, during all this time I was feeling good, and I went to the Cape for the rest of the summer. I happen to have a place down there and. . . . Let's see, about in the fall of '71 my back started to get stiff. It was in February of '71 that I had the operation. Like, when I'd get out of bed it would get stiff, and I'd wonder whether I could get out of bed at all. Kinda stiff. And then getting in and out of the car was kinda rough, too. I didn't think much of it, and I went to the doctor and he said, well, you know, it's probably just, maybe I just strained myself. Probably I did something. Well, of course I was doing a lot of things down at the beach. We were painting, painting trim on the house. But you know, things like that are kinda fun when you're at a beach place. But I had been doing things I don't ordinarily do, like a little gardening, waxing floors, washing windows, things like that . . . refinished some furniture. So I thought, like you know, maybe I did get a little stiff doing it all. So anyway. The stiffness continued, but then the next thing was my knee, which is still a problem, really, today. I started getting a pain in my knee and a pain in my hip, and I developed more difficulty getting in and out of the car. To get in I was like picking my foot up, you know, lifting it up. Even today it's difficult. But nevertheless, I was driving and doing everything . . .

What did you think was going on? I mean not being able to lift your leg?

Well, like I said. I thought possibly . . . I really thought I had strained myself down at the Cape, because among other things we laid a flagstone walk. [Laughs cheerily.] And that was a little out of my line. It came out beautiful, I will say that for it. But just the individual flagstones. We didn't put the cement and all that bit in, you know. There were four of us that did it. Talk about an invitation down at the Cape. [Laughs.] I own the cottage with another girl and we invited two other girls down and that was the week we laid the flagstone. They really had a swell time that weekend. [Laughs.] But anyway, they seemed to enjoy it. I thought that I had done too much, strained myself. So anyway now it's coming up to December '71 and I'm still stiff. Even around Thanksgiving I was still stiff . . . the car was a problem. But I was the driver at home and I had to drive, so I did the driving. And it was getting worse, and by February I was still stiff. So I went to the doctor and he said to take some Bufferin, and maybe the kinks would work out . . .

Didn't anyone notice you were having some trouble?

Oh, yes, my parents. But they're in their eighties, and they think it's just that I strained myself. I don't think they realized the seriousness of the whole thing. In April, I guess it was, I went to the doctor again. By this time, he's kinda nervous. I mean kind of concerned about all this stiffness and the fact that I can't walk too well. . . . I'm having a great deal of difficulty getting upstairs. Oh boy. Stairs. [Smiles, shakes her head.] Really a problem, and I hate to tell you how I was getting upstairs. I was like leaning on the banister with my arm, pulling myself up. And so I had X rays, and once I had X rays he knew what the problem was, because he knew then it was my vertebrae.

What was your understanding of it all?

Well, it was uh . . . I'm trying to think how he described it . . . let me see . . . called it the . . . well, it was the vertebrae anyway. But I'm trying to think what that expression was that uh . . . wasn't a weakness, and wasn't a pain. . . . Well, primarily . . . well, essentially what it was, the disease had spread apparently into the vertebrae. That's generally what the meaning of the medical term is, I believe. With that the problem doesn't seem to be in my back insofar as the pain is concerned, it's in my hip and my knee. Right now, at this point, at this moment, I have no pain in my hip. I have a little pain in my knee, not too much but maybe an hour from now I'll have a greater pain in my knee, but it'll never last that long.

Well, then he put me on pills, pain pills, and a hormone pill and a muscle relaxant. Gee, I don't know, there seemed to be eight or nine pills coming every day. And then on top of that I ran into difficulty, an upset stomach, so I had to take other pills. One has to offset the other, I guess. Anyway, to get back to the X rays. They showed up the problem in the vertebrae. That was really frightful.

Had you had any idea that anything like that was possible?

Well yes, of course. I knew it was *possible*, but I didn't realize it had happened at the time, that it had *spread*. You're bound to think that it could.

Ever scare you?

Well, I think anything like that is pretty frightening. Once I found out the results of the X rays that, of course, was pretty definitive . . . that was really very bad news.

Do you remember what it was like on that particular day, getting the bad news?

Oh, I remember because I was unemployed and had decided that just to keep myself occupied until I found something I would do some volunteer work over at St. E.'s, because years ago I had done some. Used to go over there nights and work in the coffee shop and help them out. So I went over there and did the volunteer work. The day the doctor talked to me . . . yes, I was over there that day and he had the results of the X rays. So he just came out in the lobby . . . I was in the lobby working, and he told me.

Right in the lobby?

Yes. You know, because it was very bad. The disease had spread to my back. [Her voice drops.]

Do you remember what you did the rest of that day?

Oh, gee. Well, naturally, to tell you the truth, I went right back to the lobby, I went right back to that desk and continued answering the phone and talking to the people. I mean you've got to keep your sanity, I guess you'd call it. [Laughs nervously.] It isn't easy, but you just got to [her voice drops] . . . well, you just feel you're an adult and you should control yourself. That's about what it amounts to . . . try to control yourself, if possible. So that was it. I thought the best thing for me to do was to go right back to that desk there and . . . and answer that phone. I was telling the people who called how the patients were feeling, that's the kind of volunteer work I was doing. They call it patient information. Say things like . . . same, critical, poor, danger, out of danger, bad, good, expired, whatever it was. I pushed myself.

Was the doctor nervous at all? A little bit upset by it?

Well, gee. I think the doctor must be . . . doctors must. . . . I mean, you're a doctor, I'm not. I imagine doctors are pretty much able to do . . . to . . . I don't know. I guess give that news to people and do it in such a way that they can soften the blow as much as possible for some people . . .

Do you remember how it was with your doctor?

Just stood in the lobby of the hospital. That was it. Right out.

Sounds pretty casual.

It was. Casual or not, the news is the same. It was a casual approach, but I can't say on the other hand . . . when you get right down to it, how do you tell somebody? Bad news. I think it's one of the toughest jobs that doctors have. . . . Anyway, the upshot was that I went into the hospital right that day, and I was there for five weeks, then I came over here. I'm in a wheelchair as you can see, but my therapist Lorna says I can get around with just a cane, and I can do it, and I should do it more. But you know, the whole thing is confidence . . . and I guess you've got to have guts. What was that song, something . . . you got to have heart or something? They used to have that song. Well, you just got to push yourself, that's what it amounts to. And I should be walking more, getting away from this thing, because I want to get out of here in a couple of weeks . . . I hope to, I really do, and I don't want any more than a cane.

What's the worst part of all of this for you?

Well, I think the worst thing, in addition to the pain that you have, which is most unpleasant. . . . I think the inactivity, the fact that you're not working. If I had my health and if I get it back I certainly will go back to work because I do not care for inactivity. Boredom sets in, for one thing. I don't know whether it's the pills or me, but I could sleep here easy, right now. I've done a lot of reading, but I haven't done much more than that, to tell you the honest truth. I haven't even looked at that much TV. TV doesn't interest me really at all. [Laughs.] That seems to be getting worse all the time, as far as I can make out. I don't know whether it's me or the TV. The programs. They're just terrible . . .

It was more of an adjustment coming in here. For one thing, the location I was put in . . . as Miss Reardon there knows. I was put up on the third floor. I suppose I should consider myself fortunate to have been admitted to the hospital so soon, but you know it really is an adjustment when you're put in a room with people who are about to. . . . Well, I don't know, the average age was, I suppose, around eighty, and uh . . . most of them with very little mind. Worse than my aunt, she's eighty-five and in very excellent physical condition, it's just that her mind is gone. These people . . . their mind is not clear, they have no control over anything, kidneys or anything like that [her voice drops] and no conversation, naturally, could take place. One didn't speak English, and it was, you know, very. . . . You feel sorry for them, naturally, and you want to do something for them, but on the other hand I do think if you're going to try to help people it's best to try to put people in rooms where there's going to be some . . . compatibility. In fact, it was so bad that even the nurses up there were sympathetic with my case. They tried to do what they could. Well anyway. Sickness is generally a trial, and a struggle, and it's a hard thing to go through, and you have to face it. If you're not facing it with yourself, you're facing it with some relative who's close to you. Sometime you're going to face it, sometime or another. But that third floor was kinda rough.

It must have made you think you were dying.

[She laughs lightly.] No. No. Not quite. Not quite. Not quite that bad. No. No. Not that bad.

How do you do it?

How do I do what? [Laughs.] I don't do much of anything. What do you mean how do I do it?

Well, you've explained that it's really very difficult to face inactivity, someone as active as you've been.

Well, I don't know. I guess you just have faith and hope that things'll be better. I don't think you ever give up hope. At least you shouldn't. Maybe some people do.

We do it on bad days, don't we?

Yes. [Laughs.] And over silly things. I don't know. Meaningless things. Losing a streetcar, being late for work, annoying things that are so meaningless, really, in the total picture. But what I hope is that I'll be able to get out of here at least in a two-week period. I don't know. Without faith you wouldn't have a desire to live. It's really a case of setting your mind in a certain path, and you don't want to get off it onto some side road that's gonna lead you [laughs] to sadness and . . . oblivion. You want to stay on the main track where you figure there's hope. I don't have regular prayers. I go to chapel when I can make it. I've had so much trouble with my stomach lately that I don't make it often. I should say, though, that I haven't had trouble with the food. The food in the hospital is very good, I can say that much for it . . .

We'd better make sure we get that on the record.

[Laughs.] Yeah. Get it down. No, really. It is. I just talked with Dr. Connelly and I said, look at my feet, they're swollen. And he says, oh, they'll be down in a little while, that's nothing, you know. I said, look at this. [She runs her fingers over her cheek.] Looks like adolescent skin coming back. I'm not that young, you know. Oh, that's just one of the pills, he says. Everything has a simple explanation, but it's an annoying thing just the same. It may be simple to him, but it's annoying just the same. But, it's just something you have to put up with, I guess, as long as I take these pills. I'm afraid of putting too much makeup on for fear of getting infected. . . . I'd be great for color TV, wouldn't I? [Everyone laughs.]

How about the people here, the staff?

Oh, just fantastic. You know I have Lorna. I'm sorry I can't recall her last name. She is . . . just outstanding. You know, she's the type . . . I might go down there of a day and I'll say, oh my knee is terrible today. Now, never mind about your knee [she raises her voice], we'll start the walking right away. Oh, gee, I'll say, playing the dying swan bit, I don't know . . . I can feel the pain. Well just get up and get that cane out and get the kinks out, she says, and start your walking. Oh, you think you're going to die. But she's terrific. And you just have to . . . you have to put your shoes on down there, and I can't see putting swollen feet into shoes, and I had a new pair of shoes, I had Lorna examine them to be sure they were okay . . . Hush Puppies . . . and she liked them and all, and I put them on by myself. They're fine shoes. Well, tying a shoe is a problem to me. Well, to get my foot up there to tie that shoe is . . . well, it's a problem. I might have a pain in my knee for a half an hour afterward. You don't think that was going to bug Lorna though? [Laughs. Everyone joins in.] That shoe was going to be put on by me and tied by me and believe me it was. It took me fifteen minutes to do it, and about another fifteen minutes of groaning and grunting and whining and complaining about the pain in my knee, which is . . . which she's ignoring. [Laughs.] But she really is terrific, it's the only way to be, really, if you're a patient. You'd get no place with your patients if you listen to their complaints. [Everyone laughs.] She's magnificent. No sympathy. Don't have any heart at all. No.

What about nurses. What qualities should they have? What's important for them to know about the care of people?

Oh, well, that's a little different situation. I think they really have to be quite considerate, kind and gentle and forceful, too, at times, as far as taking pills or doing whatever the doctor prescribes. But I've seen a lot of nurses in action these last two months and I think I've seen a lot of things in nurses that I don't like, and I've seen a lot of things I did like. One of the things I've seen that I don't like in a nurse is uh . . . I won't mention what floor it is, I don't want to pin anybody down . . . but she. . . . Now, for instance, many patients have got to be moved. They're constantly moving them because of bed sores and different things. Well, some of them will come along and you'd really think they were dealin' with a leg of lamb or cattle or something. I think there is such a thing as being a bit humane with a patient. And then on the other hand, some patients are looking for attention every minute. Those people really need to be straightened out a little bit because you can't do that constantly, either. Nobody has the help for that . . . to give constant attention to one individual . . . because it just means that somebody else is suffering if one nurse is going to be devoting 90 percent of her time to one person for silly little things like fluffin' pillows and movin' beds up and down, and makin' the water colder and like that. But all in all, I think nurses are quite dedicated.

What would you say about medical students, young people who are studying to be doctors?

[Long pause.] Boy, that's such a rugged life, such a long, hard struggle. I guess you just have to be very dedicated and work hard and keep up with all the latest changes, and certainly that's a problem in itself, trying to keep up with all that's changing today. I don't know as I'd have any worthwhile advice for a doctor. Who am I? Some of them are never going to have the patience to deal with patients that need help. Some may never have that. And he's got to be firm. And he's got to be a little bit abrupt, too. Some patients will come in and sit down all day just talking about some little ailment, and after all he's got to [laugh] keep 'em movin'.

Frank Sage, 79

He is wearing a red robe over striped pajamas, and lies propped up on the bedsheet, hands folded on his stomach, rolling his thumbs. Four of us are seated around the hospital bed.

I went to the war, and then I come back. I took good care of myself, and I did what I wanted to do.

You sowed a wild oat or two when you got back?

Oh, yes. That was my middle *name*. I was a pretty swifty kid, see? Little heavier than I am now. Most I ever weighed was 193. Three years ago, my legs started to bother me, so I started to reduce, and I took, uh, K for breakfast every morning. That's all and that pulled it down. Until I got sick, last year, and now I'm down to 140.

What was it three years ago? What kind of sickness?

Well, I had different things. My main thing was the bottom of my bladder.

The bottom of your bladder?

Yeah. Trouble with my bladder. I can't talk too good today, I ain't got my teeth in. Broke, waitin' to get 'em fixed. So.

What was the problem with your bladder?

Well, first thing it was I had trouble passin' water, couldn't pass it. Then they took me and put some tubes in me. Had them in about six weeks. Then they said they'd operate, so they operated, and five weeks after that they said I guess you're all right, so they took 'em out. But it was just the same as before, didn't help a bit. Took me back and operated a second time, and after the operation a second time it was the same thing.

No better?

And the third time neither. I went and they said see we have to cut you open up to here and bring your water out through here, and that's what they done.

What was the trouble exactly? What did they tell you?

Well, I tell you, I don't know them words that they said, but it was an awful funny thing to me and I can't really remember but it was an awful experience, a long time in the MGH, and I come out and went home, and I was home about five weeks and I had to go back again, and they sent me to that home or somethin' over by the river. And I stayed there about three weeks. Then I come back home and I started up again, only this time it got so bad I couldn't walk, couldn't walk at all.

What was causing that?

That I don't know. Never asked 'em, they never told me. I couldn't walk. Nothin'. They called me from the MGH, wanted to know whether I'd go, and I said I'll go anywhere so long as I get better, so that's why I'm here, over at this place now. And I've had it pretty tough. First week was rough. Three weeks since Monday I been here. I've had all kinds of troubles. I can't tell you more. All kinds. First it was one thing and then somethin' else. All had somethin' to do with . . . it was all the same thing. See, a man went around the way I did, it's a wonder I'll live. I've often, sometimes, think, Frank, you're a lucky guy.

You think all this had something to do with the way you've lived?

I wouldn't do it again if I was back the same age of twenty-six. Wouldn't do it again if you give me a million bucks. I wouldn't, I swear it . . .

Do what?

What I have done. Things I have done. And all like that. It's kinda tough. I hope to get outta this so I can be all right for a while, and I think I will, I do. Doin' pretty good, too. Done pretty good this week, I can almost walk, can stand up by myself, move around in front of a chair, but I wouldn't take no chances walkin' alone though.

Sounds to me like the way you connect the early part of your life with getting sick that you look at your sickness as some kind of punishment.

Well, doc, I'll tell you, that's a real hard question to answer. I don't know whether I do or not. Hard to answer. 'Cause the way I want to answer it . . . if there was only men here I could answer it fast, just like that, but not when there's women here, I wouldn't do it, you couldn't pay me to do it.

You don't think they'd understand?

Oh, they might understand all right, but I ain't going to let them 'cause I ain't going to tell 'em. Nothin'.

But they would understand more, I think, about how you look at it. Sometimes we do things in life and later we look at those things as the cause of why we get sick.

Well, that's what I say, that the cause of my trouble was what I done after I was twenty-six years old. I really do believe that's what truly caused all this sickness, the way I went and the way I traveled, oh boy, I tell you I could write a book. But I don't like to say things too much.

Book'd be a best seller?

[Laughs.] Might be, for some people I know.

Did the doctors ever give you any indication that there was a relationship between the way you lived and your illness?

No. No. They never told me none of that. Sometimes I asked 'em questions like that one time, but they never answered.

You have asked?

I have. But they never answered. Never told me nothin'. I asked them sometimes about the bladder and the tubes,

I did ask them about that. And he just said, oh never mind you don't want to know.

The doctor said you don't want to know?

I don't want to know. Said you don't want to know. That's all I got. Nothin'.

I don't understand that.

Well, I don't neither myself. He didn't want me to understand so he didn't tell me. But I have an idea, see, I have my own idea. What I done and the way I traveled, that's what done it. You know, a man goes out at night and comes back in the mornin' and runs around with four, five women at a time . . . that's too much, too much for any man.

Do you believe that's what the doctor didn't want to tell you?

I believe that's what it was, I do. Because that was my middle name. Oh, I was smart. I was a good-lookin' boy, dressed good, and I used to make all my points, and I didn't miss nothin' and that's the truth. Standin', sittin' and lyin' down, that was my name. Tell you. How I'm here today I don't know myself. Hard thing to understand. I wish I did really know what it was all about, but I don't.

Do you think that maybe you should have died at an early age, what with all your traveling?

I guess I'd been better off. Mighta been anyway.

You really think that?

Well, I wouldn't be in nobody's way. Wouldn't have all the sickness.

Are you in anybody's way now?

Well, I think I am.

Who?

Well, all my family.

How?

Well, I can tell. They don't want to bother with me. [His eyes moisten.] Only one wants to bother with me is my daughter. Wife and the rest of 'em don't want to bother with me. She was here yesterday, my wife, but she only comes for to get the money, what she can get.

Tell me about your wife?

[No response.]

How old's your daughter?

Think she's around fifty.

And she doesn't think you're in the way?

No. Not her. [Laughs lightly.] That's my pet. 'Nother one died young. I have one boy, and I taught him the ropes. Told him don't do what your father done, 'cause you ain't goin' to be here if you do. You ain't got the stuff in you, I told him.

Did he take the advice?

So far I guess.

How old is he?

Thirty-nine, forty. Somewhere in there. Married, got three kids. He was here day 'fore yesterday.

How are things between you and him?

Fine.

You think he looks at you as a burden?

Well, I don't . . . well, he don't pay no attention to me, that's all. You know what I mean? He don't come around to see me much. May come once in two weeks, in three weeks, now and then.

You mentioned someone, a child, who died?

Well, I had one died. She was twenty-eight when she died.

What happened?

She had a lung . . . collapsed lung or somethin' like that. I was workin' on a Sunday mornin' and I'll never forget that. I lived across the street from them. Her husband comes over and says I'm goin' to send her to the hospital. I said you got a car, why don't you take her? And he said no, the ambulance is comin' for her. I was on my way to work, I worked at Stop and Shop so I went on to work. I got back home about one o'clock and all this stuff is goin' on, so I said what's goin' on, what's the trouble? Said Hattie died, she was dead on arrival. No more than I thought. I just knew it, I thought it.

You thought it?

Yeah. I was in her house just 'fore I left for work. Seen her in bed. And I knew she didn't have long.

How did you know that?

I don't know. It just come to me. She couldn't speak, nothin' like that. She was another good one.

Must have been a tough blow.

[Sighs.] I think of it sometimes yet. I can't keep it out of my mind. Got her picture upstairs at home, and brought one with me, too. [Tears run down his cheeks.] She was the second child, boy was the third. Can't even remember their ages, and don't even know their birthdays half the time.

Awful tough to be sick, isn't it?

It's a hard thing. You get down. I know where I've been.

What's the hardest thing about it?

Now there's a question. It's like bein' in a jailhouse, and you can't get out, can't go nowhere. Have to do as you're told and that's a hard job for me, always was.

Got a mind of your own?

Well, I thought I did, but I found out I didn't. Thought I could do what I wanted and nothin' would happen, but it turned out different. See, now I can't do what I want to do. See, I used to be a terrible man, used to drink a lot and all. Wouldn't stop at the end of no quart, either. Maybe wouldn't even stop after that, only when I went down. I don't know. I tell you the truth, I don't know how I'm livin' today. I stop and think and I look back, I don't know, and I'm tellin' the truth, so help me.

So you label yourself a terrible man?

I was. But I found different when I hit seventy.

You noticed changes after that?

Oh yes. I've changed. You see, you couldn't get me to . . . wouldn't touch a drink, only thing is I smoke a cigar now and then, and I suppose I'll be quittin' them, too. See, one thing, I always ate good, always had plenty to eat. See, when I used to work first thing I'd do, 'fore anything'd get done, was go down to the big market and get all the meat, and I used to eat, boy did I used to pack it in there. Been a better man, though, if I'da taken care of my money, should be now a man of about twenty, twenty-five thousand. So I got a coupla cents, nothin' to amount to much. Yup, shoulda saved some of it. Older you get, more you think about it, more you think, and more you forget. I forget a lot. I can't remember nothin'.

What are the parts you're trying to remember but forget?

Oh, buddy, I couldn't . . . 'cept the things I done, I . . . I really regret the way I used my first wife. [He starts to cry.] It was . . . my downfall. She never knowed what I . . .

How old were you when you married her?

Married her in 1917. That was the night. . . . I was in the service, and I went over to France. Over there two years. That's when . . .

Do you ever see her, talk to her now?

Oh, I see her every so often. She lives in Boston, by herself.

Still love her?

Huh. Now ain't that a question. [Tears streak his face.] You get out, you get yourself free a little bit and you think, oh boy this is it for me, and you don't know what you're gettin' into. And I really got into it . . . still into it pretty good . . . never be out of it. Was talkin' to one of my . . . talkin' to my daughter the other day and I told her I don't know what I'm goin' to do when I get out of here because of the things that come of what I got into, what I left back over there.

What was that that you left?

[He shakes his head.]

So you don't know what you'll do when you get out of here?

No. Well, I can go back to my home, to my second wife, but I don't know if I want to. No. I don't want to. It's hard trouble. I tell you, you don't know about it when you're talkin' about it, Doc, you got to be into it, like I am. There's a whole lot I don't want to say. This wife I got now, if she says somethin' to me I'll answer. But if I don't answer when she thinks I should, she'll run up an argument, big fuss, and I can't go arguments.

You've had it rough. How do you stand it?

I tell you myself, Doc, I don't know how. But I just got a idea now that I'm gonna be all right by the time I'm eighty years old [he sobs]. I plan to be all right then, I do. I do.

Ever get scared?

No. No. Never was ever scared in my life. So, there it goes.

I've got a hard question for you. How come all the nurses like you so much?

[Smiles.] Mind my own business, laugh sometimes, and so on. Wish sometimes . . .

Wish what?

Oh . . . just things. Wish, too, that there was more men around than women so I could talk better.

Stay with it.

Doc, I got to. No way I can turn back.

It s been pleasant to have you with us.

Well, it's been nice to be here with you. But like I say there's things I like to say that I can't.

So we'll have a stag group next time.

Doc, I wouldn't . . . I wouldn't do what I done again. You know, there's a lot up in this noodle, it's a small piece but there's a lot in there, and the only thing I can say is take care of yourself and don't do like I done, 'cause if you do you're goin' to end up on the wrong end.

John Casey, 47

I'd say it was about two years ago this April I broke my arm in work and there was a tumor in the bone so they removed the tumor and the bone was healing very well. According to the doctor it was healing beautifully. And it got to a point where there wasn't even a sign of the fracture in the bone, and the following week my arm started hurting me again. So I called the doctor up. . . . It was the same pain I had before I broke it, you know. I had a pain in there, incidentally, for six weeks before I broke it.

I was going to ask you that. You'd noticed the pain before it broke. Any swelling or anything like that?

No swelling. No. It was, well, right near where your muscles . . . and I figured I had pulled a muscle because the first day I noticed it we had been moving a freezer and I just thought I had pulled a muscle. So it got progressively worse until I was favoring my right arm, you know. I wouldn't use my right arm like to open an elevator door or anything like that. It would hurt me to do it. It was sore, so I finally decided to go and see the doctor, and the day I decided to see the doctor was the day I broke my arm. . . . And I broke it just walking up the stairs. I stumbled, and I tensed my muscles to catch my balance, and that broke the arm. I didn't touch anything, I didn't touch the banister or nothing. I was on my way up to my boss's office, because he had just called me, and I was going up to his office. Well, I had to lean against the wall, like, and I had that solid surface to rest my arm against, and it quieted down some. Then I went into my boss's office and told him I wanted to go to the hospital to have an X ray, so he said, how'd you do it, and I told him I just stumbled comin' up the stairs, and when I tensed my muscles to catch my balance I said I felt this thing, this terrific pain, I didn't know what happened. I just couldn't imagine my arm had broken, because I, you know, I always thought you had to really hit it, you know. So anyway, we went to the hospital and had X rays taken of it and the doctor told me that the arm was broken and he showed me the X rays. But he said the reason it broke was that there was a tumor growing on it. So, like I say, they removed the tumor the following day, I guess, and, uh, I was on the road to recovery, and I had gone back maybe two or three times for X rays and the doctor was very pleased with what he saw. And after the third time my arm started achin' again. So like I say I called the doctor up and he said that it's too soon to tell anything. So he says come in Friday and we'll X-ray it again. So when I went in Friday they X-rayed it, and he was very disturbed. He told me that the tumor was growing back and that I'd have to go in the hospital and have something done about it, you know. So, in the meantime he got all the info on my case and I went into the hospital, and he discussed it with some experts like and they all came to the same conclusion, that the arm had to be removed. So, by this time I was in the hospital, and he come back and he told me that the arm had to come off.

How did he tell you that? How did he break that news for you?

Well, I could see that it was really botherin' him. He's a nice person anyway, this doctor, and he just told me, says the tumor is growin' bad, we can't take a chance on where it might go if we don't, says there's only one thing that we can do and that's to remove the arm. So I asked him how high they'd have to remove it, you know, and he said all the way up to the shoulder, which I wasn't too pleased with because I'd rather have had a little stump there, you know. But, I really don't know . . . like why they had to remove it all the way up to the shoulder still. But I figured that they'll remove an arm and save a life, like I was willing to trade.

What did the doctor say exactly to you, do you remember?

No, I don't. All I know is that he told me that the arm would have to come off. I think he told me he had already spoken to my wife about it and she already knew it, you know, but, uh, he just said it had to be removed, that's all.

At any time before that, when they first told you you had a tumor, were you scared?

I guess so. Yeah. Well, to a certain degree I was. I really didn't know that much about a tumor, you know. But, uh, when the arm was healing so well, naturally I was very pleased with it. Like I say, I really didn't know what it meant to have a tumor. And, uh, when they explained to me that they cut the tumor all out, I just figured it was somethin' growin' on the bone but they had taken it all off now, so I didn't have to worry about it anymore really, and that's what I figured. Course I was mistaken there.

When he told you it was growing back, what was that like for you?

Well, that was a shock, really. See, it was a matter of a couple of days from the time my arm started botherin' me until they took the X rays and I think that I had practically decided for myself that this was happening.

You mean you yourself figured it was coming back?

Yeah. Because it was hurtin' me just like before and there wasn't any reason for it to hurt. So when I went in to have the X rays he said the tumor was growin', it was growin' wild, you know. In other words, it was growin' fast. Well, that scared me. There's no question about it. But at the time I was out of the hospital, and I had to go back in again, a course, and have my arm removed. But after a coupla weeks in the hospital recuperating I went home and I went back to work. I had the arm, uh, removed the first of July, I think, and I went back to work sometime in August, and even though I wasn't able to do my job the way I did it before, you know, because I'm a licensed electrician, and I take care of all the air conditioning and electrical work in this plant. . . . An awful lot of little things come up with one arm that I couldn't do, like, you know, I couldn't zip my zipper, and I finally learned how to do it by pullin' my jacket over and goin' to a corner and restin' against the wall and then hookin' the zipper in there and then zippin' it up, and, uh, things like that.

Do you ever get mad about the arm being gone?

No. No. I just felt that I was so much better off to have an arm gone than a leg. See, I think that if it was my leg I'd have been . . . I'd have felt a lot worse about it because, you know, you're usin' your legs continually to get around and all, and your arms, well, uh, anyway that's the way I felt, and I'd rather have an arm gone than a leg, and rather have them take the arm than the chance of the tumor . . . travelin' through my body, like. So, like I say I went back to work and I was back to work till this past April. One Monday morning I got up and I went to work and my legs didn't, uh, function the way that they normally do, you know. I didn't have complete control of my legs. They didn't want to do what I wanted them to do. So I managed to get through the day anyways and, uh, the next morning I told Bea. . . . I woke up and they were worse, and I didn't go to work, and I told Bea to call the doctor. Well, he went to look for a hospital bed, I guess. Then he called back and he told me to go to the hospital the following day, which was a Wednesday. So I went in there Wednesday afternoon and they took X rays and so forth and they didn't have any trouble findin' the tumor. It was on my spine. So, they operated, and I was under the impression they removed the whole tumor but apparently they didn't. They said if they removed it all there wouldn't be anything left in there. I, uh, still can't comprehend this. If somebody drew me a picture of it maybe I could, better. But, uh, anyways they left part of it in there so they wouldn't have to open the bone up, I guess. I don't know.

They thought it would be dangerous to take it all out, is that it?

Apparently, yeah. It woulda been, uh, well, I don't really know. I, like I say, I really don't understand the complications that it woulda made.

What went through your mind in April, when you developed the trouble in your legs?

Well, the confusion. I guess that probably more than anything else. I just didn't understand it, really, you know, and, uh, well I don't know. I forget really exactly what went through my mind, but I know it wasn't anything pleasant. You know I . . . I assumed I was going to be in for some trouble, like.

Any idea what kind of trouble?

Well, like I was worried about my legs, you know? Like whether they'd be able to . . . stand up. In other words,

I didn't want them to be weak. Insofar as I can remember, that was the only thing that bothered me.

Do you remember what the doctor said when he told you he was going to remove the tumor from your spine? What did he say to you, how did he tell you about that?

I don't think he said anything to me. This was a different doctor I never seen before in my life. He was a specialist, and my own doctor called him in on the case, you know. The doctor had never seen me before in my life. But I remember that he had . . . the doctor had such a pleasant disposition, you know. He was always calm and considerate and so forth. He just told me that they had located the tumor in my back and he says, well, we'll take it out today.

Today?

Yeah. That was the day they removed it. Yeah.

That's kind of short notice, isn't it?

Well, he said either this afternoon or tomorrow morning. Actually, they took it out the next morning. Said if we get . . . these were his words . . . said if we get an opening in there this afternoon, we'll go in, if we don't we'll have to wait until tomorrow afternoon. So I guess they took it out on a Friday.

Did they tell you anything after surgery?

I don't know. Normally they just come in and ask me how I was doin', how I felt and all. Felt pretty good, really.

I guess what I was wondering was whether someone had come in and said to you that the whole thing was removed. Did anyone say . . . ?

No.

So there was no misinformation, just the lack of information.

It was just the lack of information.

The lack of information. As you look back do you wish that someone had told you that?

Definitely.

Mrs. Casey interrupts at this point: "Well, I could elaborate a little on that. It was Dr. Simmons we were dealing with and his attitude was that he would only answer as much as the patient asked. In other words, John was not asking enough questions. And he would only give as much as the patient asked. This was his whole theory."

How do you feel about that, Mr. Casey?

I don't go along with that at all. I . . . I . . . like to say I assumed that there was a tumor there, they removed it all. Beyond my wildest dreams that they only took half of it . . . I never knew they could do anything like that. Course like I say I didn't know much about tumors anyways. But I feel he should have told me more . . .

Feel kind of angry about that?

Well, I don't know if I was angry about it, but I know it disturbed me a little, and I thought I'd be better off if they had told me. I don't know what their idea was not telling me. . . . I was under the impression, naturally, that I'd get better, you know, in a matter of, well, whatever it took, coupla weeks, coupla months, and I'd go home. But you know, actually, there was a friend of mine that's a doctor that told me that . . . that they didn't remove the whole thing.

How did that come about?

Well, he's an elder in our church and he came around to talk to me one night. And, uh, he thought that I should know the whole story, so he just told me the whole thing that night. . . . Essentially, all he said was that they hadn't removed all the tumor yet. Now, I don't remember whether he actually said anything besides that or not. But that was the essential part of it, they hadn't removed all the tumor and the reason they hadn't was because it would have left an opening or somethin' in the bone. In other words, there would have been a space there. So I was . . . I was really disturbed when I heard that because this put a different slant on things now, as far my going home and all, you know. Course I didn't feel that my legs were responding to the physical therapy I was gettin' over there, and I still can't operate my legs, today. Now, I don't understand why I can't operate my legs, whether they damaged the nerves or the spinal cord or what. All I know is that they just . . . they feel . . . I mean I can wiggle my toes and like that, and they feel like all they need is a little physical therapy, some exercise to bring 'em along . . .

Do you do any worrying about that?

No. I guess I'm not a real worrier. I have a very great faith in God, really. I feel God has a plan for my life, and

I just let his plan take its course, and let him do what he will with my life.

Ever think of what might happen?

Sure. Yeah. I think that I might be called home, you know.

You think you might die?

Sure. In fact, I'm of the opinion *now* that the only thing that could save my life would be a miracle, really, and I have a. . . . I feel that a miracle is not, in other words, outside of probability, you know. In other words, if God wanted to cure me today or any day he could. But I really feel now that other than that I'll never . . . that the only way I'll get cured is with a miracle right now.

How are you able to think of things like that without getting scared?

I dunno. But like I say I just put my trust in the Lord and let him carry the ball. Because there's not much I can do about it anyways.

What's the hardest thing about the whole business for you?

Well, I really think that the hardest part is . . . my family. My wife and my children. For her and for them. In other words, you know, that they have to endure this . . . this illness that I have, and the fact that I may never come out. And I . . . I think it's much harder for them than it is for me. Because I know when I die I'm going to heaven, and that's a big help, boy. I know positively that's what's goin' to happen. But I definitely do worry more about them. My wife has to come in here, you know. . . . She doesn't have to but she comes in here twice a day and she's been comin' for nine months pretty nearly every day, twice a day, and that's no picnic especially with five kids at home. All I know is that it helps me to have my faith, it does. My wife and I had a spiritual experience approximately five years ago, and my wife had this . . . experience first. What they call bein' born again, that's a biblical term, according to the Bible, you know. . . . And when I became born again it made all the difference in the world in our lives. It just changed our lives completely.

How so?

Well, I don't really know. It was just. . . . God was watchin' over us more or somethin'. I don't know how to express it. But it's like in the hospital now. In other words, I have put my faith and my trust in the Lord and, uh, he says bring all your troubles to me, you know, and I'll take care of 'em. So that's what I'm doin'. . . . I don't feel like I, uh, am able to do anythin' for myself right now anyways, so that's all I do, put my trust in the Lord.

Of all the troubles you have, then, the biggest one is your worry about your wife and your children. What's number two?

Well, number two is, uh, naturally . . . I don't think anybody wants to die. It really wouldn't bother me that much, like I say, but I think of all the . . . different things that I'll be missin' out on as far as my family is . . . my family goes, you know? Like my children's graduation and weddings, and grandchildren and all. This is somethin' I've looked forward to, grandchildren, for years, you know. So I think that, uh, that really . . . that bothers me a lot.

Find yourself thinking about that?

Yeah. So naturally I'd rather live 'til I was seventy-five, that's all. But, uh, like I say, it isn't what I'd rather do that's not what the deal is here. Life is like a trip to the store, you know. Your mother sends you to the store for loaf of bread or somethin', uh, in other words that's how fast it goes. In ten minutes it's over and you're back and I compare this life . . . this average sixty-five, seventy years, to a ten-minute trip to the store. . . . It's really not that important.

But it can be awfully tough during that short time, can't it?

Sure can. Yeah. But it isn't that important, when you come to realize it, you know? It isn't as important as we think it is. We think nothin's important, more important, than ourselves, and I tried to explain that to my kids, but I don't know whether they understand that or not, and can gather it in their minds or not.

You've talked to them about it, all five?

About what?

About your life, and the shortness of it?

Lord, no. No. I haven't spoken to them. No. But I think they understand somethin' . . . I mean I couldn't very well tell 'em I'm not goin' to live very long and then turn around and live. [Everyone in the room breaks into laughter, and Mr. Casey and his wife join in.]

Well, we wouldn't object, you know.

Right. But like I say the only thing that'll save me, really, is a miracle. . . . Right now I don't have any pain. Things could be a lot worse, I guess. [Sighs.] I try to . . . look at the good features, though, of life. Because I guess I haven't given it up yet, really. I haven't, like, got angry yet, but I have got discouraged a coupla times, like when the doctor told me about the thing on my back, you know. I was discouraged for about a week or two weeks then.

What kind of thoughts go through your mind when you're discouraged?

Well, the thought that was going through my mind then was really that I wasn't . . . going to heal. And from what he told me I just wasn't going to heal up and go home, like everybody else does in the hospital. So every time I thought of it, naturally I was unhappy about that. But like I say, I try to trust in God in that I put it in his hands. Because there's nothin' I can really do about it myself.

Mrs. Casey, he was saying he thinks it's a lot harder for you than it is for him. I wonder how it is for you?

Well, actually, it's rather amazing how it is when I think back on the last nine months. It's not as bad as I co ld possibly imagine. And it has to be our trust in Jesus Chrı . There's no other answer.

You had some periods when it was pretty bad?

Well, I can remember when I was first told he had cancer. It was an awfully overwhelming experience to say the least, and it showed me that life isn't always like we see it in the movies. I was sitting in the house alone the day the phone call came in. . . . The doctor called me and I was alone, and it was just earth-shattering, to say the least. And now it's waiting for calls, too, and I have a friend who'll come up with me . . . you're always expecting the call, fearful of what they'll say. I can remember the day of his amputation, and the doctor didn't really tell me the day before that he was going to operate. And I can remember walking to the hospital that night and praying that that's all it would be. As he said, it would be his arm and his life would be spared. I didn't want him to lose an arm, but that's what I had hoped it would be, just that. And I can remember walking to the hospital, out of my mind, and when I went in he said I have something to tell you. He told me himself that his arm was going to be amputated. I was . . . shaken up by it but no more than that because I had hoped and prayed it would be just his arm, and that God would spare his life. . . . One doctor on the staff there thought it was rather disastrous when he saw it, but when he sent the biopsy to the medical center other doctors didn't feel quite the same way. But he felt it was quite serious right from the start.

Did he share that with you both?

Well, when he called me on the phone he told me he thought it was disastrous and he was going to send it away, and that was the later report that it was all right. But on a second time around he called me then and told me that it was definitely cancer. It was real.

When he told you that did he share the same thing with your husband?

No, because this was when he called me on the phone, called me at the house right after they got the reports and all.

You mean it was kind of something that you knew but . . .

John didn't. But I knew. It was cancer.

What do you think about that? Do you think that's the way it ought to be, that you ought to have the information and he didn't?

Well, as I look back on the past months, it's sort of hard to evaluate. I think it sort of depends on the type of people you're dealing with. Some people can accept this kind of news and others just can't and I think it just narrows down to that. Some want to be told and some don't.

Were you glad, Mrs. Casey, that he told you?

Well, I can't say exactly but I'm sure that sooner or later he couldn't have kept it from me. But I guess . . . like John says, I trust in the Lord and I'm sure that the Lord prepared me all the way. I firmly believe it, I firmly do. I do, really.

Was that the word the doctor used, "disastrous"?

That was the way I can remember his putting it. He put it pretty . . . it was . . . he was very open and all.

Did he say it was a malignant tumor?

No. He just said he . . . like I say, he said it was disastrous looking, but that he was going to send it to the medical center. Next time around he said there was no question.

Do you think it was better that your husband didn't know?

Well, it was hard for me to say. That's a very hard thing for me. . . . I went through weeks of searching. I prayed about it so that the Lord would lead us, lead me to know what was the best way to go. I discussed it with one of the elders of the church, the doctor that John mentioned, and he felt that John being a born-again Christian and knowing that if he died he would go home with the Lord that he should know the truth. And this was the conclusion we came to, so I asked him to go and tell John. We felt that it was best for him to go in and tell him. The doctors figured he wasn't asking enough questions . . . so . . .

What was your sense of your husband, since you know him better than anybody else?

It's hard to know. I wasn't quite sure myself. The fact that he didn't ask a great many questions. . . . I didn't really know myself, otherwise I would have known sooner how to handle it, and I wasn't quite sure whether he truly wanted to know or not. So it was a difficult decision to make, and like I said I prayed and spoke to the elders and we decided . . . that really he probably did want to know the truth. If he were to face death, then he should know. . . . And after the elder told him, John and I talked about it, in the days after that, because we just . . . just . . . first of all, we didn't have a cemetery plot, so we talked about those things. I mean, it was things like the average person does, they put all those things off and never have them done and we talked about them and I had it done and all. We had a will made out because I was warned it could be very confusing.

Did all that make it harder for you?

I don't know. I seemed to have got through it. I don't think it was the most pleasant thing to do, but I don't think it was all that difficult, really. Do you think it was, John?

No. No. Course I didn't have to do anything 'cept . . . sign. And, you know, stay here.

Well, you talked, John.

Yeah, but I mean like this guy is buying the plot of land out to the cemetery, makin' the will out and all, I didn't have anything to do with it, really.

Yes, John, that's right, but we talked about it being the thing to do, and talked those matters out, and later agreed what should be done, didn't we? And going back to the children. I told my children from the beginning, I told them the truth right from the beginning. I figured my children, they're from eleven to twenty, ought to know and I told them the truth. Because he was sick, so sick at the time we didn't know how long he might have, and I figured how

337

can you hide such a thing as that, so I told them the truth, and my eleven-year-old child was just absolutely beautiful, her attitude was unbelievable. She has committed herself to Jesus Christ also, and she said, well if Dad is called home he'll go home to be with the Lord and if he stays, and she said, he'll be sicker. We'll miss him, she said, but that's because we're selfish. That's what an eleven-year-old child said. Unbelievable. And she's absolutely right. She knows that we can trust in Jesus Christ. We will have a home in heaven.

What's the hardest thing for you, Mrs. Casey, of all of this?

I don't know how to answer that. The Lord has done so much for my life in these months that I think I could write a book. I began to realize that I had not, this was before, that I had not really taken Jesus as the Lord of my life, and that means to live for Jesus. And I asked the Lord for a closer walk with him. That was just about a year before all this hit us, so when this hit I said, Lord, is this part of my closer walk with you? And he's shown me so many things in these months that. . . . The Bible teaches we all have tribulation, and this is for the believer and the unbeliever. But that's how we grow, through tribulation.

What are some of the things you've learned, Mrs. Casey?

Well, I've learned to have compassion. I have not had an easy life. I don't think John really has, either. In our younger lives, we were both from large families. His father sort of had an alcoholic problem. My father was sort of a gambler. There was other problems in our home, and I thought I had it pretty rough then, and learned a lot about life then in my first twenty years. The next twenty were raising our children. Then this. I never had compassion for the sick. I can't drive now down the road without even just . . . my eyes now just flick to anybody with a pair of crutches or. . . . I'm so aware of the sick that it's just unbelievable. And now, in this crisis, about 75 percent of my thinking is on Jesus Christ, and it wouldn't be so if I wasn't going through this trial. When things are going good we don't always look to the Lord.

So during your day, actually 75 percent of your time . . .

Absolutely. And the things that he's done in our lives.

For example?

Well, like we had a kitchen that John started to remodel and it wasn't really finished, and Christians came down from our chapel and spent three or four different nights there, and they took the wood that John had bought, took it home with them, and made up the cabinets, finished off those cabinets, even put up the ceiling. I've got a picture right here in my purse now. The kitchen is completely finished . . . it's really beautiful. See, here it is, you can see it. Beautiful, isn't it?

How long had you been working on that project, Mr. Casey?

Well, I spent a lot of time on it, but I wasn't that far along, there was quite a bit of work on it to go, actually. It was years. I was a good planner, though. Like I had everything drawn out and all. I'm not a very good drawer, an architect I'm not, but I had everything drawn out, the whole thing, the ceiling, the cabinets, as far as the space they'd take up, and the number of tiles that I'd put down on the floor and so forth. I never finished it . . .

Antonia Faliconi, 62

"Today," explained the psychiatrist, "what we are going to do is talk with one of the patients here in the hospital, and with her husband, too, who has agreed to be with us. I gather many of you know Mrs. Faliconi here. So, Mrs. Faliconi, you're among some friends."

"Yes, I know."

"Who do you know here?"

"My nurse. She's right over there."

"And do you know some of the other people, too?"

"I can't seem to recognize them."

"And how do you feel about coming to talk to us?"

"All right."

"I'd like to hear from you something about yourself and your illness, how you came here. What can you tell us?"

"I don't know. What would you like me to tell?"

"Well, how long have you been sick?"

"I been sick now for four years."

"Four years. How did you first recognize that there was something wrong?"

"Well, the first time the blood showed up in my urine, and I knew there was something wrong. I went to the doctor and he told me I should go into the hospital as fast as I could. So . . . they found out that I had a tumor in my kidney."

"The doctor told you that?"

"Oh yes."

"And that was four years ago?"

"Yes."

"And what happened?"

"I had an operation."

"And what was that like for you?"

"An operation is an operation."

"Was that the first one you ever had?"

"Yes."

"Was that a frightening experience?"

"Everything is frightening when you go under the knife."

"I'm sure it is."

"Even if you go in for a toothache, that's frightening, too."

"How did you get through it?"

"Well, you make up your mind, and I have my faith. I always say what's going to be is going to be. So that's what I generally always say and that has carried me through a lot."

"What was it like for you after the operation?"

"Oh, I got better fast, and I seemed to be on the road to recovery."

"Until when?"

"Well, until . . . afterwards I had a dizzy spell. The doctor said I had a . . . like a shock, although all I thought was that I was dizzy. I didn't recognize it as a shock. So later I had to go to the hospital, and they had me X-rayed, and they found out that I had a tumor in my brain, so I had to get operated on my brain."

"That was how long ago?"

"Nicky, how long ago was that?"

"That was in '69."

"That's right, and until that I was perfect. The week before I was in Utica for a funeral."

"And this occurred suddenly."

"Everything occurs suddenly with me."

"And what was that like, the brain operation."

"That was scary, too."

"And how did you do with it?"

"Well, when I came the doctors explained to me exactly what it was going to be, and when they explained it to me I wasn't afraid because I knew what it was going to be. That's the one thing that I like, is when they explain. I'm that type. I want to know exactly what's what. Some people are afraid. But I'm not. I want to be told."

"So they told it all to you."

"Yes. They told me what to expect. They told me I could be paralyzed the whole one side. But they couldn't predict what it would be . . . how bad . . . whether it would be. Afterwards, I was coming through it nice with therapy. It was exactly like they said it might be. I was not able to move these fingers, then my arm and everything, one leg, my left leg. . . . I couldn't move . . . but therapy brought it all back to me."

"And that was in '69. How have things been since?"

"Well, it was all right for a while and afterwards I started to be sick again."

"When was that?"

"Nicky?"

"That was early in '70, around April."

"What did you first notice then, in April?"

"My back. I thought I caught a cold in my back. And I didn't think anything was wrong except that I had a cold in my back. And that's what I treated it as, a cold. But it came . . . too fast, and I found out I was wrong. And I had radio . . . radium treatments."

"What did the doctors tell you when they gave you radiation treatment?"

"They keep saying that it'll be all right, that'll be all right, everything'll be all right."

"They say that."

"Yeah."

"Did you believe them?"

"Well, I believed them at first. But afterwards when I saw that they were beatin' around the bush I didn't believe them anymore. So naturally when a doctor beats around the bush you know yourself that it's worse than anything else. So I made up my mind . . . there was only one thing, that God was calling me home. And I was wishin' that he'd do it as fast as he could. It wouldn't be too fast for me."

"When did you decide that? When did you wish that?"

"When I made up my mind that there was no hope."

"When did you do that? When did you make up your mind that there was no hope?"

"When I was having the radio treatments. Instead of getting better I was getting worse. I could navigate around. Afterwards I couldn't even do that."

"But that was a long time ago, wasn't it, that you had those treatments? And you've had no hope for how long?"

"For quite a while. Nicky. When did I start givin' my things away?"

"Oh, about four months, three months."

"Well, I decided there was no hope about, say, six months ago."

"Did the two of you talk that over?"

"Yes. I told him, but he didn't want to believe it. But I told him that I felt it. That there is no hope. And I asked him if they told him anything . . . he wouldn't lie to me.

343

And he said nobody told him anything, what to expect or anything. And that's somethin' I have against. . . . A doctor should know his patient. . . . There's some you can tell and some you can't tell, and I believe in telling the truth to the ones that can take it."

"How can you tell who can take it and who can't?"

"A doctor knows. When you meet people and treat them like that you have that . . . intuition. What do they call it? The seventh sense?"

"So you wanted to know."

"That's right. I'm a person that didn't just ride around aimlessly when I used to drive. I had to have a destination in mind and I knew where I was going and what I was going to do. And when I was going to come back. And that's the right way to do it."

"What's it been like for you, Mr. Faliconi, being with your wife, seeing her have all this trouble, seeing her lose her hope?"

"It wasn't easy."

"What did you go through?"

"He felt very bad. But I told him what's to be is to be."

"Is that right, Mr. Faliconi? Is that your philosophy, too?"

"Well, yes, I feel . . . I suppose it is. You do have to be practical."

"And being practical means what?"

"Like I told him, what's to be is to be."

"Is that right, Mr. Faliconi?"

"Yeah."

"How did you feel about her decision to give away her things?"

"It's her business. Personal possessions. She can do anything she wants with them."

"I made sure that the ones I wanted to get my things were the ones who got them. And there's different instructions that I left with my husband to give them other things away."

"When she told you that she gave up hope, what did you say?"

"I told her, don't give up hope so soon. Doctors keep tellin' her they'll help her, this'll help her, this therapy'll help her, this treatment'll help her . . . it's all they've been sayin' over there."

"What happened when you told her that?"

"She says she knows she's all done. What could I say?"

"What did you say?"

"He didn't say nothin'. There's nothin' left to be said."

"Do the two of you talk a lot to each other?"

"Oh yeah. He and I we understand each other perfectly."

"You've understood each other for years?"

"Yeah."

"Could you tell me about your marriage, and your years together?"

"We've been very happy. He's a nice, considerate, truthful man. That's why when I asked him did the doctor say anything to him he said no and I believed him. And that's another thing that's wrong. If you don't believe your patient can handle it someone else in the family should be told. You've got to prepare these things. It isn't easy for the doctor, I know, but it's the truth that's important. . . ."

"You know, what puzzles me is that although, you know, you have a serious illness, as you know, how it was that you decided to give up hope?"

"I believe in what's to be. And my faith, like I say, I believe in it. If God meant for me, meant this for me, this is what it is. You can't do anything about it. It's the way of

life. We come one way and we're going to go one way.
There's no two ways about that."

"Have you done a lot of thinking about that?"

"Well, naturally."

"And?"

"Well, you think a lot before you give up all hope."

"What did you think about?"

"Well, the main thing is, life is sweet, but if it isn't to be
it isn't to be. That's all."

"How did you deal with losing people in your life?"

"I used to feel bad about it. But then again . . . I never
lost anyone who was on the young side. My mother was
quite old when she died."

"How old was she?"

"Seventy-nine."

"And how old were you then?"

"Gee, I'd have to count back. My brain doesn't go that
far back."

"Just about."

"Nicky, that's how many years ago?"

"Seven years ago."

"What was that like, for you to lose her?"

"Well, anybody'll tell you what it is to lose a mother.
And my mother was a wonderful woman."

"What was she like?"

"I was a lot like her. Socially minded. Mixing with people
and everything. We always mixed."

"Was it a time you cried, when she died?"

"Naturally. I cried bitterly."

"For how long?"

"Well, there's different times. And even now . . . when
. . . I think of her, I cry. My mother . . ."

"What do you think about when you cry?"

"Mostly . . . her."

"What kinds of memories come up then?"

"All kinds of memories. From the day I was a kid. How good she was to us. My father died when we were very young, so she brought three up herself."

"How old were you when he died?"

"I was in the first grade of grammar."

"And he died suddenly?"

"Yes."

"You were the oldest?"

"No, I was the middle one."

"And what was that like, growing up?"

"Very happy. We were too busy to be otherwise."

"Busy with what?"

"With chores. We never had idle hands. I had to take care of the cooking and everything. My mother worked. My brother had to do the man's chores around the house. My sister was young. She was always treated as the baby."

"And when you think about your mother, you still do cry."

"Oh, yes."

"As you've been sick here in this hospital, do you cry?"

"For my mother?"

"For anything. For your mother, yourself."

"For my mother I cry because I'm selfish. I miss her. For myself, what's there to miss?"

"You're not sad?"

"No. I was sad when I first found out. But now it makes no difference. I'm just waitin'. I can't wait to be fast enough home. For good."

"But you were sad when you first found out?"

"Everybody is then."

"Could you tell me about that. What you felt when you first found out."

"I felt like it couldn't be, but then it is, so what's to do about it?"

"And what was the sadness that you felt?"

"Everybody feels sad when they'll have no more life."

"That was when your back started to bother you."

"Yes. When I started to have the radio treatments, and instead of gettin' better I got worse."

"And that's when you cried."

"Yes."

"Was that when she did a lot of crying, Mr. Faliconi?"

"She didn't do much cryin'."

"I cried to myself. By myself. He has a nerve problem, so I never like to shoulder him with troubles. He had enough to do, enough worries as it is."

"And when you cried, what memories came up, what thoughts?"

"No memories. No thoughts. The only thing . . . that life is sweet, but when you have to go you have to go. God has somethin' else in mind for me. And like I say, I'm just waitin' and askin' to be home, that he'll take me as fast as he can. I hate this lingering."

"Do you feel you are lingering?"

"Yes."

"What do you call lingering?"

"Wasting my time."

"What are your thoughts about the future, after death?"

"It's going to be sweet, no more problems. No more troubles, no more nothin'."

"And what happens then?"

348

"Well, what more do you want? No more responsibilities, no more nothin'."

"Where will you be?"

"If I could tell you that I'd be the richest woman goin'."

"Well, in terms of what you believe, what do you think?"

"I guess I never went that far."

"Do you think about it much?"

"No. No. I take each step as it comes along."

"And you consider yourself a religious person?"

"Yes."

"Could you tell me what religion has meant to you?"

"It's meant a lot to me."

"When you think about dying, do you think about any people you'll see in the future?"

"Oh, I'll meet every one of my old buddies."

"Who in particular do you want to meet?"

"My mother."

"Are there things you want to say to her?"

"Children . . . always want to say . . . to talk to their parents."

"What would you say?"

"Who . . . knows?"

"I have a sense that you can cry about your mother, as you are doing now, but I have a sense that you don't let yourself cry about the sadness of being sick and seeing yourself so downhill."

"I'm down, so what's there to be sad about?"

"But you began to be sad, you say, and then it went away. So what happened to it?"

" 'Cause I made up my mind, like I said, that what's to be is to be."

"Do you ever feel angry?"

"What for?"

"I don't know."

"That'll do nothin' and nobody no good."

"Are you a person who ever gets angry?"

"I have a temper, same as everybody else."

"What's your temper like?"

"It's good."

"Well, when does it come up?"

"When I'm frustrated."

"And what will make you frustrated?"

"Nothin' now."

"Nothing now. What used to?"

"Oh, different things. Like not being able to do this and not being able to do that. Now I know I can't and that's it."

"You mean not being able to do things when you get sick?"

"No. Problems. Everyday problems."

"Do you ever feel cranky?"

"I'm still human. Everybody does."

"Can you let people know when you feel cranky?"

"I try not to."

"Why is that?"

"Because they have enough problems. They're tryin' to do their best. After all, they only have two hands, two feet, and two can't be doin' six."

"I've asked you a lot of questions. Would you like to ask me any?"

"You've asked them all. But I'll tell you, Doctor, I'll put it straight to you. What should I expect in the future?"

"You're asking me a question that you can't answer. How should I be able to answer that one?"

"Well, see, we put our faith in the doctor, and we expect him to know these answers."

"Well, what are your concerns about the future?"

"Nothin'."

"Well, when you talk about the future I'm not sure whether you're talking about after death or the point up to death."

"No, Doctor. No human being can tell you about after death."

"So you're talking about . . ."

"Before. What's to expect? How long do you think I'll last?"

"Well, you know, obviously those are questions that I can't answer, because I'm not sure any doctor can . . . and I really don't know your medical problems that well. But I'd like to know what your fears are about the end, what you're afraid may happen."

"Doctor, I just don't want no pain."

"Have you been having much pain?"

"No. So long as I keep up with the needles I'm all right."

"And you ask for the needles?"

"Yes."

"Any other fears?"

"No."

"So it's a comforting thing to know that up to now you haven't had pain. Do you feel that the nurses are responding to your needs about pain?"

"They're very good. I couldn't ask for no more."

"Do you think that if you do have any fears as things come up you could let people know?"

"I suppose so."

"That is important, isn't it?"

"It is."

"You've been a very straightforward person, so maybe you can let people know when fears come up."

"I'll try."

"I think that's very important."

"Yes. Because a person doesn't know what a person feels unless they're told."

"Exactly. What's it been like for both of you to sit here and talk to us like this?"

"Well, if it's done any good for anybody, I'm glad. But all I can say is have complete faith in God. And that's the most important thing, that's about the only thing."

"Well, it's been important for me to talk to you and I want to thank you both for coming here."

"Thank you, Doctor, you've been kind, too."

"Thank you, Mrs. Faliconi."

POSTSCRIPT: The patients Hennessey, Casey, Sage, and Faliconi died within a few months after the interviews. Mrs. Whitehead and Mrs. Jackson are alive at this writing.

Afterthoughts

You need things like this to happen to you every now and then to make you put things into perspective. It makes you forget about all the day-to-day Mickey Mouse things you worry about.

> — Boston Police Officer William Johnston, rescued after 16 hours in a small boat that had drifted 24 miles out to sea when the engine failed

I think death is sort of beautiful. I've learned to love people. I'm not afraid to say, "Hey, I love you."

> — Lyn Helton, twenty, of Denver, who died of cancer

During and after the writing of two books on death and dying, I learned something about people and something about myself, but nothing at all about the ultimate reality, which should surprise no one, least of all the snotty MIT engineer who, like so many others who misunderstood the endeavor, said, "Oh, books on death and dying? You've been there?"

He was expressing not only the frustration that besets most of us when we are faced with the subject, but, more important, there was the common confusing of death with dying. As we muddle the drink with the drinking, the lay with the laying. Death is the light gone out, and we dwell inexorably on the extinguished and not enough on the extinguishing because it is less demanding, less tedious, to view a result than the often slow progression toward it. And because dying, we have been conditioned to believe, is but a bad passage to an undesirable end, the road becomes the somewhere to which it leads.

Dying and dreaming are kindred spirits, and they are real. Perhaps it is their associated nouns, death and dreams, that are unreal, or less real. One comes to that understanding rather quickly when dealing with the terminally ill or with those for whom death is a likely possibility. That, at least, was how my interviewing dying patients (or being present while they were interviewed by their physicians) and those who care for the dying affected me. I became less interested in death itself, the noun and its aftermath, than I had in the past, and more in the dying process. I did not seek, nor did I find, what a clergyman's wife wrote of in 1914 after an experience in which she believed her soul fled her body and returned: "It was gone in an instant, leaping out, a joyous light and exhilarating release of the very essence of life into space. My form remained the same, but the substance had utterly changed. It was not a translucent vapor, capable at my will of going immediately to any place. I possessed all my faculties, imagination, will and memory. I was among the clouds, knowing the joy of flight. Then I came down and hovered over the city, saw the people and wished to be able to reveal myself to some to let them know that life after death is beautiful." No one I talked with had that experience, nor did I see it in any of the dying eyes into which I looked. A curiosity about death, of course, still remains, and I doubt that that will ever leave me. But I can make no definitive statements about death, not even a negative one such as that tacked up on a bulkhead aboard an aircraft carrier on which I once served: "Death Sucks." To do so would be as presumptuous as a clergyman's saying that one should not act in a certain way because it will displease God. I have yet to make out a will. I am not sure how I will face my own death, if it comes slowly, although I hope the alternatives presented here will help. Nor would I presume to tell others how to face theirs. I did not know what to say when a grieving relative, during the funeral of close family friends — a gentle elderly couple killed in a highway crash in Canada during this writing — asked me in a tone of voice that suggested I could make some profound statement: "Well, what do you think of this?"

While I do not understand death any better, I do understand the needs of the dying as I never did before. Focusing on the subject has also taught me that most people do want to talk about death, in spite of the denial that we acquire, and it is not only the dying and their caretakers who want to. It is almost as if the people I have met while writing this book were waiting for an opportunity to unburden themselves. They invited me to wakes. They asked me how I would cope with my own. They sent me poems by John Donne and Edna St. Vincent Millay. They asked me if I had read Sylvia Plath. They slipped notes under my office door, offering to write essays on happy deaths stemming from guiltless and fulfilled lives. They sent me newspaper clippings about dying people who set examples of courage by their resignation to their plight. They sent me copies of the Fire Fighters' Prayer: "And if according to your will, I have to lose my life. . . . Please bless with your protecting hand, my children and my wife." They asked me to address local chapters of memorial societies, groups banded together "to obtain dignity, simplicity and economy in funeral arrangements by advance planning." They phoned to say one of their relatives was dying and would I want to talk with him. They told me they thought of me when people were murdered or died tragically. They called me a death freak, but even those who did were magnetized, and they talked about it eventually. They asked me to speak to the children to whom they could not speak. And I read most of the things they sent me, and I talked to most of the people they invited me to talk to. And the more I did these things, the more possessive I became of the subject. I was angry whenever a new book on death was issued. I was critical when they received favorable reviews. I quit listening to the speeches of thanatologists. I grew impatient with people who were discussing, for the first time, the attitudes of the dying patient, whether passive euthanasia is permissible, or when death actually occurs. And I swung between worrying that I was into something that was going to have a long-lasting and disastrous effect — that maybe it was better to hide behind the good old healthy defense of denial — and between the awareness that facing mortality spurs creativity and whets the appetite for life. And the last won out, for never do I want to say, too late, too late. Like missing a bus. An opportunity. A chance not taken. A horse not bet, an offer of love not accepted.

And they asked me why I chose the subject, such a morbid subject, in the first place, and what it had done *to* me, never *for* me. And I knew the answers to those questions, I had convinced myself, and I answered the questions casually, confidently. I am a reporter, I would say, whose job is to inform, interpret, sometimes entertain. I simply do interviews and research. No, the experience did nothing to me because a reporter avoids entanglements, hiding behind a carefully built barrier in the interests of impartiality and objectivity, advocacy journalists notwithstanding. I was a witness, and no, I would say, I could not afford to have the wall breached. The subject was just a subject, like organ transplantation and human experimentation, and the only thing that bothered me a little bit about it was that being a newsman for so many years gives you this awful awareness of irony, and all I could think of was that I was going to die of something during the writing, and it would be just like that underwater survival expert who died in the research submarine off Key West, or the scientist-uncle of mine who worked for years on Meniere's disease at the Massachusetts General and later came down with it, and it's not something you catch.

I went to this party in a New York City apartment. The man who lived there wasn't an architect or a draftsman but he had a drafting table with lamps suspended over it arranged hugely in a corner. The stereo was playing Greek or Syrian music, and there were an Italian TV director in dark glasses, arranged in a leather chair, patting the head of a girl sitting at his feet, a caged bird named Onan, the host told me, because it spilled its seed on the floor, and cocktail glasses that said FUCK YOU on them in pseudo-Hebrew characters which you could read by holding them upside down, and a copy of a sex manual by Alex Comfort on the coffee table. The host was paunchy, in plaid slacks and blue button-down shirt and red knitted tie, and he quoted Freud and Jung and told us about Esalen and his friends at the *New York Times*, and I figured they just had to be advertising men, and he talked a lot about how provincial New Englanders were. He asked me how old I was. I told him forty-two and he wanted to know why I was writing a book on death at that age, and that he had known a lot of newspapermen in his day and never one who wrote on death before, and I told him to read the papers again. He asked it again, why, and I told him that there was current interest in the subject, and maybe because I was hoping to dispel some of the uneasiness about the subject, and maybe to help some professionals and other people deal with the dying patient and maybe their own death in the process some day, and also because I make my living writing, and that there was obvious commercial value in subjects like that. He refused to accept any of it, except possibly the last; he laughed and said I was doing it at forty-two because I had reached emotional and physical menopause and realized that my life was better than half finished. He said there was some "deep-rooted reason sunk into your psyche" that was making me do it, and I told him, don't be silly, does that mean that every time I go out on a story about kidney disease it's because I'm hypochondriacal?

He flopped in a chair, Scotch in hand, and quoted something from somebody named Young who said something like no one can take death's portrait because the tyrant never sat, and he asked me did my father love me. Stoned, I told him I never knew my father, that he and my mother split when I was young and that when he walked out when I was nine I never saw him again, except at a distance sitting by the Charles River, looking at the water, and later my mother told me he tried to kill himself by jumping off a Coast Guard cutter during the war. And I told him too much more, how my father had died of cirrhosis on a Boston street, a derelict, a block away from the newspaper I worked at, and he never knew I was there, I didn't think. My mother who protected me from him always in my younger years, and she had me escorted to school and she never had a listed phone, and she never told me when he died until one night I called just to say hello and she said, I thought I'd tell you, your daddy's dead, and it's all taken care of, the funeral and all. And I told him, my host, that I dedicated the first book to my father because I wanted his name on something besides the police blotter down at Station 4, and the admission sheet at the Deer Island House of Correction, and the docket at Roxbury District Court, and the emergency room roster at the Mass. General and the door of the alcoholic ward at Boston City. He put his head in his hands and he didn't say another word to me, so I walked out into the street and left him like that, and ever since I have wondered, too.

I wondered more about my father and other losses as I got deeper into the book, and that is natural when you talk to dying patients for two years. I was Mrs. Faliconi who told of how she cried when she thought of her mother, and of the memories that came up, all kinds of memories, from the day she was a child, how good her mom was to her, and how she brought up three herself, and I have thought a lot since then, since Ned Cassem put it so neatly, that the last loss is a reminder of all the losses one has had, that the caretaker must try to be alert to this not only in the patient but in ourselves so that we can better share the dying person's problem with him. Once I went to the file and pulled out a letter I wrote in 1965, that I thought at the time was ballsy because it was to Pope Paul VI, and attached to it was a lovely card I received in reply one month later, embossed with the words "The Secretariat of State of the Vatican is pleased to inform you that His Holiness appreciates your thoughtful communication."

My letter said that it was written by a Roman Catholic who sympathized deeply with the mental anguish which must have been his over the decision he was called on to make regarding contraception. It said I was not a theologian and therefore would not dare to solve the thorny problems which lie in the theologian's domain. It said I did, however, have an intensely personal interest in the birth control issue and that I felt I had much to tell theologians, if some would listen. I cited the case of my wife and me, nine years married, seven pregnancies, an Rh incompatibility, the first a miscarriage, the second a healthy child, a son, the third a severely jaundiced and sickly daughter who required several complete exchange transfusions before she recovered, the fourth a son who died a week after birth, the fifth a daughter whose life fluttered for weeks before it took hold and she pulled through, the sixth a son who died, the seventh a son who died, and I could not, because it had not yet occurred, tell him of the daughter who died a few years later, shortly after she was born. I implored His Holiness to consider cases such as this, and I was asking for a listener to share a problem, just as my wife and I had shared it and worked it out, in hospital rooms at two in the morning after brusque or perplexed or uneasy residents or obstetricians told us it had happened the first time, and again and again and again, and in bed at night after each burial, with repetitious, shattering, comforting, tearful talk. We finally grew up without him in Rome and all those who answered with no answer or with embossed cards or with a murmured "His will be done," and found the answers in ourselves and in some who were unselfish enough to hear and brave enough to speak.

I have realized that if I could be reminded of previous losses by listening to the dying talk, and not dying myself, then the wall must have been breached, that meticulously constructed wall not only between me and them, but between me and It. I found I could talk to the patients after the tape ran out. And I have wished many times over that the wall had been breached before my grandparents, who helped raise me, died. For I know now what I would have done. When my grandmother died, I was in my early twenties, and she died at home. We were friends, and she was the best I ever had, and she used to make me heaping plates of homemade *gnocchi* and *polpettes* as big as oranges, and we would talk while I ate lunch each day with her before I got on the subway to college. She had these great aphorisms. "He who has bitter things in his mouth will never spit out sweets." "Sheep, priests and women never have enough." "Marry for love without money and you'll have happy nights and bad days." "A cask of wine works more wonders than a church full of saints." "It takes nine Jews to make one Neapolitan." And she talked about death often, but never in awe, never with fear, because her heritage had taught her simply that it was a part of life. There were aphorisms about that, casual peasant words. "Laugh and you remove a nail from your coffin." "He who digs a grave is the first to fall into it." "Marriages are for weeping and funerals for laughing." But when she died, I stood in the living room as her life left her, and I refused to go in to see her. I loved her and I had laughed with her, and at her words about death. But I was afraid of the look of death in her darkened room. The oxygen tent, the olive oil of extreme unction on a table, the candles, prayerful relatives, and I could not enter that room, and she died without me. My grandfather, too, died in the same house, a few months later, in the same room, and his sons took turns changing his colostomy bag. I did not help, but wept by myself in another part of the house. I went into his room only once before he died, and only after he asked to see me, and I found it difficult to respond when he touched the pouch at his side and said, "Vado in seconda classe, Giovanni." Today I hope that neither of them died thinking of me.

RC
49
,L36

RC
49
.L36